AF574266

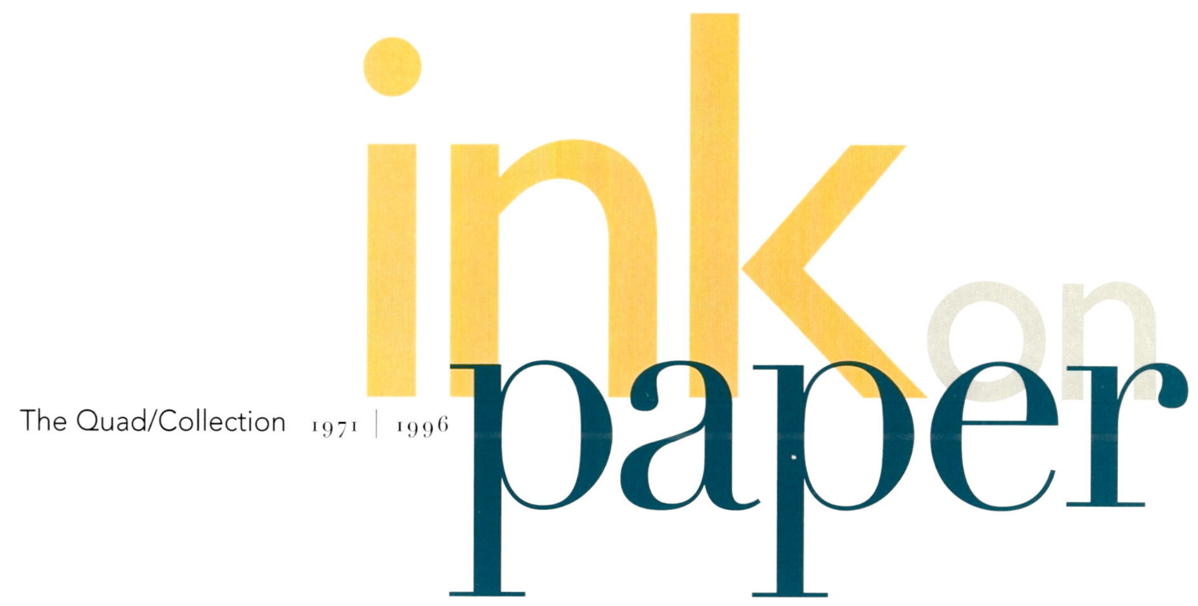

The Quad/Collection 1971 | 1996

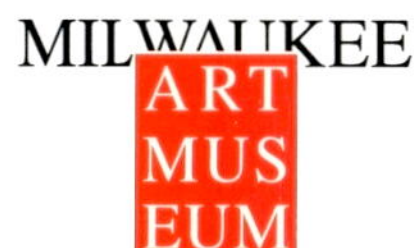

Ink On Paper: The Quad/Collection, 1971-1996
Milwaukee Art Museum
Milwaukee, Wisconsin
and
Quad/Graphics Gallery
Sussex, Wisconsin
August 23-November 3, 1996

Published by the Milwaukee Art Museum,
Milwaukee, Wisconsin

ISBN: 0-944110-52-5
ISBN: 0-944110-55-X

Library of Congress
Catalog card number: 96-77777

Curated by Joseph Ruzicka
Design and Production by Quad/Creative
Printed by Quad/Graphics, Pewaukee, Wisconsin

Cover: Jim Dine, *Piranesi's 24 Colored Marks*, 1976 (see p. 55)

contents

foreword

Ink on Paper: The Quad/Collection celebrates one of the primary corporate collections in the state of Wisconsin and one which provides a model of enlightened corporate collecting for the entire country. Founded in 1971 with a commitment to applying the latest technology to high volume, high quality printing, Quad/Graphics saw the basis of its business as "ink on paper." Building on that core interest, and committed to creating "an environment for excellence" and educational opportunity for its employees, Quad/Graphics began a collection of limited edition prints in 1974. Since the 1970s the company has grown into an international concern with 17 plants in North and South America and offices in Europe and Asia; the collection has grown to an extraordinary 2,500 pieces distributed throughout that international network. Quad/Graphics still believes deeply in the value of art in the business environment, stating in a 1996 publication, "The fine art prints on our walls inspire us to strive for excellence." And further: "Artwork on the walls ... is the most tangible way we remind ourselves to stop looking at our shoes and start looking at the stars. When we challenge our imagination and intellect, we create countless opportunities to look anew at the processes we work through everyday." I can hardly think of a more eloquent statement of art's importance in the workplace or, for that matter, in our lives.

As part of a philanthropic commitment ranging from involvement in social, educational and cultural institutions to caring for the environment, Quad/Graphics has a long history of major support for the Milwaukee Art Museum. In 1980-81, Quad/Graphics provided the matching funds for a grant from the National Endowment for the Arts to purchase prints by living American artists. Among the works added to the collection through that program were prints by Willem de Kooning, Sam Francis, Jasper Johns, Roy Lichtenstein, Richard Estes, Frank Stella, Robert Morris, Brice Marden, Elizabeth Murray, Susan Rothenberg and many others. In some cases, the purchases marked the first representation of those artists in the museum's graphics collection. This extraordinary support for the museum's collection was followed by a sequence of support for exhibitions and programs which is unparalleled in our history. From 1983 to 1985, the Scholastic Art Awards exhibition of works by outstanding high school students was sponsored by Quad/Graphics; for the last decade that exhibition has been supported by *Milwaukee Magazine*; in 1989 and 1990 Quad/Graphics and *Milwaukee Magazine* co-sponsored two major exhibitions which dealt with prints or the printed word: *The Modern Poster: Selections from the Museum of Modern Art* and *Word as Image: American Art, 1960-1990.* Since 1982, Quad/Graphics has sponsored a Quad/Graphics Family Day at the museum bringing in more than 1,500 employees and their families each year. We have been fortunate to have the direct involvement of both Quad/Graphics founder Harry V. Quadracci and Betty Ewens Quadracci, publisher of *Milwaukee Magazine*, in all these events and programs. Also, Betty Quadracci served on the museum's board of trustees from 1981 through 1990 and again since 1994.

The Milwaukee Art Museum is very pleased to be able to present a selection from the Quad/Collection of fine prints. The works shown at the Milwaukee Art Museum are presented in conjunction with a larger portion of the selection shown at the Quad/Art Gallery at Quad/Graphics' Sussex plant. The joint exhibition, which celebrates the 25th anniversary of the founding of Quad/Graphics, also connects fortuitously to the presentation of the museum's major exhibition *Landfall Press: Twenty-Five Years of Printmaking.* Acquired in 1992, the Landfall Press Archive provides an opportunity for the in-depth study of prints and reflects the museum's continuing commitment to the printmaking medium. We are very grateful to Quad/Graphics and the Quadracci family for the support of this exhibition and its publication, part of the continuing exceptional support they have provided for the museum for almost two decades.

I would like to thank Harry and Betty Quadracci for the extraordinary personal commitment they have shown both to art in the working environment and to the museum. They are truly an example to our community and beyond. I would also like to acknowledge Judith Ramazzini, curator of the Quad/Graphics collection and an integral part of bringing all the information for this exhibition together. Finally, I would like to thank Joseph Ruzicka, curator of prints and drawings, who, with a major commitment to the Landfall Press project already on hand, found both the time and the dedication to bring this exhibition and publication to such a successful conclusion.

Ink on Paper is truly a cause for celebration: of Quad/Graphics' 25th anniversary, of the company's overwhelmingly generous record of support, and of an unusually sensitive corporate understanding of the value of art.

Russell Bowman
Director
Milwaukee Art Museum

president's letter

Art. It's as much a part of Quad/Graphics' daily existence as putting ink on paper. Walk through any of our doors and you'll find our plants to be an uncommon blend of artistry and high technology.

From the time of our founding in 1971, we've used art to symbolize what we expect of employees: perfection. Art is a metaphor for performance excellence. We've learned that by surrounding people with great works of art, they, in turn, become great performers. Really, the concept is very simple: A quality environment stimulates quality thought and quality work.

Through art we have found the world, particularly because the world cannot always find us, tucked away as we are in out-of-the-way places like Pewaukee, Wisconsin, and Thomaston, Georgia. Displayed on our walls – framed or as a mural or sculpture – art has transformed our workplaces into works of art. Employees find Quad/Graphics someplace special to work. And, by working at someplace special, they become special, something more than they ever hoped to be.

Art, just as ink, is in our veins. It is our blood. We ponder it. We use it to excite the senses. We learn from it. And, ultimately, we absorb it into the very fiber of our soul. There, we feast upon it, incorporating its perfection into our performance.

That our collection should consist entirely of prints should hardly be surprising. We are, after all, printers. With this collection, we celebrate the work of the human hand and heart, knowing that printed artistic excellence comes from the partnership between the creativity of the artist and the skill of the printer.

Harry V. Quadracci
President and Founder
Quad/Graphics, Inc.

introduction and acknowledgments

One of the great privileges of being a curator in an art museum is working with a supportive and informed community of collectors. The Milwaukee Art Museum is particularly fortunate to have a broad base of enthusiastic patrons who care for art in a passionate and committed manner. Chief among them are Betty and Harry Quadracci, who have been involved with the museum for almost two decades.

In 1981, Betty was a founding executive board member of the Print Forum, the support group for the museum's Department of Prints and Drawings. Print Forum has given most generously for acquisitions of works of art on paper over the years, and certainly Betty's authoritative presence at the beginning set the right example. Indeed, in that same year, Quad/Graphics matched a grant to the museum from the National Endowment for the Arts for the purchase of contemporary master prints for the museum's collection, including work by Jennifer Bartlett, Jasper Johns, Willem de Kooning, Richard Serra and many others. For 10 years, *Milwaukee Magazine*, of which Betty is publisher, has underwritten the annual Scholastic Art Awards exhibition held at the museum, as a manifestation of her special interest in education issues. Having first sat as a member from 1981 to 1990, Betty is currently serving her second term on the museum's board of trustees.

Away from the museum, the Quadraccis have served an equally important function as major patrons and role models for other collectors. Twenty-five years ago, when their Quad/Graphics commercial printing operation was just beginning, they quickly grasped the importance of having outstanding art in every corner of the work space; Harry eloquently explains his philosophy in his President's Letter on the previous page. In an era when many corporations abdicate their responsibilities as patrons of the arts or, even worse, disband their collections altogether, Quad/Graphics continues to collect the finest contemporary prints and to share them with their staff, and more recently, the general public. The Quad/Graphics Gallery opened in Sussex, Wisconsin, in October 1995, offering the public access to changing exhibitions from the collection. This humane sense of generosity and social responsibility is rare among today's corporate leaders.

Given Quad/Graphics' sustained relationship with the greater Milwaukee community, and the museum in particular, it seemed entirely natural that the museum and the Quadraccis should work together on an exhibition and catalogue commemorating more than two decades of their informed collecting. Reflecting the spirit of collaboration, the exhibition will appear simultaneously at the Milwaukee Art Museum and the Quad/Graphics Gallery. This show does not pretend to represent the full scope of the collection's holdings, which number close to 2,500 pieces. Rather, it is a telling microcosm, with pieces representative of the intellectual and visual trends embodied in the collection.

The collection is composed almost exclusively of American prints, from 1960 to the present. In assembling it, the Quadraccis have deliberately avoided acquiring pieces using their personal taste as the only criterion. Rather, they have tried to be as inclusive and far-ranging as possible stylistically, intellectually and technically, so that a viewer's experience of prints from this era might be as complete and meaningful as possible. And while the collection is large, the Quadraccis constantly seek ways to make it more historically complete, adding work that they missed early on, and international in scope, looking overseas to Asia and Europe.

Almost every major contemporary American printer and/or publisher from this period is represented: Abrams Original Editions, A.G.B. Graphics, Arion Press, Brooke Alexander Editions, Castelli Graphics, Crown Point Press, Derrière l'Étoile Studios, Editions Schellmann & Klüser, Experimental Workshop, Gemini G.E.L., Landfall Press, Multiples, Inc., Pace Editions, Parasol Press, Solo Impression, Stewart & Stewart, Tandem Press, Tyler Graphics, Universal Limited Art Editions (ULAE) and Vermillion Editions.

Abstract, Conceptual, figurative, and landscape art all play major roles in defining the aesthetic and visual character of the Quad/Collection. And within each of these broad categories, there is a range of sensibilities in and approaches to making art.

A very rational, systematic approach to abstraction is found in Gene Davis' rigorous investigation into color relationships, Al Held's boldly colored geometric shapes ordered within the framework of a single-point perspective scheme, Donald Judd's variations of geometric shapes, Ellsworth Kelly's grid of different colored squares, Barnett Newman's minimal banding of black and white. Each of these artists takes the basic building blocks of art – color, geometric shapes, the interplay between flatness and depth – and constructs clear-cut, highly intellectual works that deal with issues surrounding their composition. In general, these are very hermetic, self-referential works of art.

Another approach to abstract art is found in the lyrical, organic work by Louise Bourgeois, Richard Diebenkorn, Nancy Graves, Howard Hodgkin, Roberto Juarez, Joan Mitchell, among others. These artists take a more intuitive approach to making art, and most of them use the forms and forces of nature as points of departure. Graves was influenced by her keen interest in botany to interject plant-like forms into her print. Juarez's experience of living in Miami Beach relates to the intense colors and tropical plant forms found in his monoprint. As a point of departure for her print, Mitchell looked to the upstate New York landscape for inspiration. In contrast to the former group of abstract artists, the latter operate in a more outward-looking, expressive manner.

Conceptual art – work that incorporates language, ideas, narratives, performance and process – also forms an important part of the Quad/Collection. Appropriately, there are many works in which printed words form the principal compositional elements. Lesley Dill prints excerpts from Emily Dickinson's poetry over fragile paper body parts as a way to discuss the ideas of vulnerability and weakness, how we use words as a way to protect ourselves and to project an exterior image to the world. Jim Dine's lithograph *Cincinnati III* is part of a large project involving paintings and other prints, in which he wrote down the names of every person whom he knew (including those in his hometown, Cincinnati). By inscribing "ELEGY" across a scene of a burly steam railroad yard, Lawrence Gipe elicits melancholy reminiscences of a specific time of American brawn and might that has slipped irretrievably into the past. Other Conceptual work makes use of humor and punning. For instance, Jonathan Borofsky's oversized *Footprint* diptych of left and right footprints plays on the similarities and differences between a literal footprint (marks left on the ground) and a fine-art print (marks left on paper). The title itself is a crucial linguistic element in the humor surrounding a print of a foot.

A sense of humor also pervades the figurative work in the collection. In Warrington Colescott's etching, *The Hunt: Counterattack,* the deer of Wisconsin turn the tables and stalk the human predators. Red Grooms takes a colorful (and quite literally, moving) tongue-in-cheek look at the efforts of missionaries among the South Sea natives. Naturally, portraiture plays an important role in the figurative portion of the collection, with work by Robert Arneson, Chuck Close, Alex Katz and William T. Wiley. These are deeply personal portraits, not cold commissioned pieces. Arneson and Wiley offer probing self-portraits, while Close and Katz concentrate on friends and family.

Various faces of landscape are also found in the Quad/Collection. There is a great sensitivity to the lyrical side of nature, found in Jim Dine's very long close-up of an iris garden, *Rachel Cohen's Flags,* Susan Hall's poetic evening-time *Orange Ball,* Wade Hoefer's still and empty *Aestas I,* Georgia Marsh's leafy three-part *Science of the Night* and Ann McCoy's study of undersea life, *Night Sea.* All of these works deal in some way with the life-giving, nurturing aspects of nature. In other work, however, there is a great awareness of its impersonal, forceful side, as seen in work of Vija Celmins, who focuses on the powerful vastness of the ocean, and Freya Hansell, who draws upon the melancholy, brooding aspects of the edge of the sea.

Finally, there is work that deals with these same kind of dualities in the cityscape, the 20th century's contribution to landscape creation. Richard Bosman and Arthur Cohen seek the poetic aspects of the odd and little traveled edges of the city. Prints by Robert Cottingham, Richard Estes and Yvonne Jacquette focus more on the vast, gleaming machinery that drives our cities and gives urban life its power, excitement and uncertainty.

The work in the Quad/Collection embraces the full complexity of contemporary society. Taken as a whole, it offers viewers a portrait of our world. A project of this magnitude requires the dedication and generosity of many people. My foremost thanks must be extended to Betty and Harry Quadracci. They opened their collection to me, put all of their resources at my disposal and underwrote the cost of producing this catalogue. It has been a most rewarding experience for me to work with two people possessing such a refined sense of quality and focused intensity. I am particularly grateful for all of the hours – clearly their single most valuable asset – that they spent with me discussing their passion for art and collecting.

Judith Ramazzini, curator of the Quad/Collection, has been immeasurably helpful, showing me all the prints, creating endless checklists, coordinating photography, planning shipping, and in her spare time, contributing entries to this catalogue. She was ably assisted with framing and exhibition design at Quad/Graphics by her curatorial assistants Robert S. Krenzke and Frederick C. Moesel III. Photography was coordinated and shot by John Ehlers of Quad/Photo.

A whole army of people at Quad/Creative played critical roles in the conception and formation of this publication. Sandy Galioto, with Sue Dezur, Mindy Benham and Signe Thiemer expertly handled all phases of the production of the catalogue. I am grateful to Charlene Mills for her sensitive and insightful editing. Maggie Marcowka is responsible for the elegant layout and design.

I owe special thanks to my co-contributors to the catalogue text: Margaret Andera, Elizabeth Fernandez-Gimenez and Jane O'Meara from the Milwaukee Art Museum, Judy Ramazzini from Quad/Graphics, and Samantha Becker from Tandem Press, Madison, Wisconsin. Earl Kittleson, of the Print Forum, contributed an informative text on printmaking. Their perceptive and critical writings are essential contributions to this volume, and the catalogue is immeasurably better because they had a hand in it.

Special thanks are due to Christie's, New York, for graciously permitting us to use their glossary of print terms as the basis for our glossary in this volume.

The preparation of this project has necessarily touched every department in the Milwaukee Art Museum. Thanks go to the museum's director, Russell Bowman, and executive director, Christopher Goldsmith, without whose support this project could never have been realized. In addition to her writing, Jane O'Meara, administrative assistant, oversaw and coordinated the many difficult details in a timely and professional manner. Rebecca Schultz, librarian, provided much scholarly research material, often on very short notice. Leigh Albritton, registrar, expertly arranged the shipment of the portion of the exhibition shown at the Milwaukee Art Museum. John Irion, exhibition designer, produced yet another beautiful installation. Larry Stadler, facilities manager, and his crew of Jo-Bob Boblick, John Dreckmann, Joe Kavanaugh and John Nicholson hung and lit the exhibition in their usual efficient manner.

Alerting the public to such an exhibition is a large and complicated task that Polly Scott, director of communications, handled in an expert manner. Fran Serlin, director of audience development, devised ingenious ways to bring this exhibition to the public. Barbara Brown-Lee, director of education, marshaled her dedicated corps of docents to do their usual marvelous job of teaching and interpreting the material for groups of visitors to the museum. Dedra Walls, coordinator of media, wrote perceptive and informative wall panels for the show.

Finally, very special thanks are due to Susan Fancher, without whose essential support, this catalogue and exhibition could not have been realized.

Joseph Ruzicka
Curator of Prints and Drawings
Milwaukee Art Museum

ES OF AMERICA AND TO THE
UBLIC FOR WHICH IT STANDS

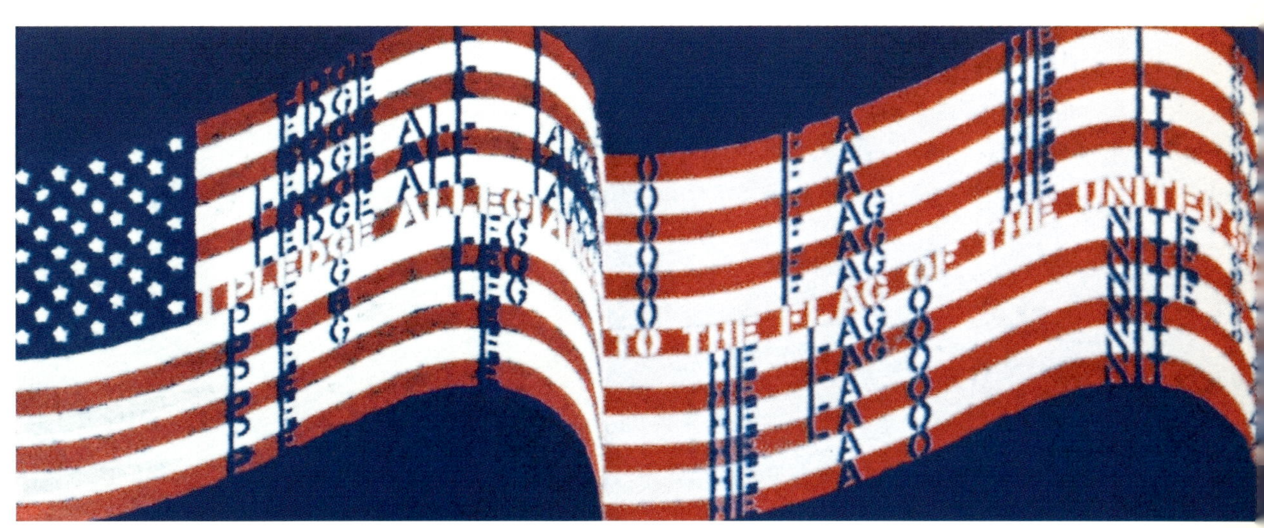
I PLEDGE ALLEGIAN
TO THE FLAG OF THE UNITED

10

VITO ACCONCI (American, b. 1940)
Wav(er)ing Flag, 1990
Lithographs
6 sheets, 18 x 24 (45 x 60) each
Jack Lemon, Barbara Spies, David Jones
Landfall Press, Chicago, Illinois

Acconci is a sculptor and performance artist who has worked on many print projects. Influenced by the scale of his sculpture, he generally makes very large prints. Here, he stretches an excerpt from the Pledge of Allegiance across the length of the flag, pulling letters up and down, out of the central core of text. Acconci creates a sort of visual noise that spotlights the fragmented, confused nature of contemporary American politics.

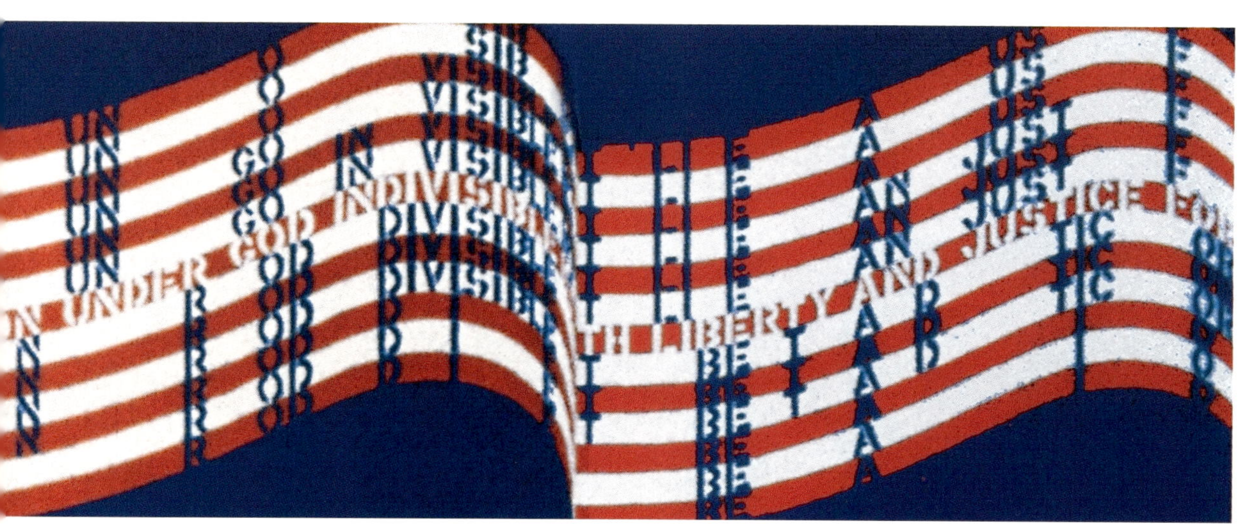
IN UNDER GOD INDIVISIBLE
TH LIBERTY AND

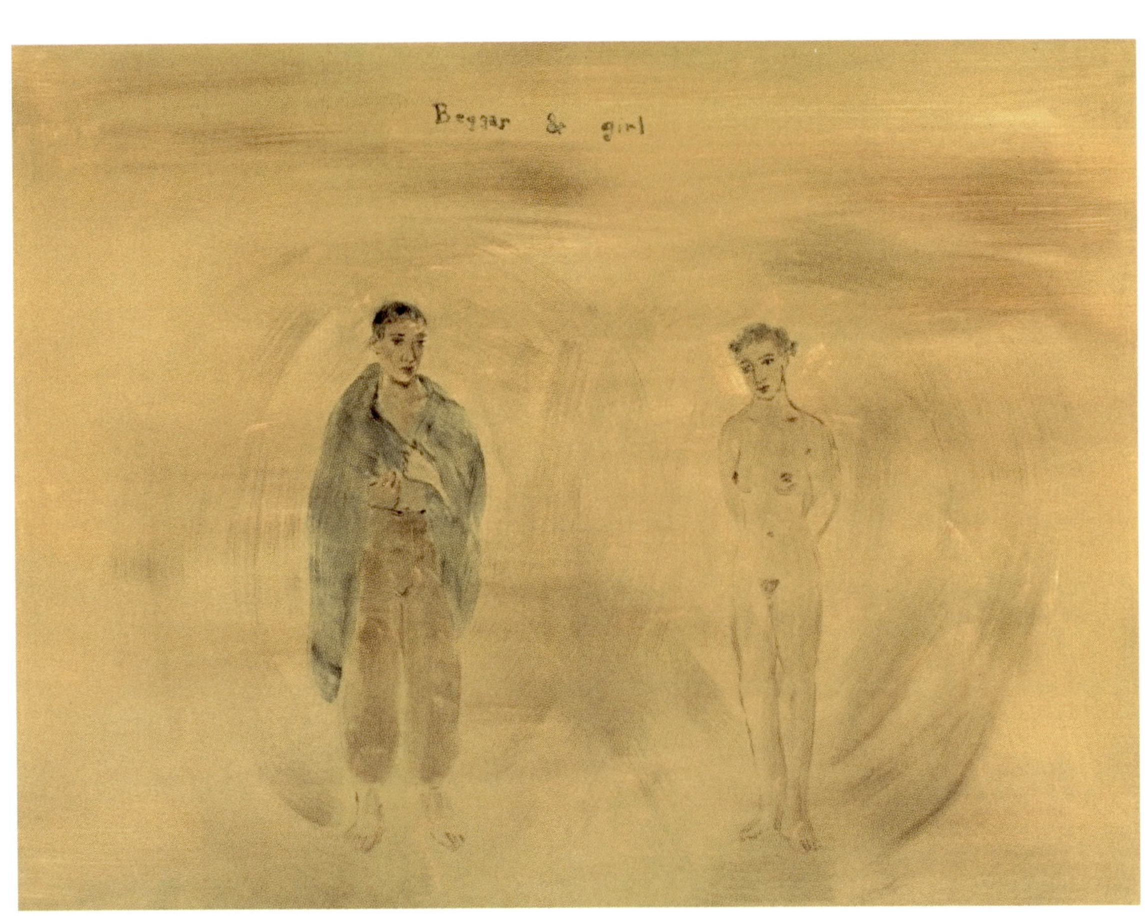
Beggar & girl

NICHOLAS AFRICANO (American, b. 1948)
Beggar and Girl, 1992
Monoprint
31 x 41 (77.5 x 102.5)
Steve Andersen
Vermillion Editions Ltd., Minneapolis, Minnesota

As a writer, Africano developed his interest in verbal and visual imagery and began sketching small illustrations for his stories. He found the immediacy of the images he had created more appealing than the words alone, and he began to use art to tell his stories. A common theme in his work is emotional isolation.

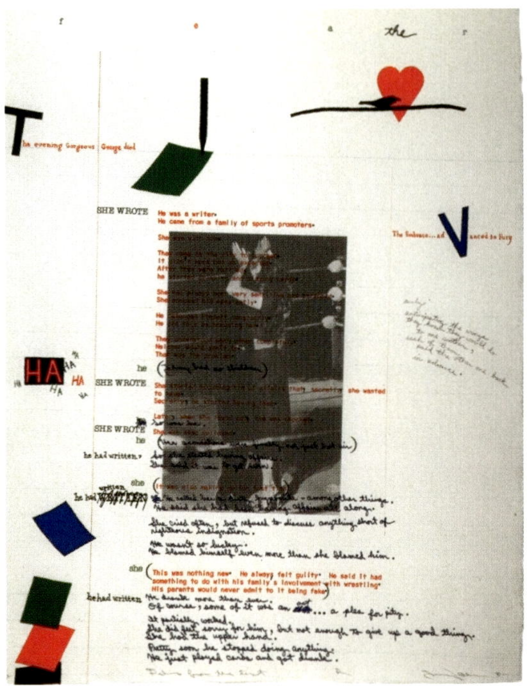

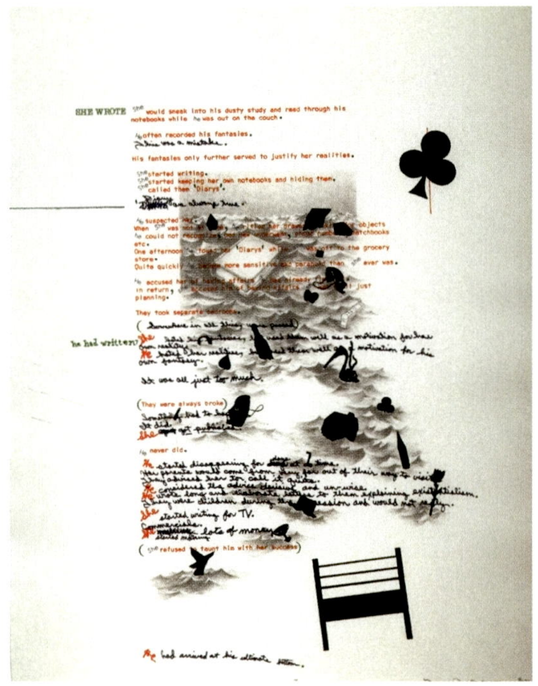

TERRY ALLEN (American, b. 1943)
R, I, N, G, from the portfolio ***Debris from the Text,*** 1981
Lithographs
4 sheets, 30 x 23½ (75 x 58.75) each
Jack Lemon, Fred Gude, Scott Russell
Landfall Press, Chicago, Illinois

Allen is a consummate storyteller who often blends images with text in his compositions. Collapse and failure on the fringes of society are common themes. In this portfolio, he recounts the story of a marriage doomed from the outset to split apart.

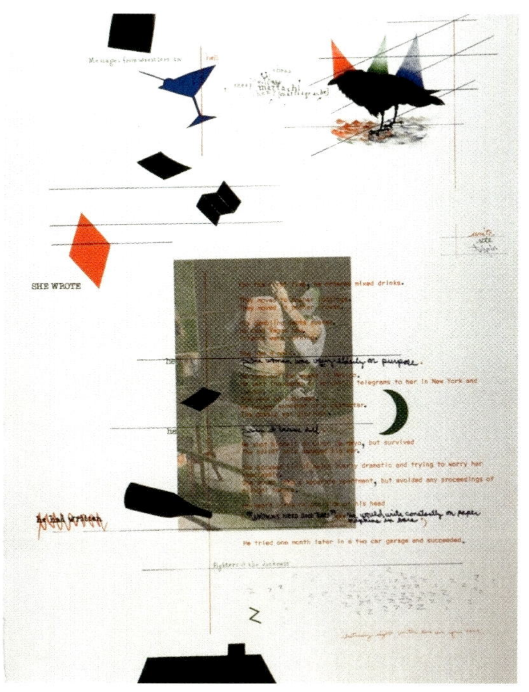
SHE WROTE
He tried one month later in a two car garage and succeeded.

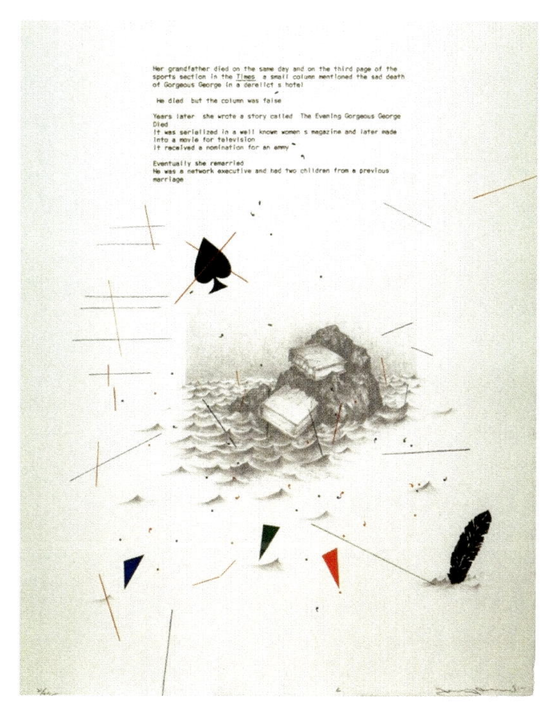
Her grandfather died on the same day and on the third page of the sports section in the Times a small column mentioned the sad death of Gorgeous George in a derelict s hotel
He died but the column was false
Years later she wrote a story called The Evening Gorgeous George Died
It was serialized in a well known women s magazine and later made into a movie for television
It received a nomination for an emmy
Eventually she remarried
He was a network executive and had two children from a previous marriage

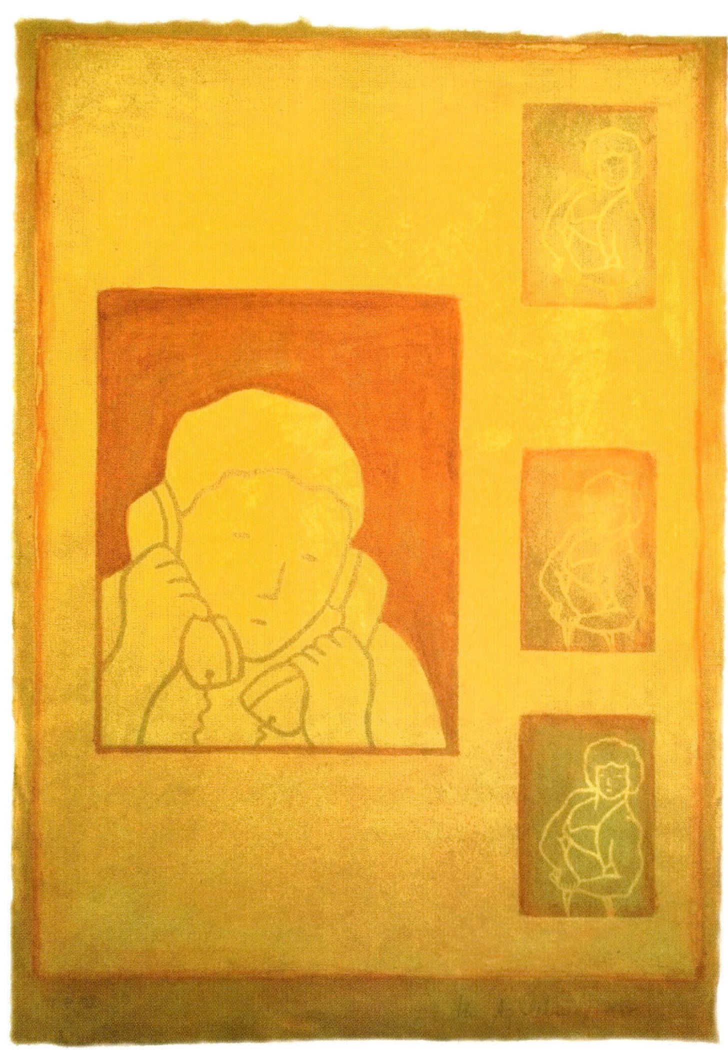

16

IDA APPLEBROOG (American, b. 1929)
Gulf & Western Plaza, 1987
Lithograph, with hand coloring
32½ x 23½ (81.25 x 58.75)
Judith Solodkin
Solo Impression Inc., New York, New York

Applebroog employs the generic style of public signage to convey the banality of corruption. Here, voyeurlike glimpses through repeated windows in a glaring blank wall suggest unsavory dealings.

SHUSAKU ARAKAWA (American, b. in Japan, 1936)
In Voice/In And Around, 1979
Lithograph, serigraph
39 x 44½ (97.5 x 111.25)
Multiples Inc., New York, New York

This Conceptual artist investigates the role of sense-transference, such as hearing distance and seeing sounds, in grasping abstract concepts. Variations in color and size fuse text with non-verbal experience.

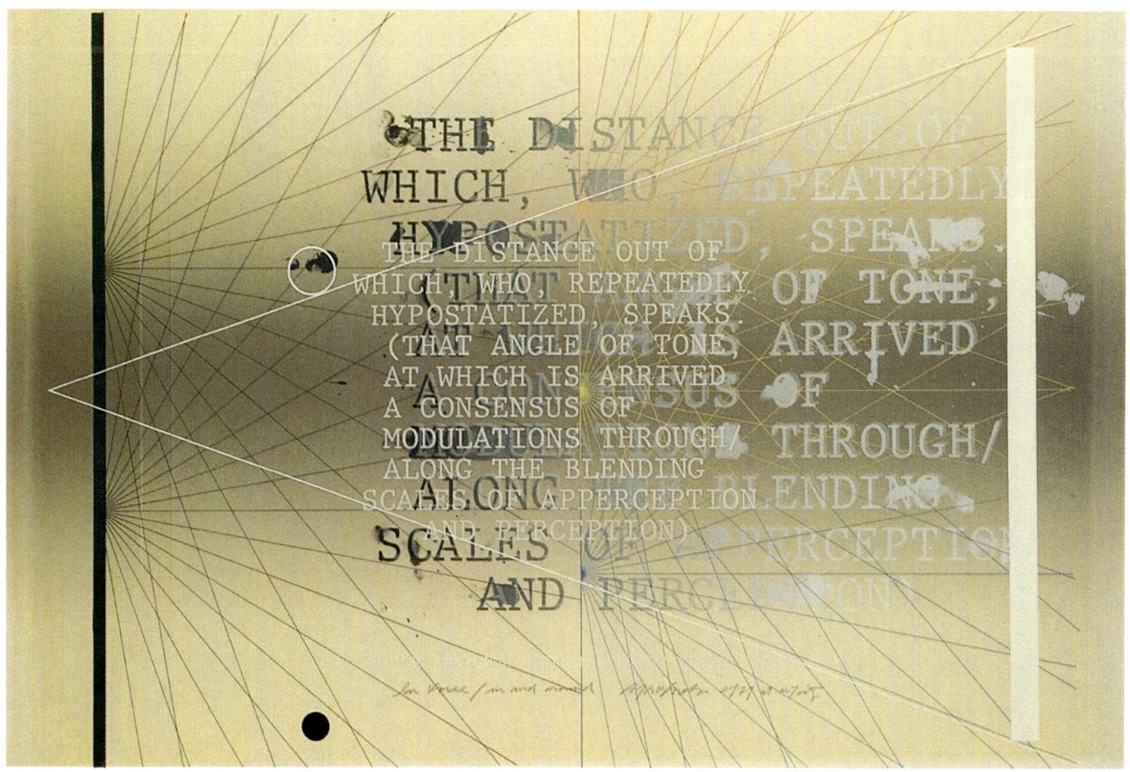

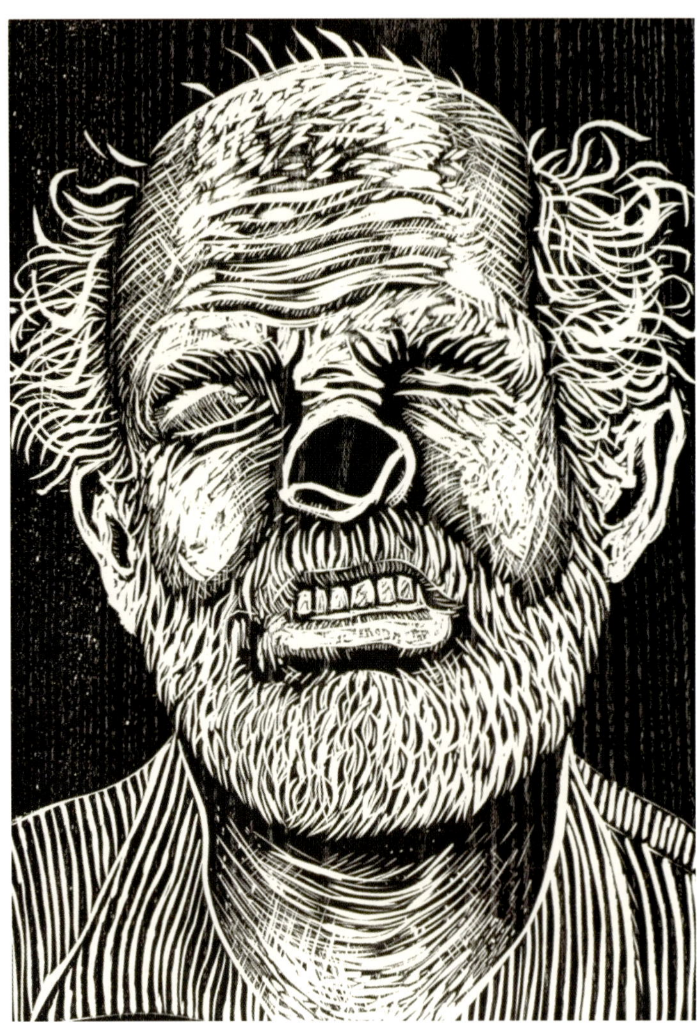

Bob

ROBERT ARNESON (American, 1930-1992)
Five Guys, Suite Of 5 (Bob, Pollock, Westermann, Picasso, Bacon), 1983
Woodcuts
5 sheets, 31 x 25 (77.5 x 62.5) each
Experimental Workshop, San Francisco, California

Arneson was known for mock-heroic portraits of himself and others. Here, a wry self-portrait, based on his drawing *Up Against It,* made while fighting cancer, is accompanied by photo-derived woodcuts of four fellow artists, famous "guys" who have been "up against it" too.

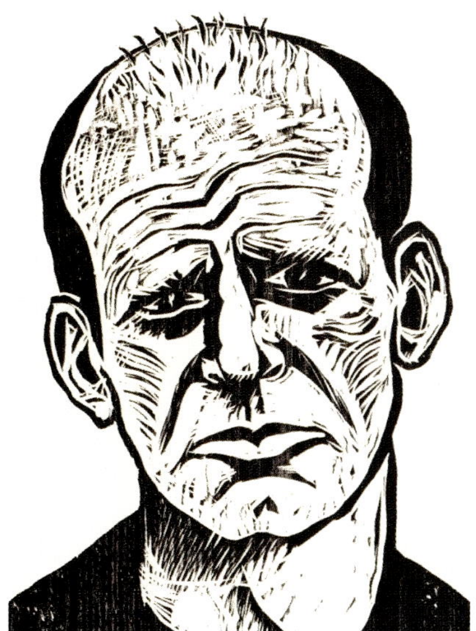
Pollock

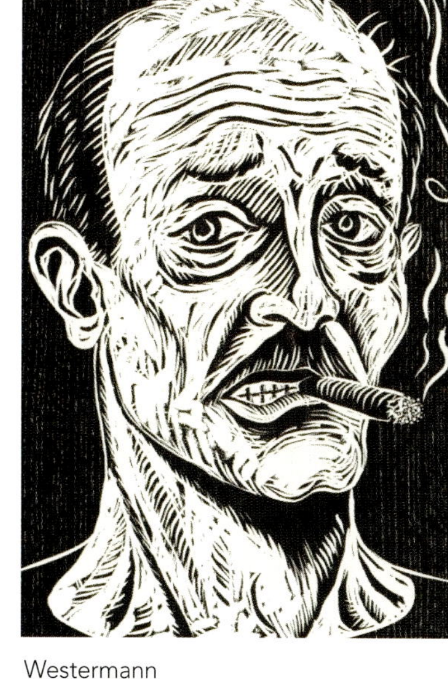
Westermann

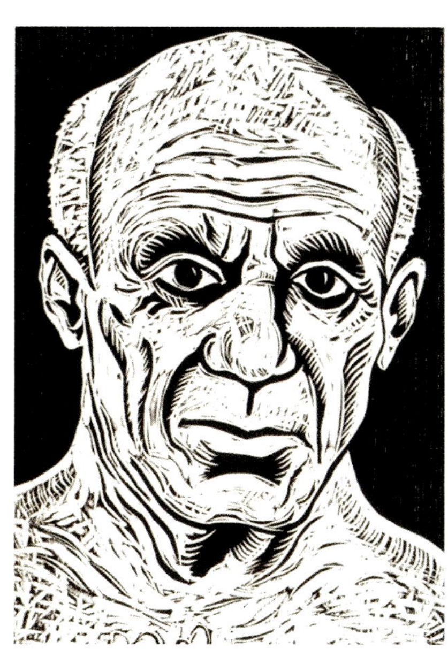
Picasso

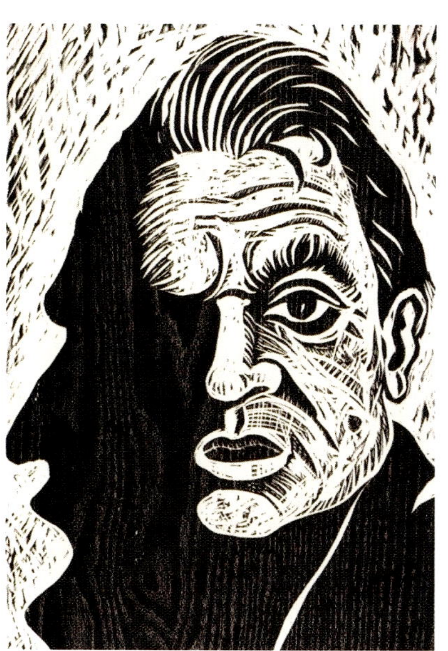
Bacon

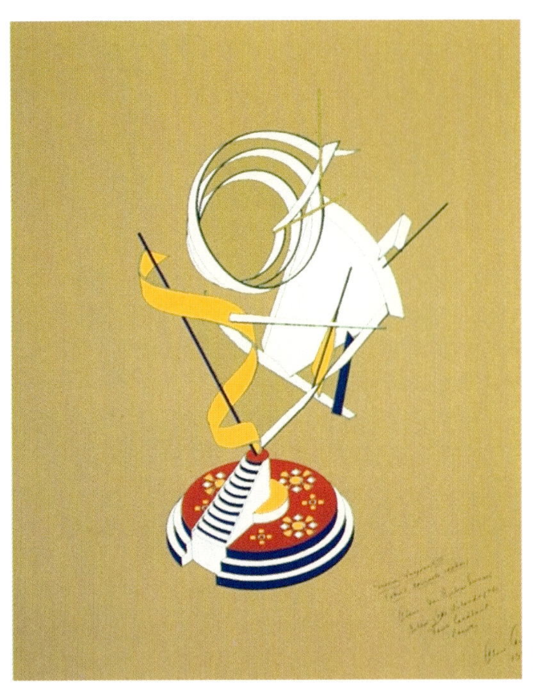

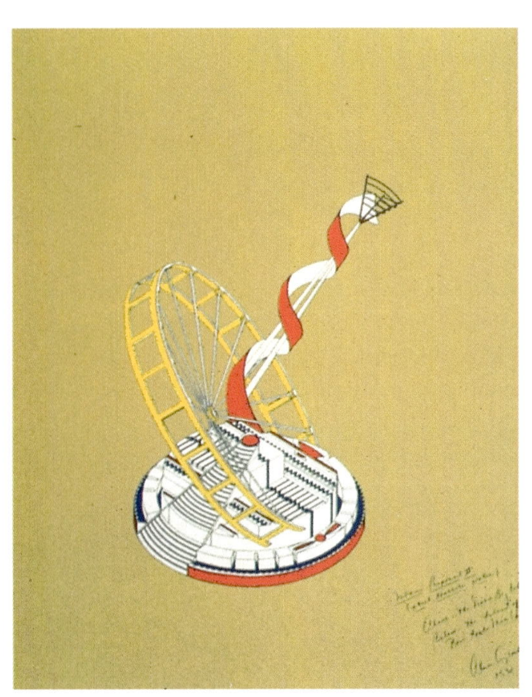

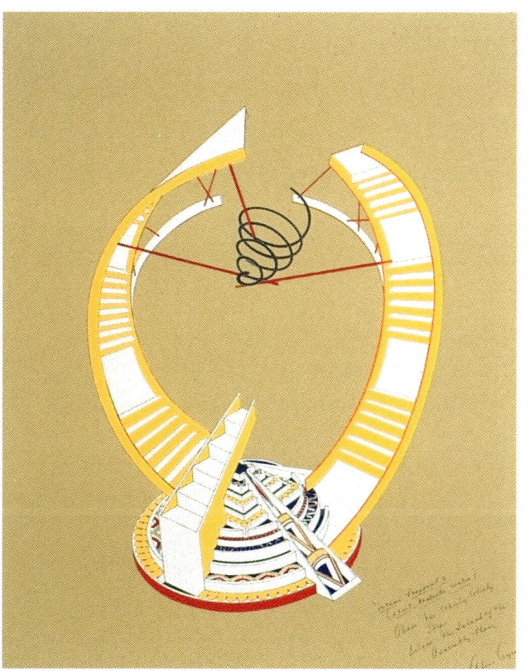

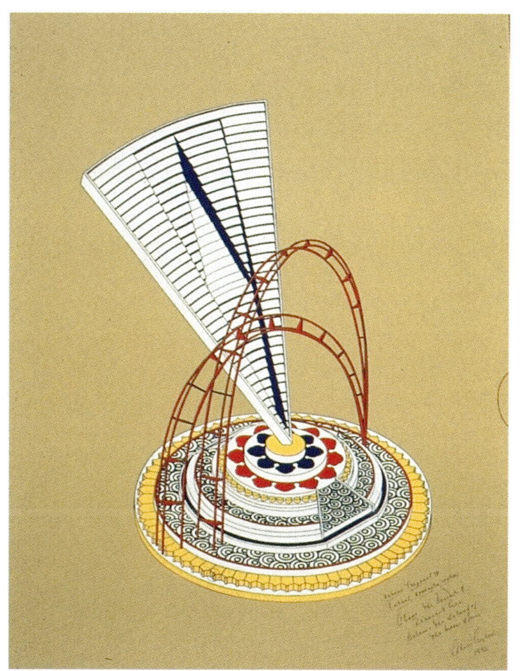

ALICE AYCOCK (American, b. 1946)
Miami Proposal I, II, III, IV, 1990
Serigraphs
4 sheets, 29 x 22 (72.5 x 55) each
Tandem Press, Madison, Wisconsin

Best known as a sculptor, Aycock created a series of serigraphs inspired by drawings she made to illustrate proposed projects for the Miami Airport concourse. Aycock gains the feeling of an architectural rendering because of the sharply defined lines and shapes that characterize serigraphs. The images suggest fantastical shapes similar to those in an amusement park.

JOHN BALDESSARI (American, b. 1931)
Cliché: Eskimo (Blue), 1995
Lithograph, serigraph
39 x 39¾ (97.5 x 99.25)
Cirrus Editions, Los Angeles, California

These Eskimos by an influential Conceptual artist belong to a series satirizing ethnic stereotypes. Anonymous faces from found photographs are masked out with symbolic blue dots. The artist's own painterly touch personalizes the image.

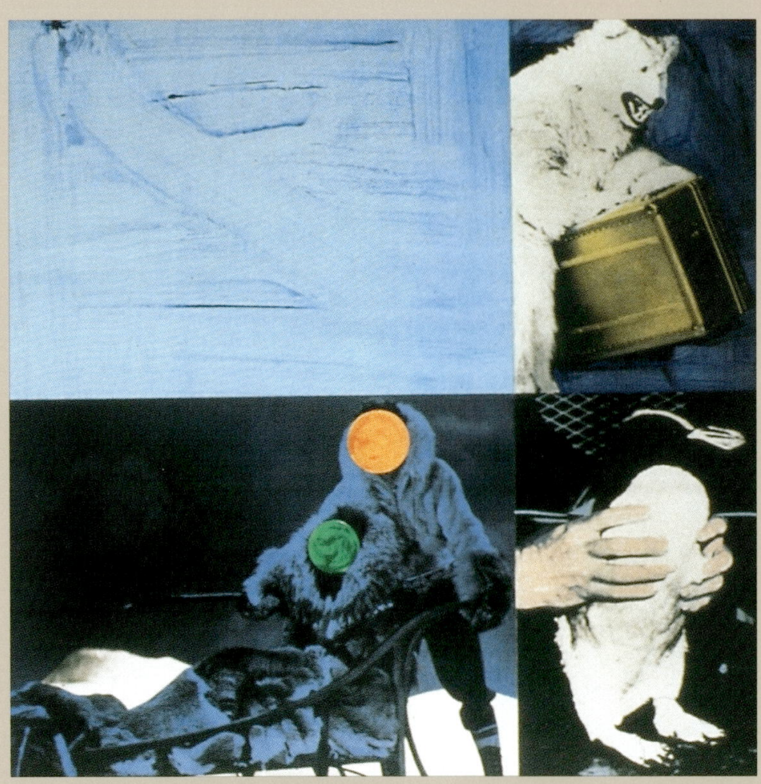

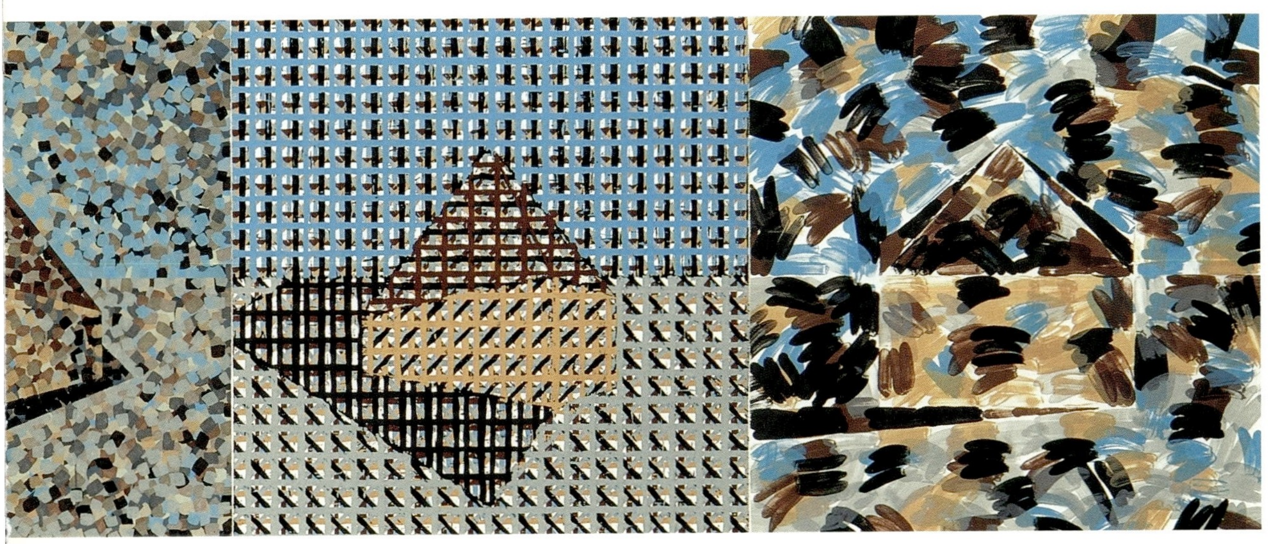

JENNIFER BARTLETT (American, b. 1941)
Graceland Mansion, 1978
Drypoint, aquatint, serigraph, woodcut, lithograph
5 sheets, 24 x 120 (60 x 300) overall
Multiples Inc., New York, New York

Translating past and present art forms and ideas into her own post-modern idiom, Bartlett repeats the simplified shape of Elvis Presley's mansion as seen at different times of day (like Monet's famous haystack paintings) and from various angles. Each of five segments demonstrates a different printing technique and style, from the impersonal grid format of the serigraph to the emotional brushstrokes of the aquatint.

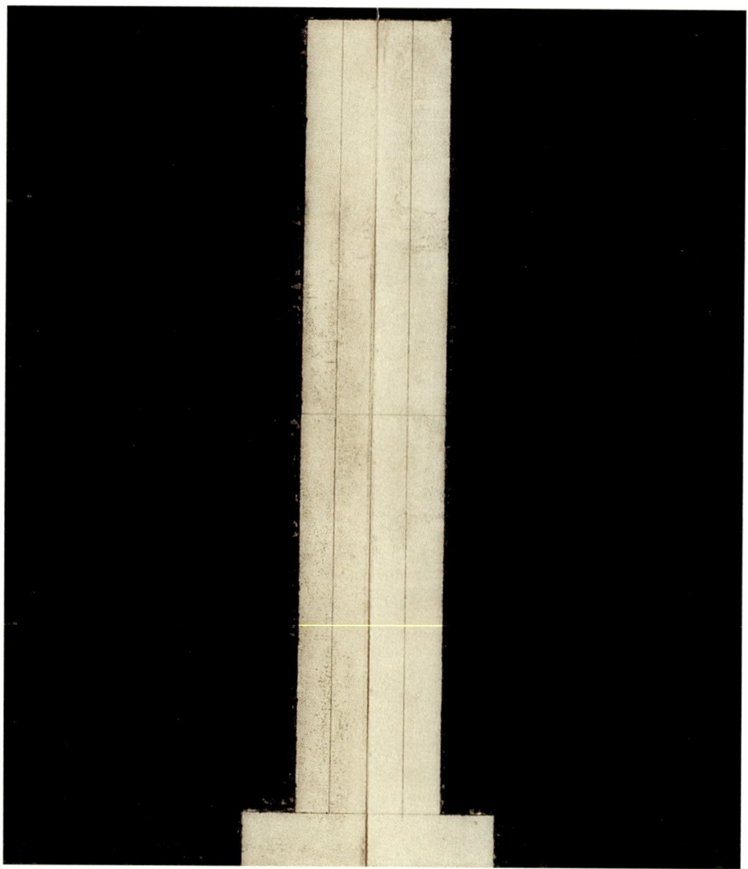

STEVEN BEYER (American, b. 1951)
Four Member Family System, 1979
Drypoint
Diptych, 48 x 42 (120 x 105) overall
Steve Andersen
Vermillion Editions Ltd., Minneapolis, Minnesota

Beyer constructs his compositions using basic geometric shapes to create stern architectonic forms. The very strong white column stands against a black background. This manner of conceiving a two-dimensional print is closely related to the way in which Beyer constructs his sculpture.

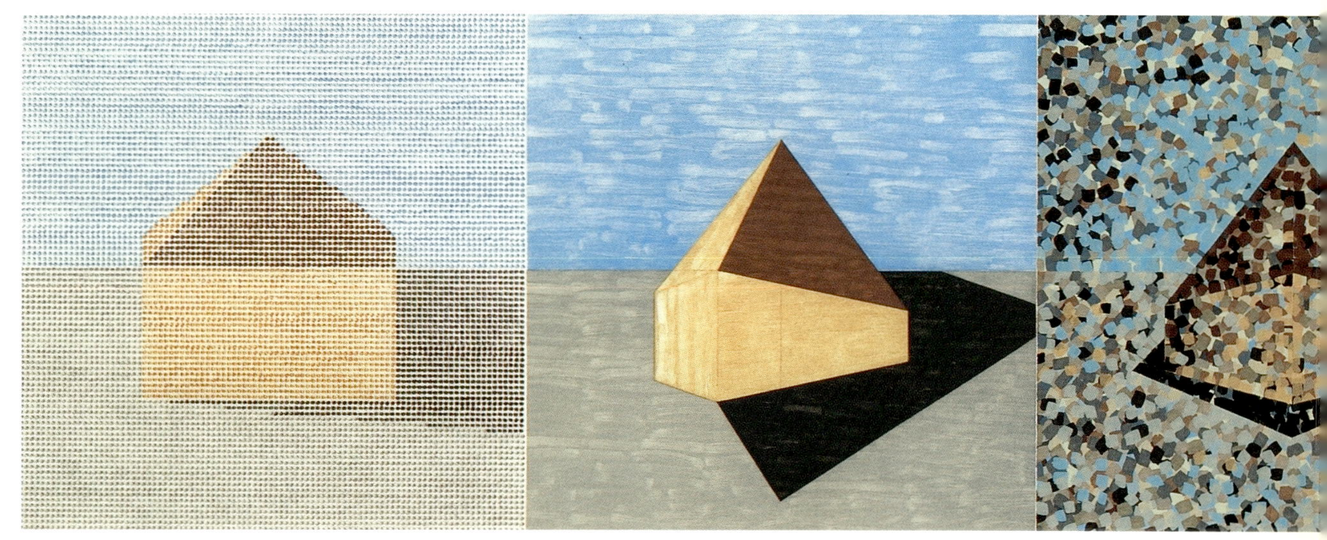

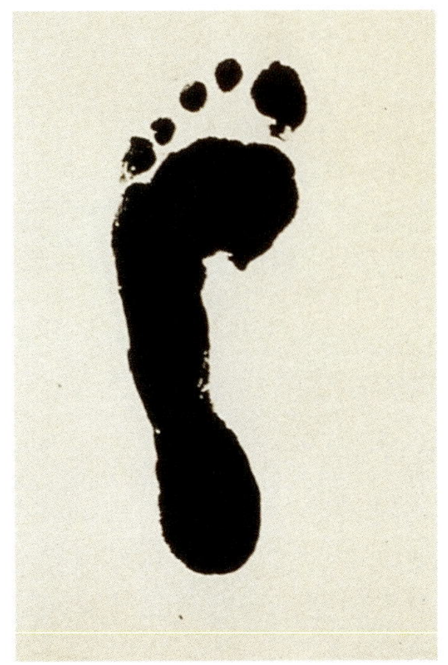
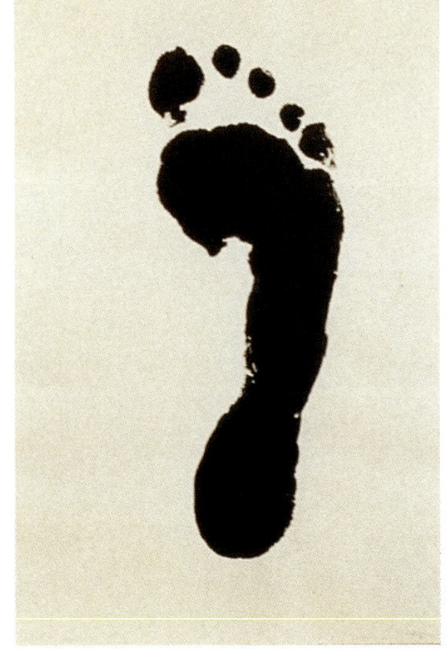

24 JONATHAN BOROFSKY (American, b. 1942)
Foot Print (Left, Right), 1986
Serigraph, with 3-D ink
Diptych, 69 x 47 (172.5 x 117.5) each
Gemini G.E.L., Los Angeles. California

Borofsky's large-scale works projected from small drawings connect concepts of the personal and global. Nothing is more uniquely individual than a foot or fingerprint, nor more anonymous. By enlarging the prints' scale and isolating them on a wall, Borofsky suggests both a newborn's first identifying marks and some archetypal giant's tracks.

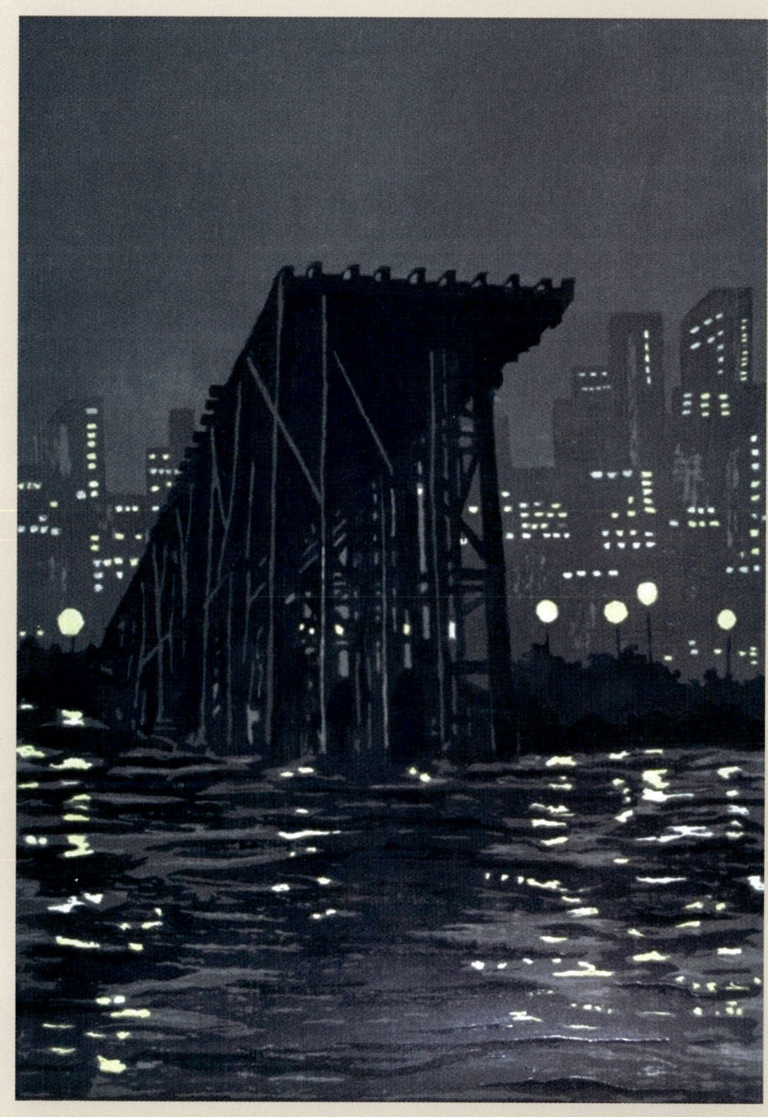

RICHARD BOSMAN (American, b. 1944)
The Edge, 1992
Woodcut
42 x 30½ (105 x 76.25)
Experimental Workshop, San Francisco, California

Interested in the interplay of "high" and "pop" culture, Bosman employs the style of a Japanese woodblock print (originally a popular art form), to what (according to the title) might be the pulp media scene of a waterfront crime. Looming over deceptively calm waters, a surreal pier in Japanese perspective implies some sinister disappearance over "the edge."

LOUISE BOURGEOIS (American, b. in France, 1911)
Storm at Saint Honoré from the portfolio ***Les Artistes pour Médecins du Monde,*** 1994
Engraving, drypoint
21 x 32½ (52.5 x 81.5)
Éditions De La Tempête, Paris, France

Widely known for her sculpture, Bourgeois' work is considered to be among the most innovative and influential in the American art world. Her work as a printmaker remained largely unknown for most of her long career. Bourgeois uses printmaking to explore, on a more intimate level, many of the same ideas and concerns she focuses on in her sculpture. In this work she is exploring her feelings of helplessness as she visits yet another spa to help relieve her mother's illness.

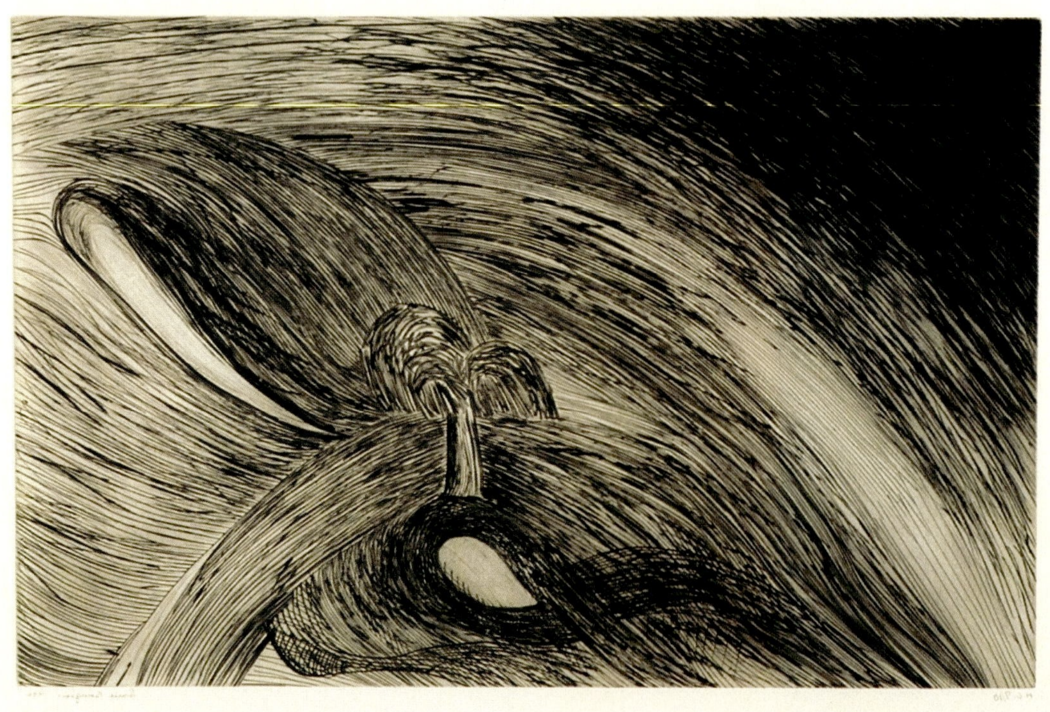

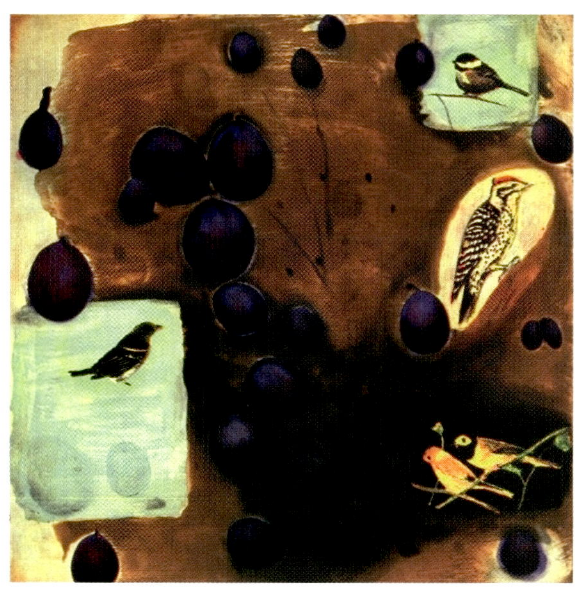

CHRISTOPHER BROWN (American, b. 1951)
The Farmer's Almanac, 1994
Spit-bite etching, soap-ground aquatint, with aquatint, soft-ground etching
35 X 34 (87.5 x 85)
Renee Bott
Crown Point Press, San Francisco, California

Brown, a painter and printmaker, typically isolates and repeats common objects, such as the birds and fruit in this print; he has been drawing birds since he was a child. Talking about the objects in his work, he recently said, "What's interesting about things at any moment is not simply what you know about them, but what you don't know about them. Part of what any artist is trying to do is to create a situation in a [work] that is revealing and mysterious at the same time."

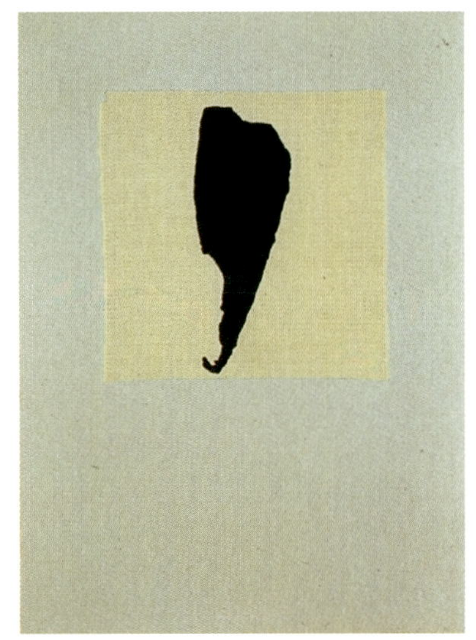
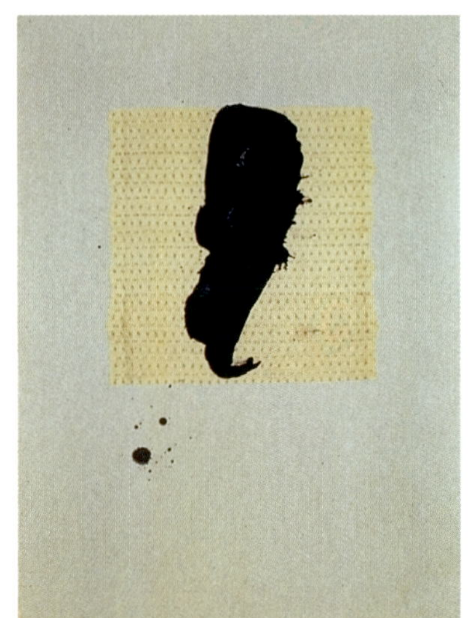
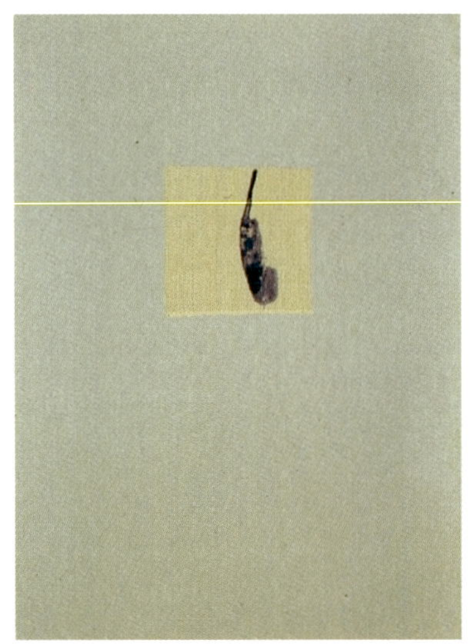
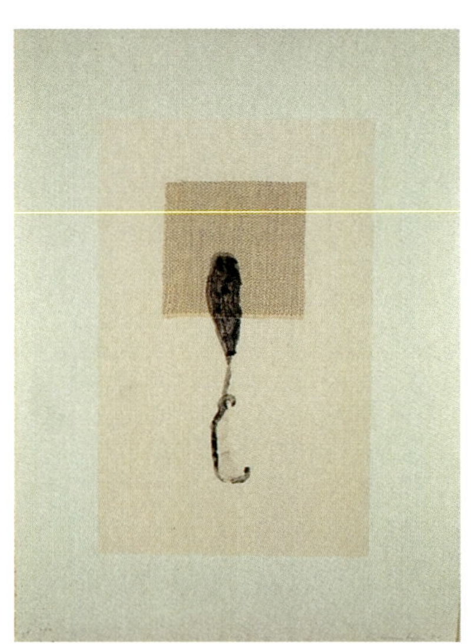

28

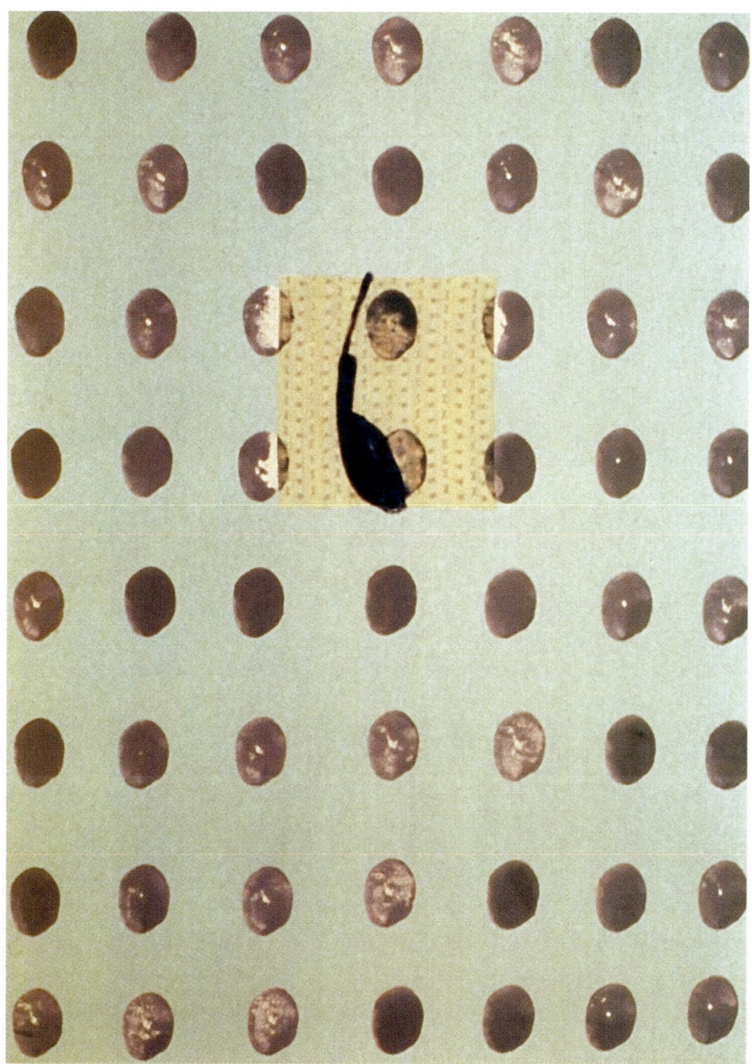

JAMES BROWN (American, b. 1951)
Salt Suite (Violet), 1991
4 Lithographs, 1 monoprint, with chine collé
5 sheets, 31 x 22½ (77.5 x 56.25) each
J. Miller, M. Sanchez, A. Yarme, J. DiJoseph
Derrière l'Étoile Studios, New York, New York

Made to be viewed in sequence, this series of four lithographs and one monoprint was printed on antique linen and paper. Salt here refers to the basic essence of the earth, what is left when all else is distilled. "Like acid eating into an etching plate, salt leaves its indelible mark within whatever it touches. It alters the identity of a thing while infiltrating its form."

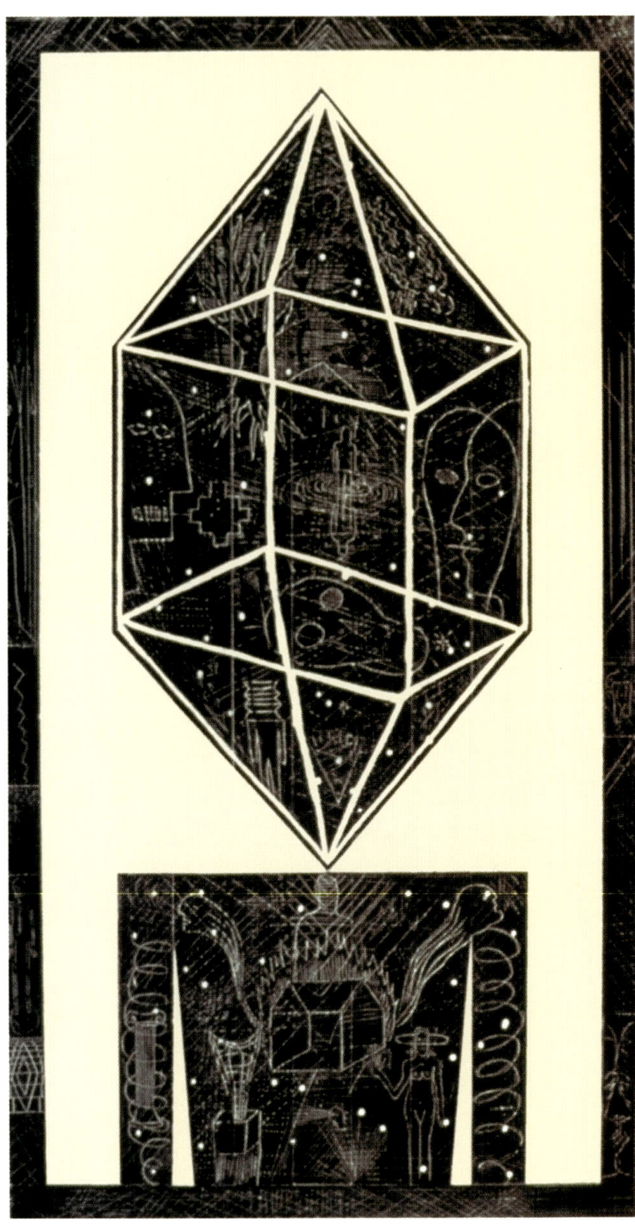

JOHN BUCK (American, b. 1946)
Tropic of Cancer, 1984
Woodcut
60 x 34 (150 x 85 cm)
Jack Lemon, Mark Genrich, Barbara Spies
Landfall Press, Chicago, Illinois

A woodcut print is a natural progression for Buck, who is also a wood sculptor. By juxtaposing various symbols, he presents ideas about nature and environment, politics and domestic life.

JOHN CAGE (American, 1912-1992)
HV2, 1992
Etching
11½ x 14½ (28.75 x 36.25)
Pamela Paulson
Crown Point Press, San Francisco, California

John Cage, widely known as a composer of avant-garde music, was also an accomplished writer and visual artist. The title of this work, *HV2,* refers to the invisible underlying grid of the horizontal and vertical. The blocky but soft forms seem to suggest buildings, fields of growing things or the sea seen from the sky.

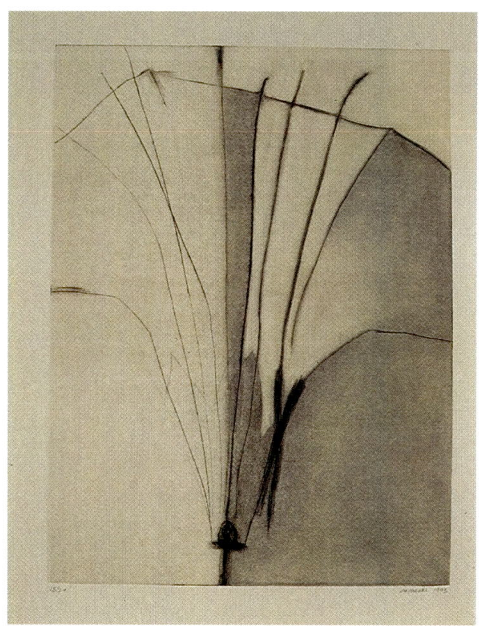

SUZANNE CAPORAEL (American, b. 1949)
Morning Glory, from the suite ***Dissection,*** 1993
Drypoint, etching
31½ x 25 (78.75 x 62.5)
Andrew Rubin
Tandem Press, Madison, Wisconsin

Caporael brought inspiration from her garden to this etching, based on a flower she grew at her ranch. The subtle brown tones of the etching create a soothing but strong image, and the flower becomes a beautiful, abstracted shape.

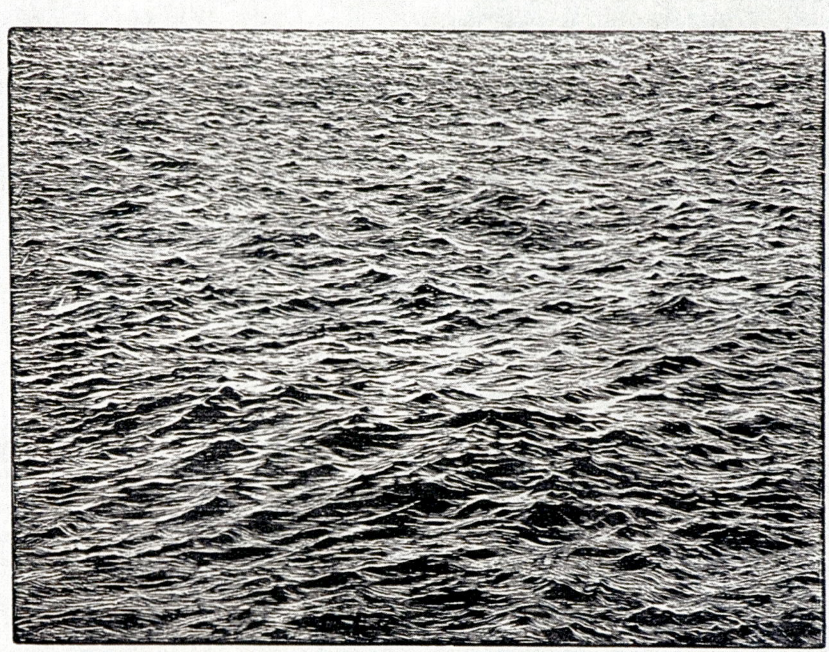

VIJA CELMINS (American, b. in Latvia, 1939)
Untitled, 1990
Woodcut
19½ x 15½ (49.5 x 39.4)
Greenfell Press, Derrière l'Étoile Studios, New York, New York

Based on photographs she took of the ocean, the artist does not include any visual markers, such as a horizon line or the place where she is standing. This gives the composition a sense of infinite space. Celmins does not intend any deep emotional reading into her subject matter: "I like looking and describing, using images to explore the process of making."

LOUISA CHASE (American, b. in Panama City, Panama 1951)
Icarus, 1991
Lithograph, with added relief elements
29½ x 40 (72.75 x 100)
Andrew Rubin
Tandem Press, Madison, Wisconsin

Chase chooses a classical Greek myth as a subject. The formalized blue block figure recalls Icarus' frantic attempt to regain his ability to fly. The static relief element of the figure contrasts with the painterly feel of the background elements.

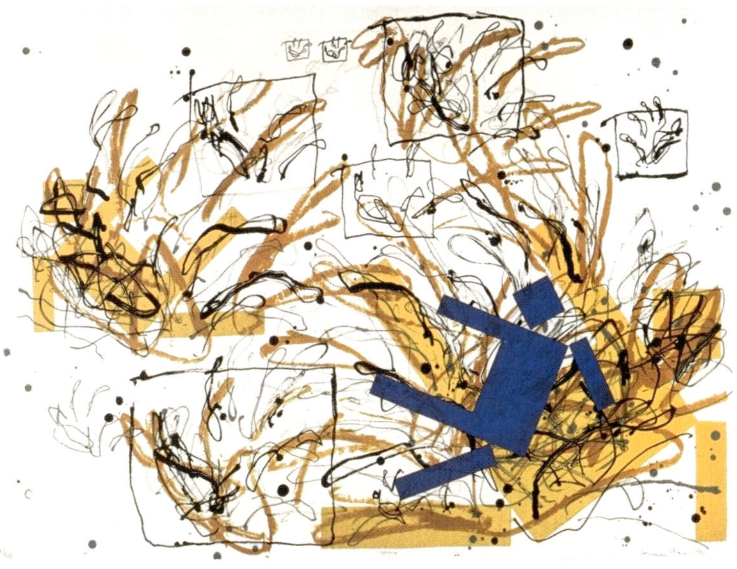

CHRISTO (Bulgarian, b. 1935)
Wrapped Book "Modern Art", 1978
Wrapped by artist in polyethylene and twine
14 x 10 (35 x 25)
Abrams Editions, New York, New York

Christo's graphic works are essentially studies for proposed three-dimensional projects. Shocking and ambitious in scale, these "installations" are often public media events that require considerable logistical coordination and many hands to accomplish. Whether he plans to wrap an island, a building, monument or object, Christo's work results in a dramatic transformation of the site. He produced *Wrapped Modern Art Book,* which is wrapped in transparent polyethylene with twine and cord, to help fund the publication of the book *Christo: Running Fence.*

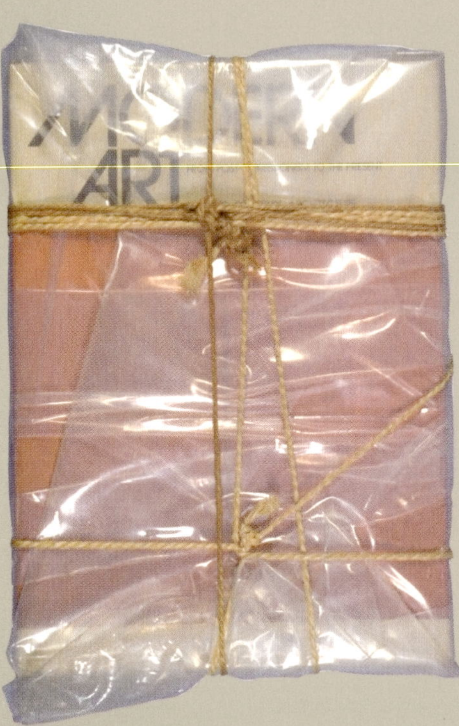

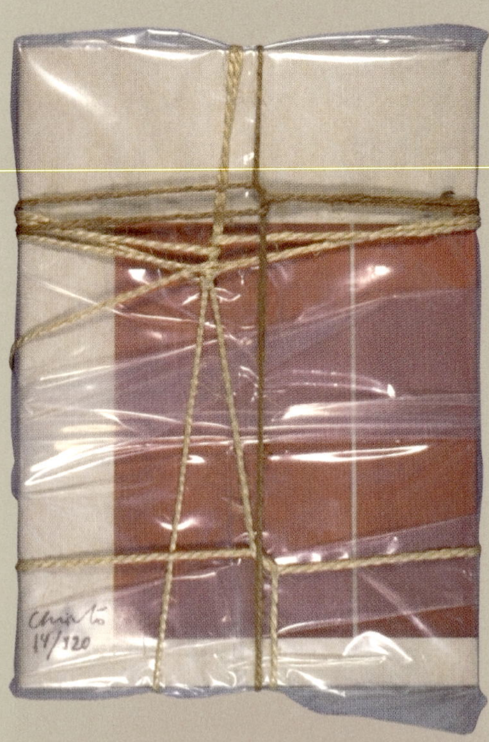

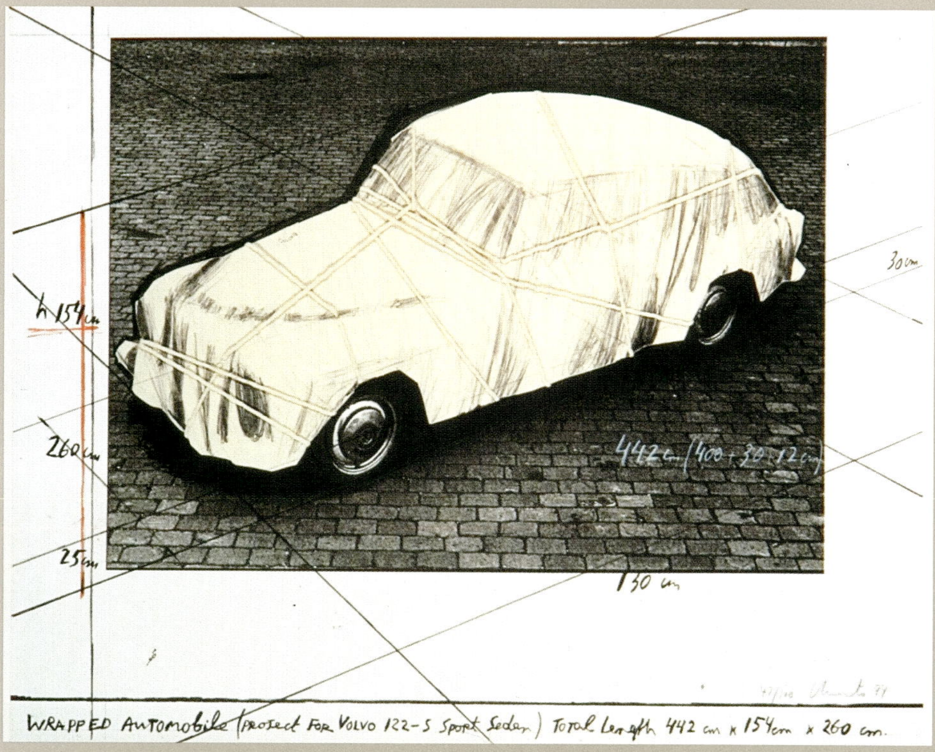

CHRISTO (Bulgarian, b. 1935)
Wrapped Automobile, Project for Volvo 122 S Sport Sedan, 1984
Lithograph, with collage
22 x 28 (55 x 70)
Jack Lemon, Michael Riley
The artist and Editions Schellmann, Munich, Germany, and New York, New York

While many of his proposals are not literally executed, the impact of Christo's concepts is effectively documented in his prints. In *Wrapped Automobile,* he retains a strong three-dimensional element by superimposing fabric and twine on the surface of the print.

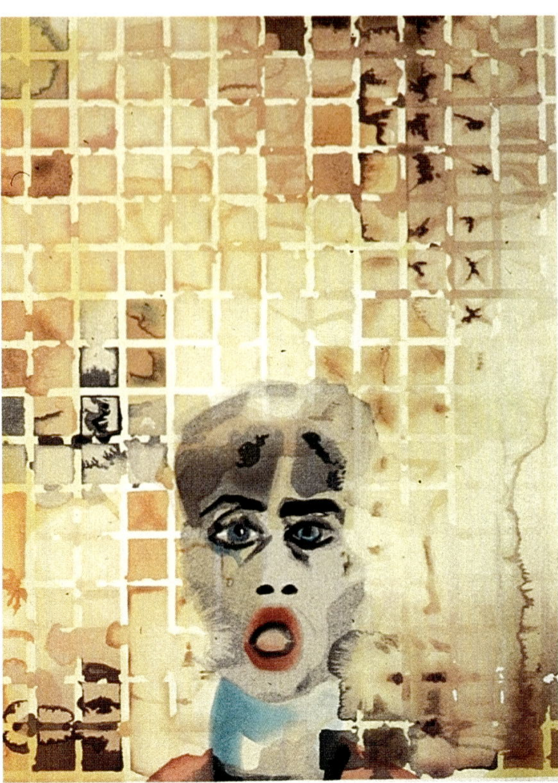

FRANCESCO CLEMENTE (Italian, b. 1952)
Self-Portrait, 1990
Woodcut
30 x 34 (75 x 85)
Tadashi Toda
Carved by Shunzo Matsuda
Crown Point Press, San Francisco, California

Clemente's art is notable for its rich diversity; he easily alternates between mediums and his work reveals a wide range of approaches and influences. Although Clemente has had virtually no formal art training, his numerous artistic endeavors and his acute understanding of mythology, religion and the occult have resulted in a remarkably vast *oeuvre* for a relatively young artist. In his *Self-Portrait,* Clemente experiments with wood blocks to create an intimate portrait of himself that shows an interesting use of color and composition.

FRANCESCO CLEMENTE (Italian, b. 1952)
Seed, 1991
Spit-bite etching and aquatint using paper stencils
45 x 53 (112.5 x 132.5)
Brian Shure
Crown Point Press, San Francisco, California

In *Seed,* the artist cut around individual letters of various sizes to create stencils that were soaked in acid and then placed on the copper plate. The letters do not form words, but rather suggest weathered stone engravings.

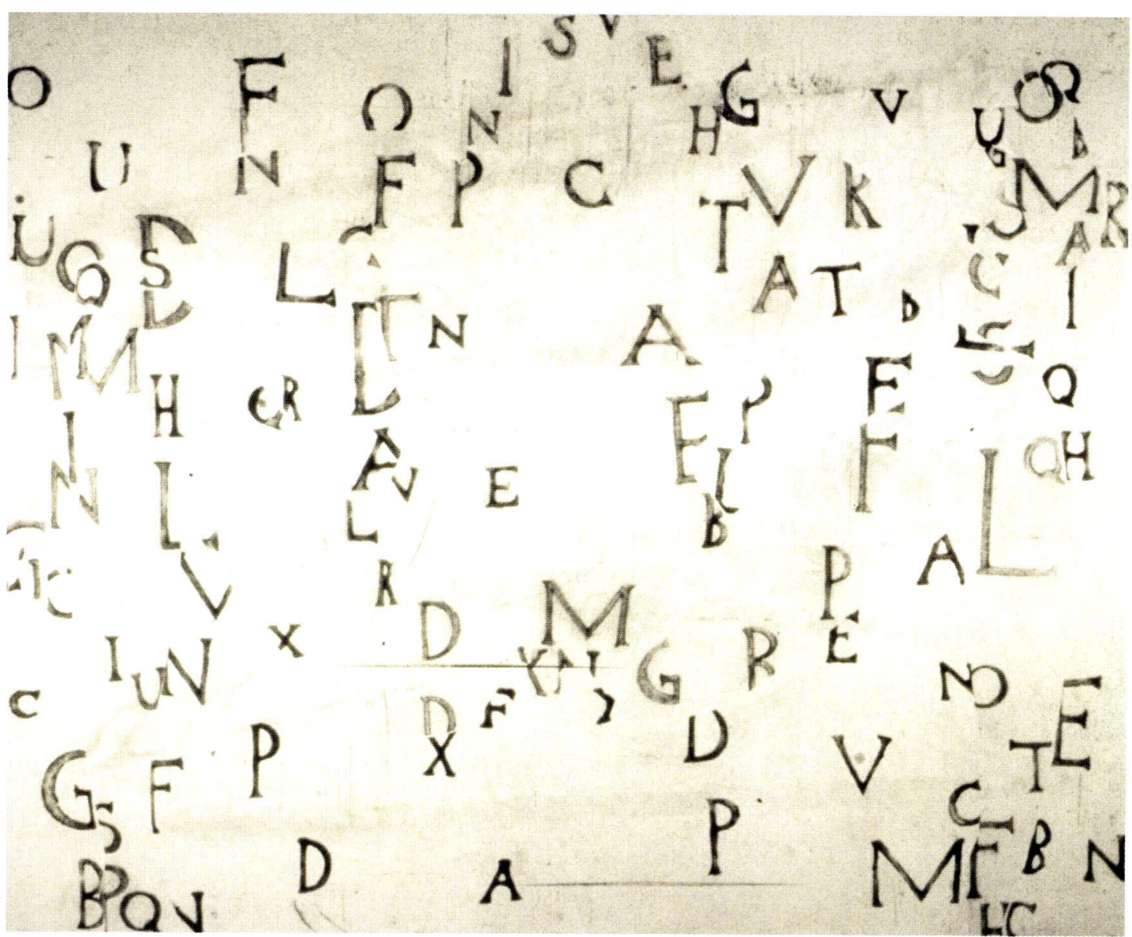

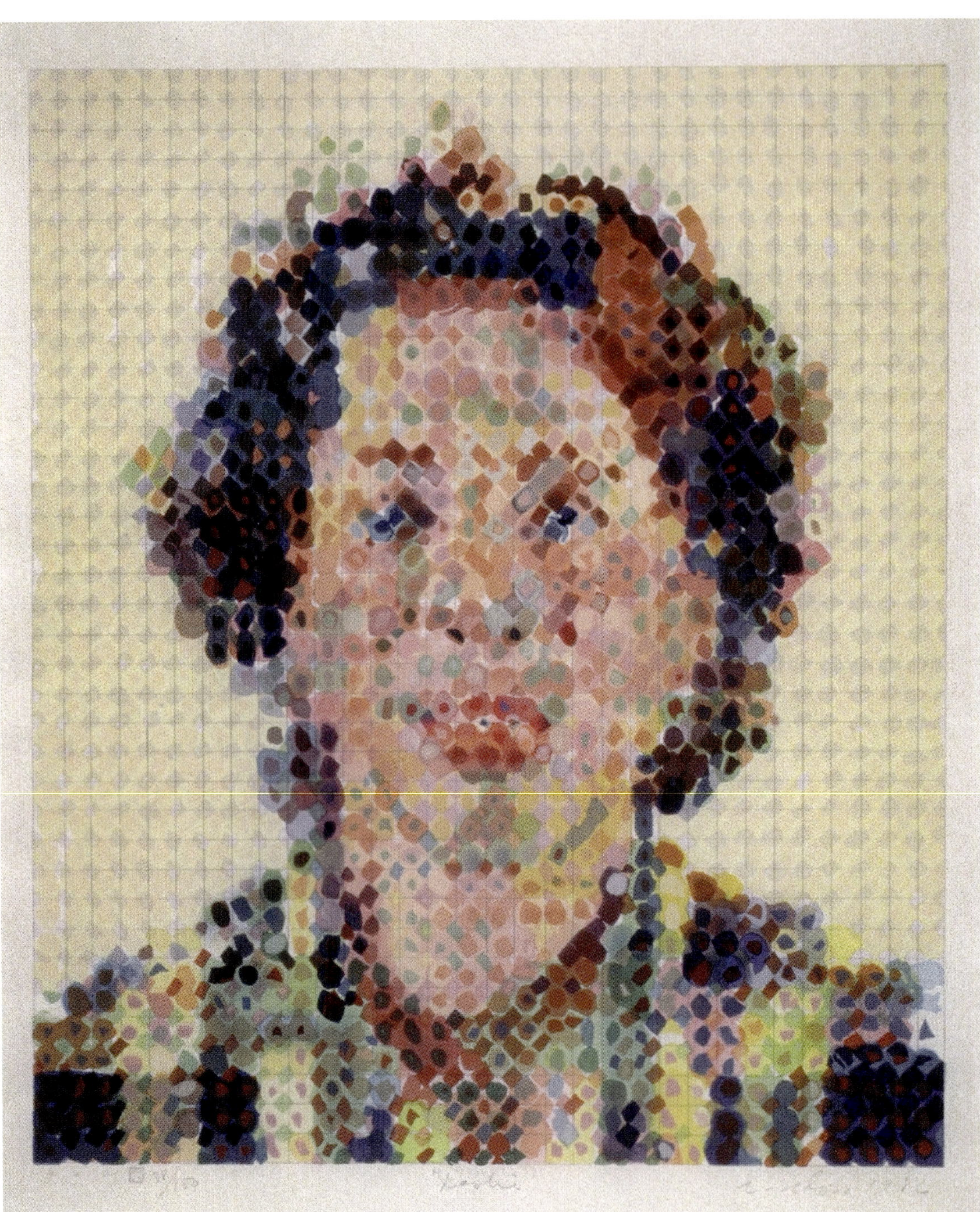

CHUCK CLOSE (American, b. 1940)
Leslie, 1986
Woodcut
30 x 25 (75 x 62.5)
Tadashi Toda
Carved by Shunzo Matsuda
Crown Point Press, San Francisco, California

Close is revered as one of the major contemporary artists today. He has spent his career doing portraits of family and friends. To make this woodcut print of his wife, he traveled to Japan to work with master printer Tadashi Toda. This print expands Close's grid format to the use of a diamond shape that worked better for a woodcut. Using a very thin water-based ink, each block is printed with hand pressure.

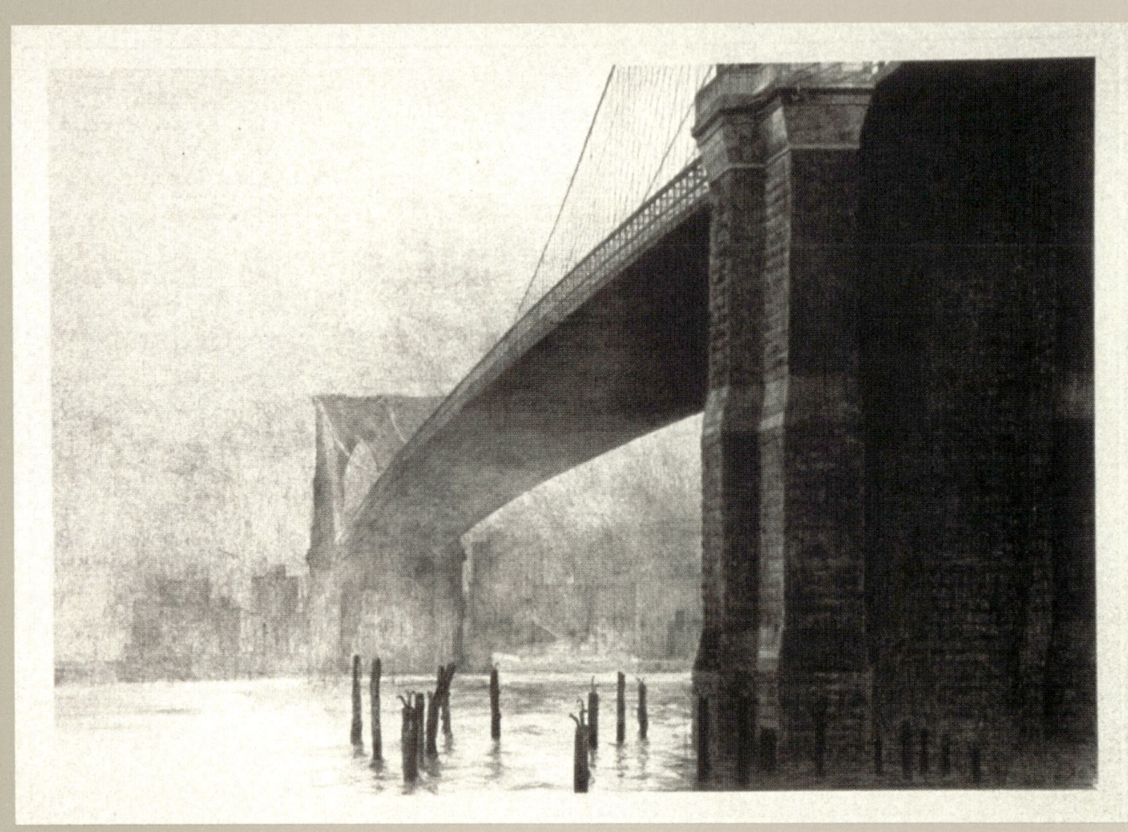

ARTHUR COHEN (American, b. 1945)
Brooklyn Bridge, 1984
Lithograph
22 x 30 (55 x 75)
Derrière l'Étoile Studios, New York, New York

Cohen is well known for his subtle and poetic depictions of water and atmosphere, and has a special fondness for the Brooklyn Bridge. Here the delicate curve of the long span is softened by the fog rising on the far side of the East River, lowering a serene hush over teeming Gotham.

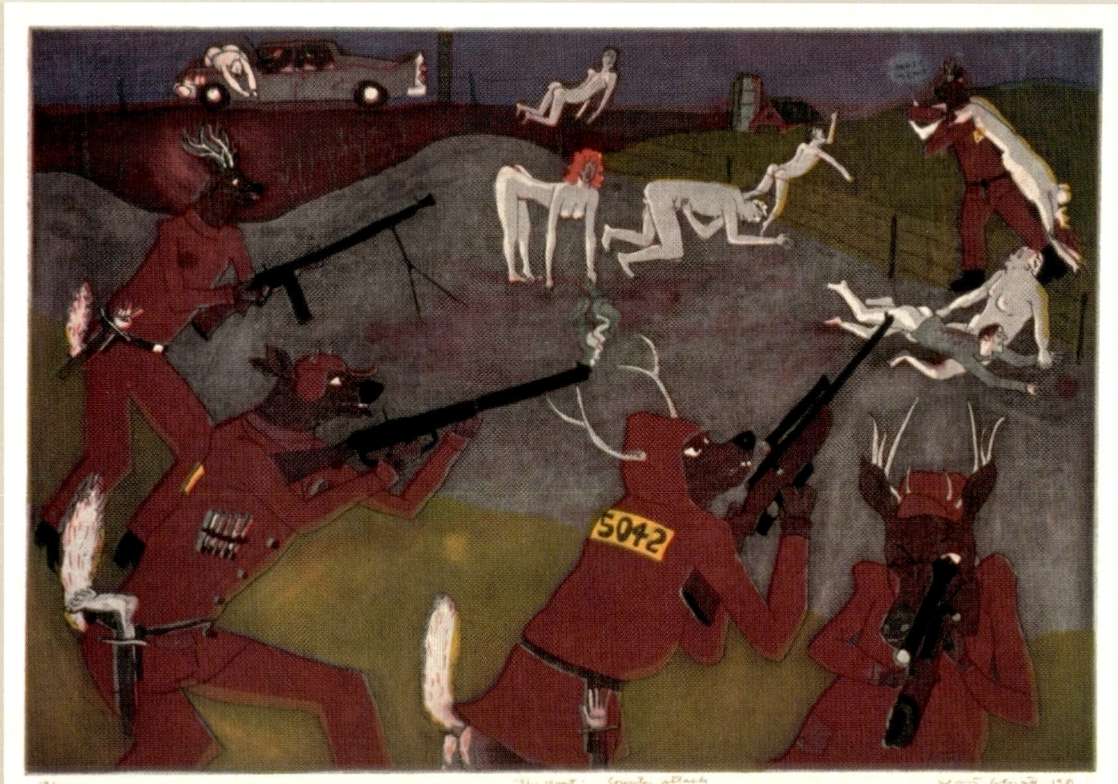

WARRINGTON COLESCOTT (American, b. 1921)
The Hunt: Counterattack, 1981
Etching
22½ x 29¾ (56 x 74.25)
Warrington Colescott, Hollandale, Wisconsin

Regarded as one of America's finest printmakers and an innovator in the development of color etching techniques, Colescott is Professor Emeritus at the University of Wisconsin – Madison. He is a satirist, poking fun at social and political institutions, historical events and cultural icons. His wit is evident in this turnabout-is-fair-play perspective.

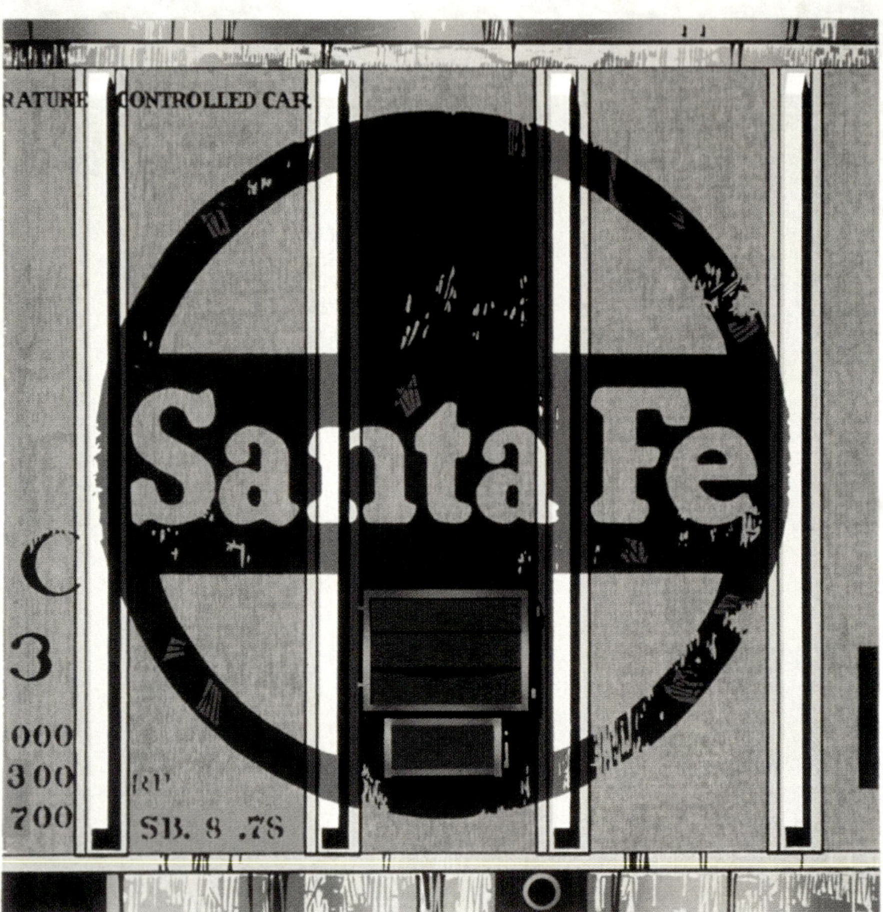

ROBERT COTTINGHAM (American, b. 1935)
Sante Fe, 1988
Woodcut
24 x 28 (60 x 70)
Karl Hecksher
Signet Arts, St. Louis, Missouri

Although Cottingham's style is deliberately photographic, the camera is just a starting point for his prints and paintings. He often manipulates the appearance of common signs, lettering and objects of the workaday environment and likes to paint things that are about to disappear. In *Santa Fe*, he celebrates the classic logos emblazoned on weathered boxcars.

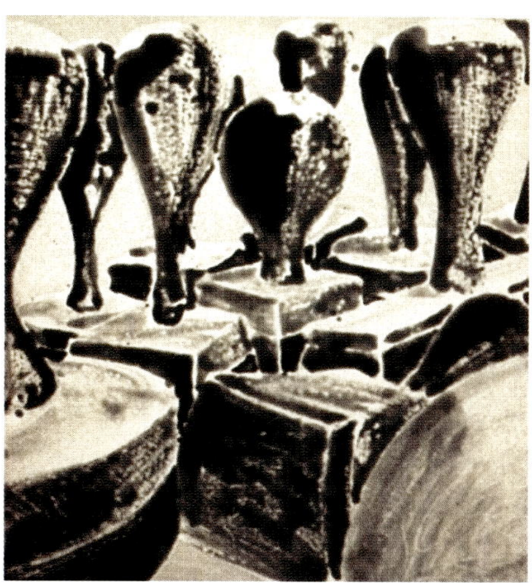

TONY CRAGG (English, b. 1949)
Suburbs I, 1990
Etching, spit-bite etching, aquatint
28 x 26 (70 x 65)
Lawrence Hamlin
Crown Point Press, San Francisco, California

Cragg transforms everyday objects, usually in terms of scale or material. In a body of related prints and sculptures, he creates giant-sized versions of common objects, such as the rubber stamps in this print. By doing so, he removes them from their everyday context, casting them in a new light. They become more abstract, as they lose the grounding of their original identity.

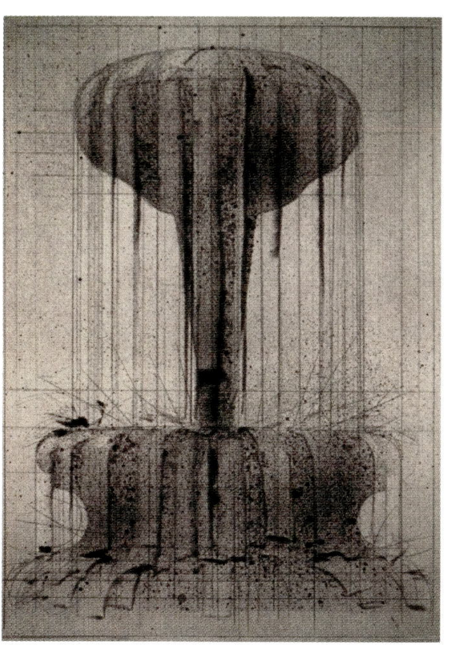

ROBERT CUMMING (American, b. 1943)
Water Above/Water Below, 1989
Monoprint
36 x 28 (90 x 70)
Derrière l'Étoile Studios, New York, New York

Cumming is known for his visual wit and interest in architecture, in this case, his interest in the structure of a fountain. "From piece to piece, there are some in which I'm the product designer, some a speculative architect, others a cosmologist; often the boundaries blur and they're all there together."

GENE DAVIS (American, 1920-1985)
Series 2, 1969
Serigraph, on canvas laminated to board
24 x 30 (60 x 75 cm)
Petersburg Press Ltd., London, England

The Washington Color School painter Gene Davis is best known for overall stripe paintings whose focus on the effects of pure color is enhanced by large scale and standard format. In this print, the identical width of the individual stripes is countered by the interesting variations created by their grouping in bands of different colors.

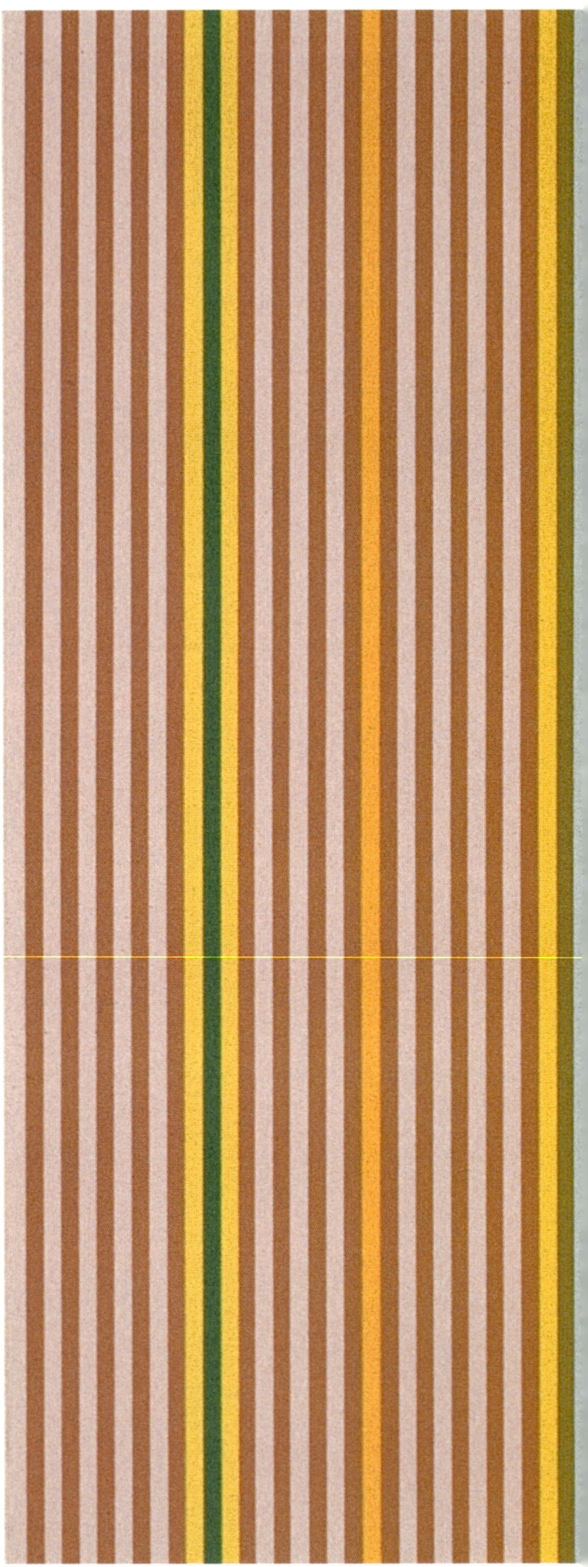

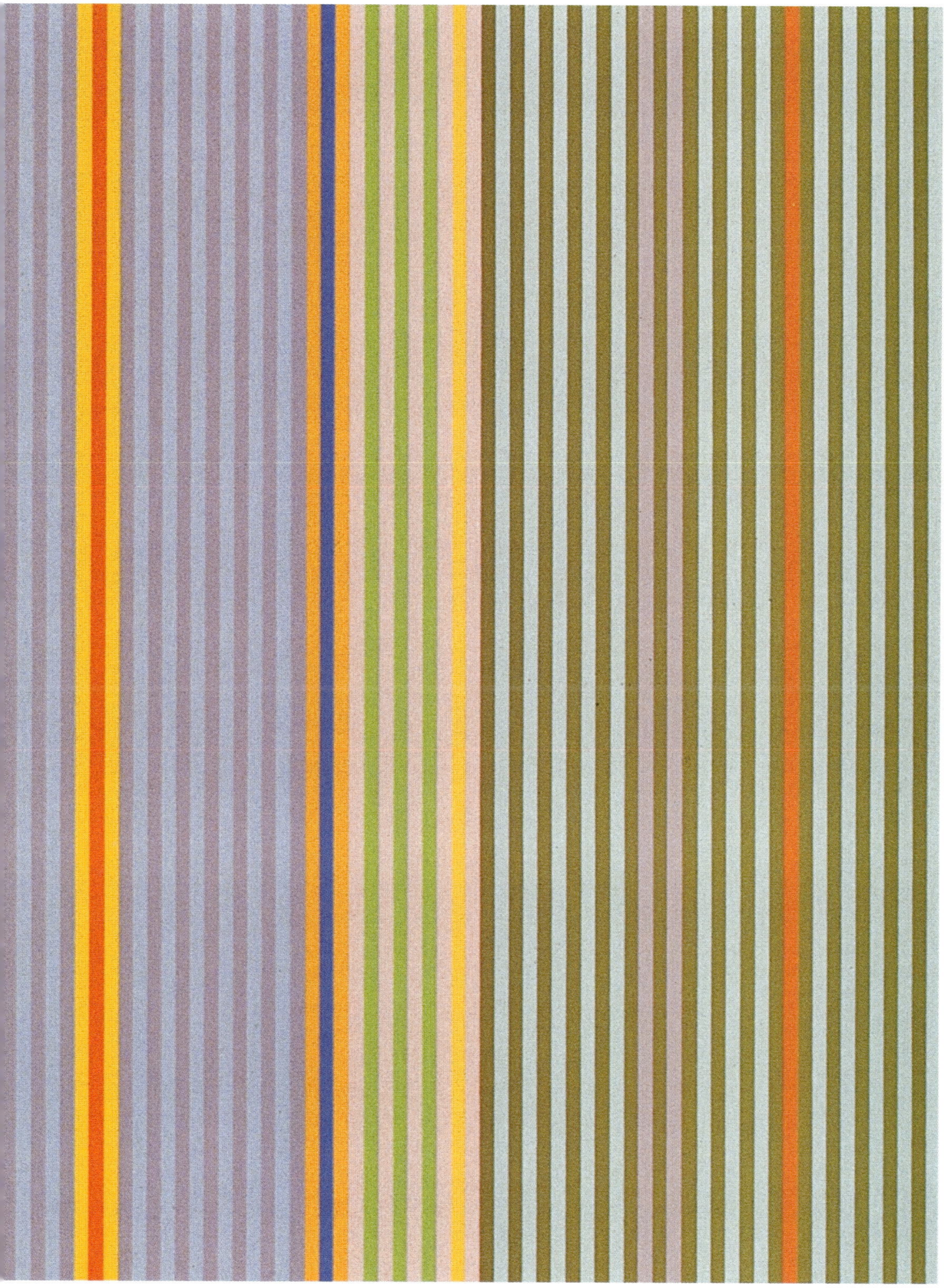

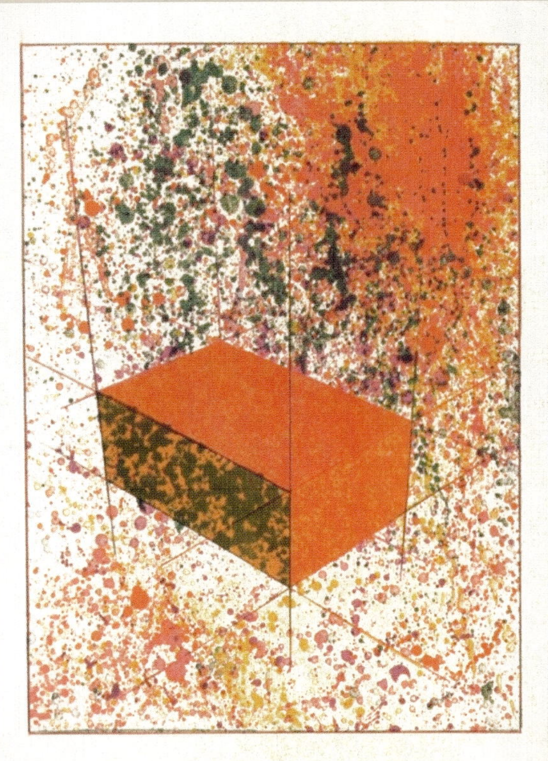

RONALD DAVIS (American, b. 1937)
Brick, 1983
Lithograph
42½ x 32 (106.25 x 155)
Serge Lozingot, Chris Sukimoto, James Reid, Richard Garst, Anthony Zepeda, Alan Holoubek
Gemini G.E.L., Los Angeles, California

Davis studied engineering before turning to art in the late 1950s. By the end of the 1970s, the artist was exploring computer-generated imagery for his art, and he began to investigate the printmaking process as a way to extend his ideas on painting. Many of his works, such as *Brick,* include a geometric form hurtling through a brilliantly colored space. In this work, the intricate textures of the planes of the brick are achieved by using three different densities of mezzotint screen, photographically applied.

ELAINE DE KOONING (American, 1920-1989)
Les Eyzies, 1985
Etching, sugar-lift etching, spit-bite etching, aquatint
30 x 44 (75 x 110)
Peter Pettengill
Crown Point Press, San Francisco, California

Inspired by the prehistoric cave paintings of Les Eyzies, France, this print evokes the irregular surface of the stone wall. Red smears suggest reflected firelight or blood rituals connected with the hunt. The print communicates de Kooning's sense of identification with the first human artists.

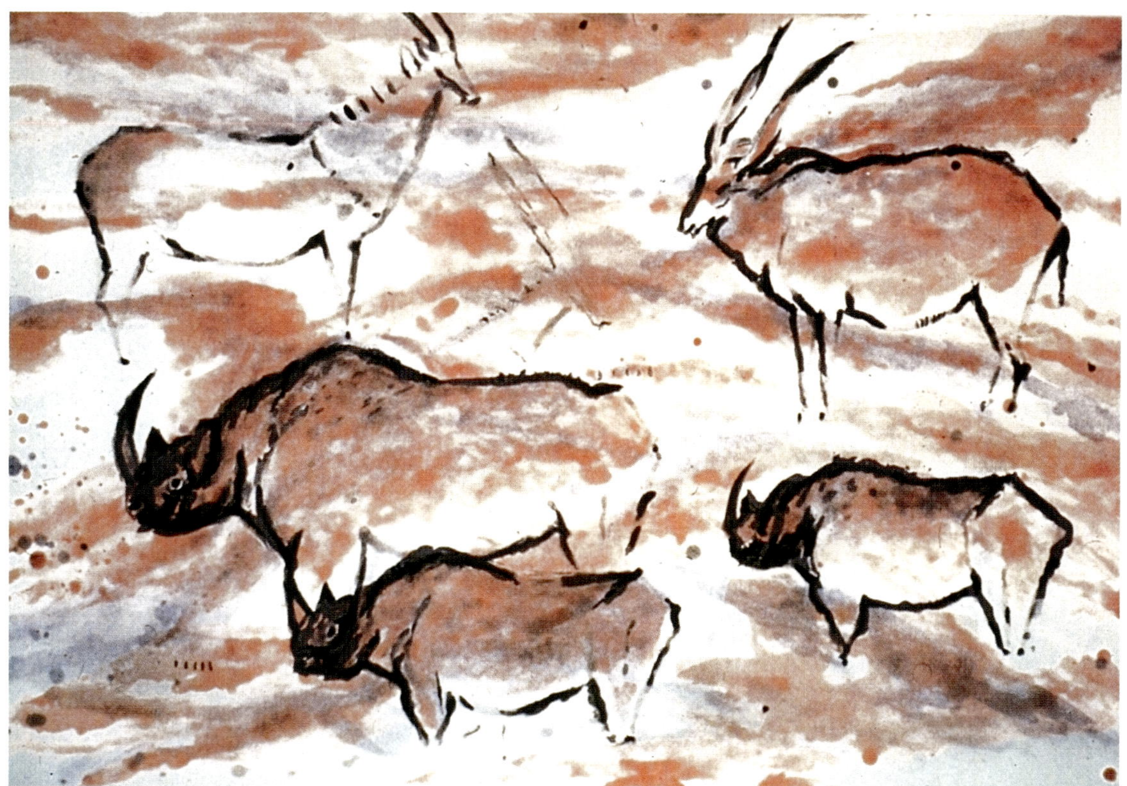

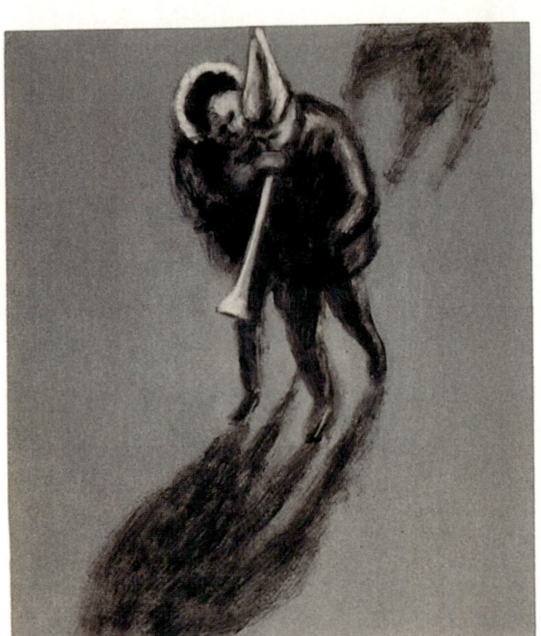

JANE DICKSON (American, b. 1952)
Revelers II, *1989*
Monoprint
27 x 23 (67.5 x 57.5)
Derrière l'Étoile Studios, New York, New York

Dickson, like Yvonne Jacquette, likes to view her subjects from above. Her studio and residence overlook Times Square and is the perfect bird's-eye view for her works. "My work deals with people who want to be entertained and yet are unfulfilled, about the failures of entertainment."

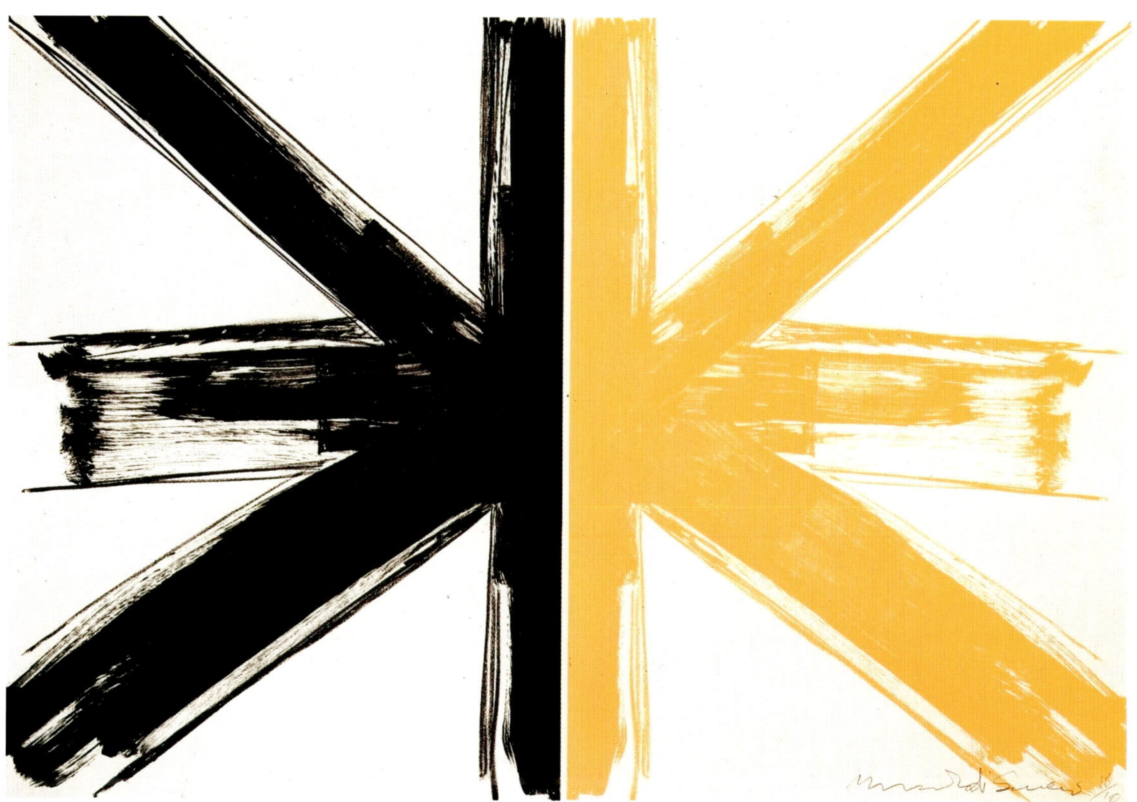

MARK DI SUVERO (American, b. 1933)
Centering, 1976
Lithograph
42½ x 62¼ (108 x 158)
John Hutcheson, Kenneth Tyler, Robert Bigelow
Tyler Graphics Ltd., Mt. Kisco, New York

The radiating, centralized composition of this lithograph relates to di Suvero's Milwaukee lakefront sculpture *The Calling*, whose outflung "arms" parallel the spontaneous gestures of 50s action paintings. The print's rough brushstrokes echo the ruggedness of di Suvero's industrial materials and, like his painted I-beams, combine the qualities of line and plane.

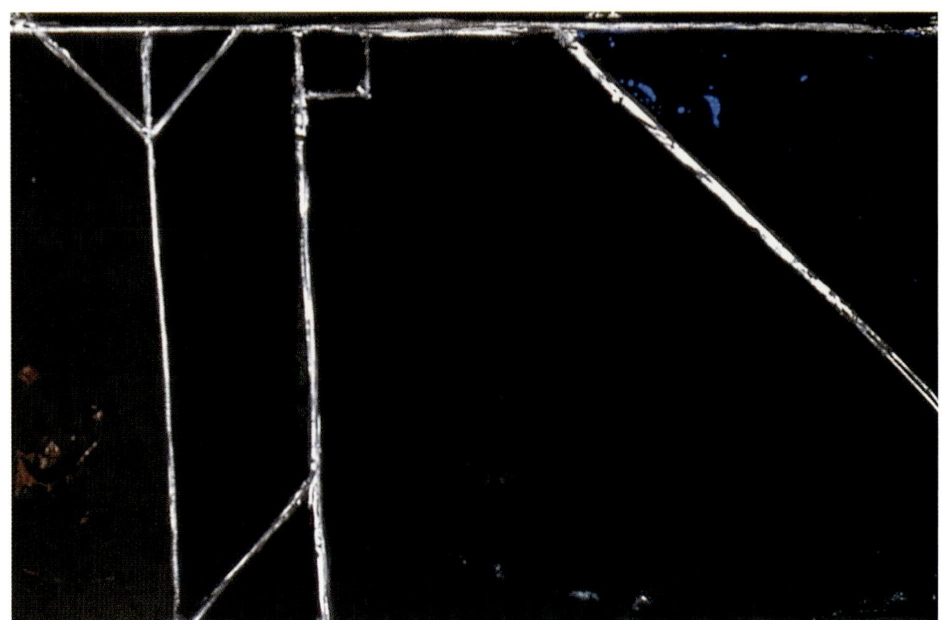

I (Black)

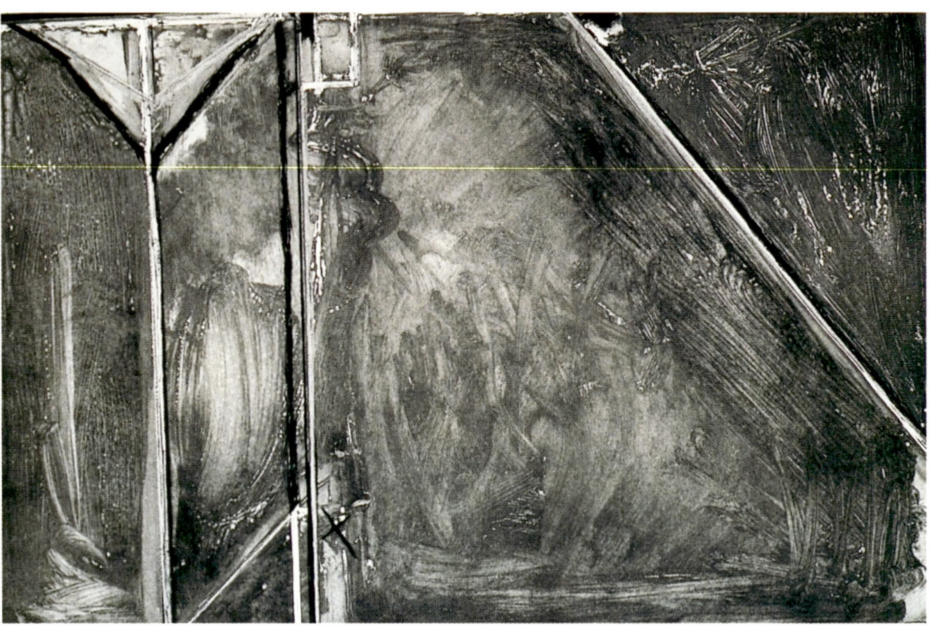

II (Grey)

RICHARD DIEBENKORN (American, 1922-1993)
Folsom St. Variations I (Black), II (Grey), III (Primaries), 1985
Etching, with soap-ground etching, aquatint, drypoint, flat bite
3 sheets, 26 x 40 (65 x 100) each
Marcia Bartholme
Crown Point Press, San Francisco, California

These prints are named after the location of the San Francisco Crown Point Press studio. The etching plates are coated with soap to produce a surface on which every mark – made and erased – by the artist during the process of creation is recorded. The prints combine a sensuous involvement in the creative process with an austerely rectilinear blueprintlike structure. Like the artist's *Ocean Park* series of paintings, they explore the relationship of line and plane as a means of balancing depth and flat space.

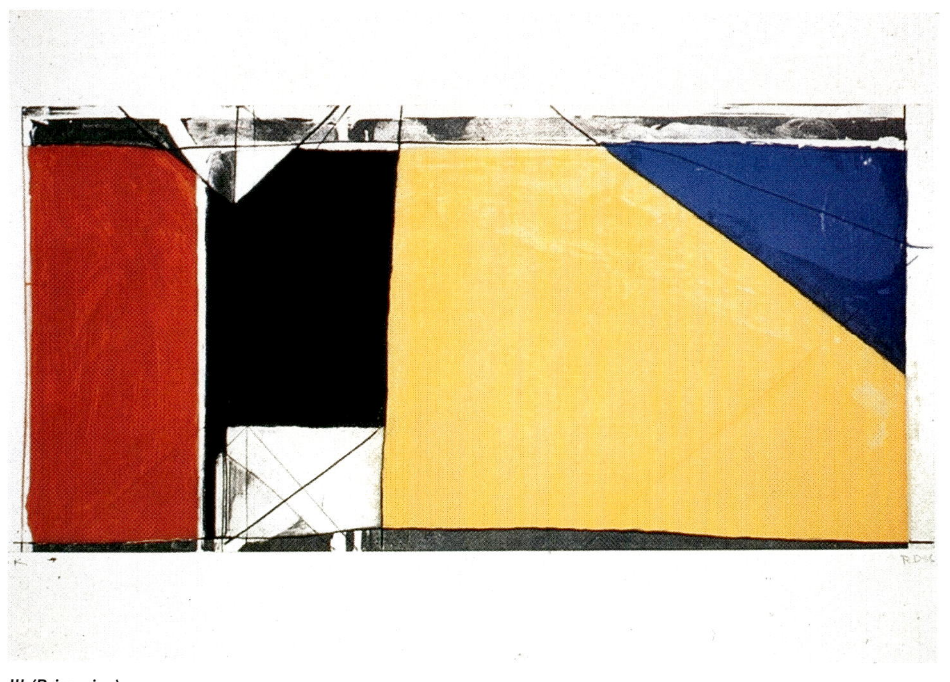

III (Primaries)

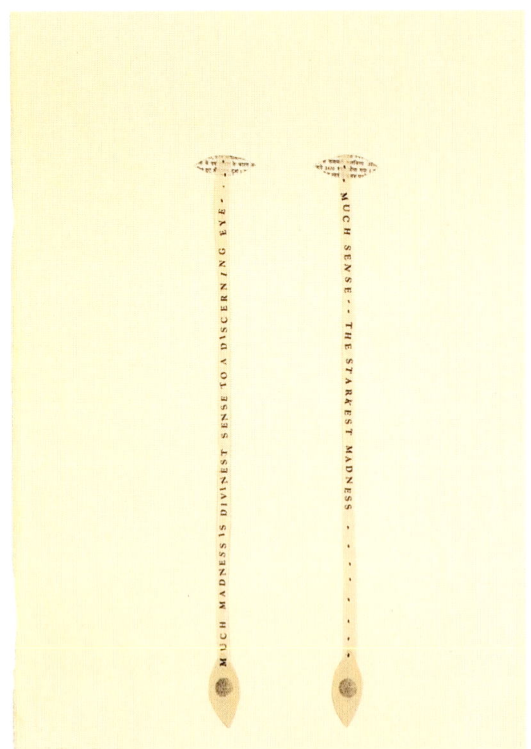

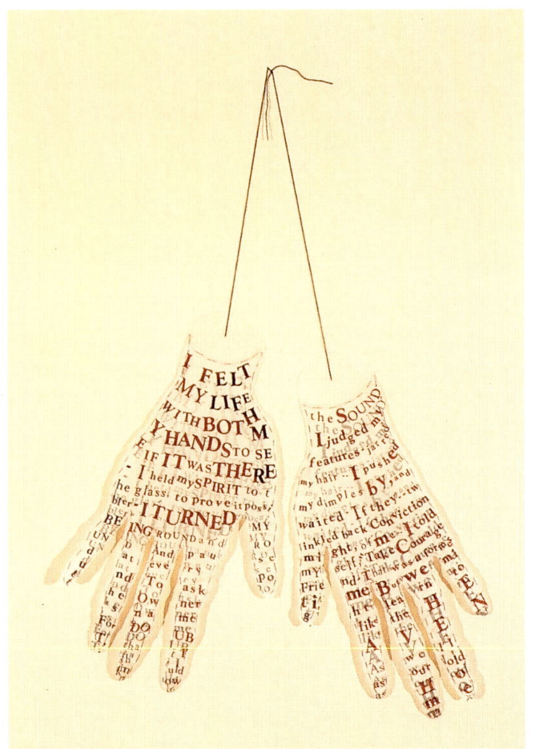

LESLEY DILL (American, b. 1948)
Poem Eyes, from the suite ***The Poetic Body,*** 1992
Lithograph, letterpress, collage
18 x 13 (45 x 32.5)
Judith Solodkin
Letterpress Printer Anne Noonan Elliot
Collage Rebecca Lax
Solo Impression Inc., New York, New York

The Poetic Body is a series of prints inspired by the reclusive 19th-century poet Emily Dickinson. To sculptor Dill, Dickinson's words are a spiritual armor, a protective second skin: "How right to slip inside words, the meaning and shape of some emotion you are feeling, and go out into life." In airy prints using letterpress type in relief, Dill literally embodies Dickinson's poetry as body parts and accessories.

LESLEY DILL (American, b. 1948)
Poem Gloves, from the suite ***The Poetic Body,*** 1992
Lithograph, letterpress, collage
18 x 13 (45 x 32.5)
Judith Solodkin
Letterpress Printer Anne Noonan Elliot
Collage Rebecca Lax
Solo Impression Inc., New York, New York

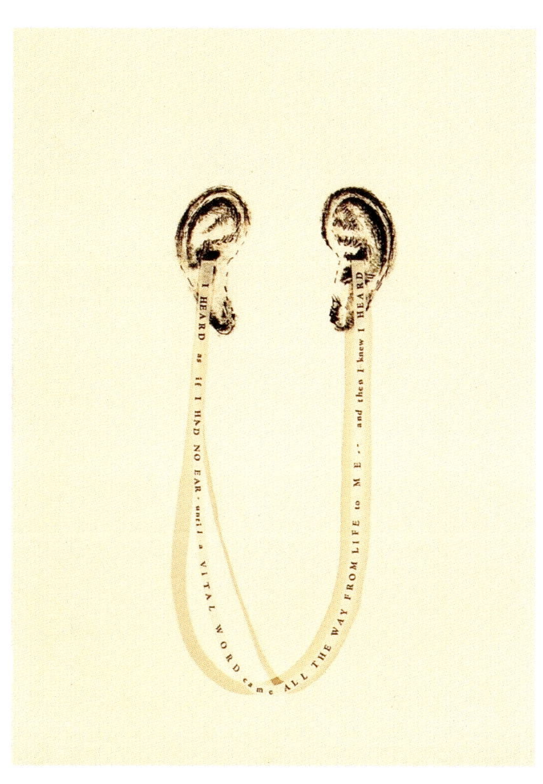

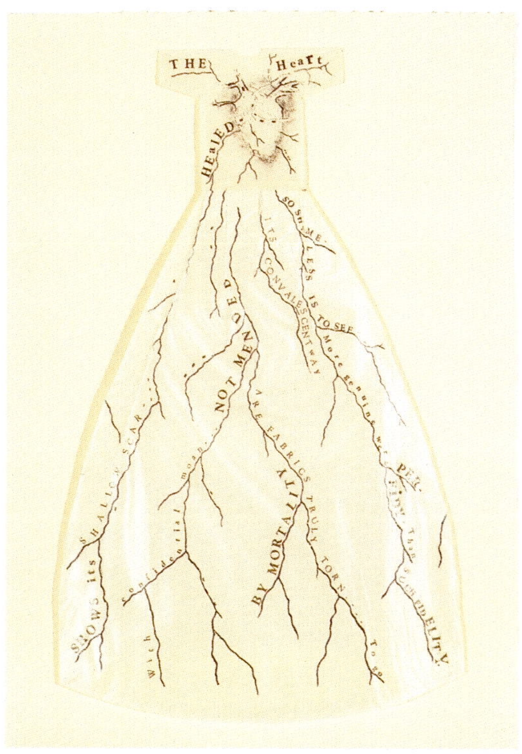

LESLEY DILL (American, b. 1948)
Poem Ears, from the suite ***The Poetic Body,*** 1992
Lithograph, letterpress, collage
18 x 13 (45 x 32.5)
Judith Solodkin
Letterpress Printer Anne Noonan Elliot
Collage Rebecca Lax
Solo Impression Inc., New York, New York

LESLEY DILL (American, b. 1948)
Poem Dress, from the suite ***The Poetic Body,*** 1992
Lithograph, letterpress, collage
18 x 13 (45 x 32.5)
Judith Solodkin
Letterpress Printer Anne Noonan Elliot
Collage Rebecca Lax
Solo Impression Inc., New York, New York

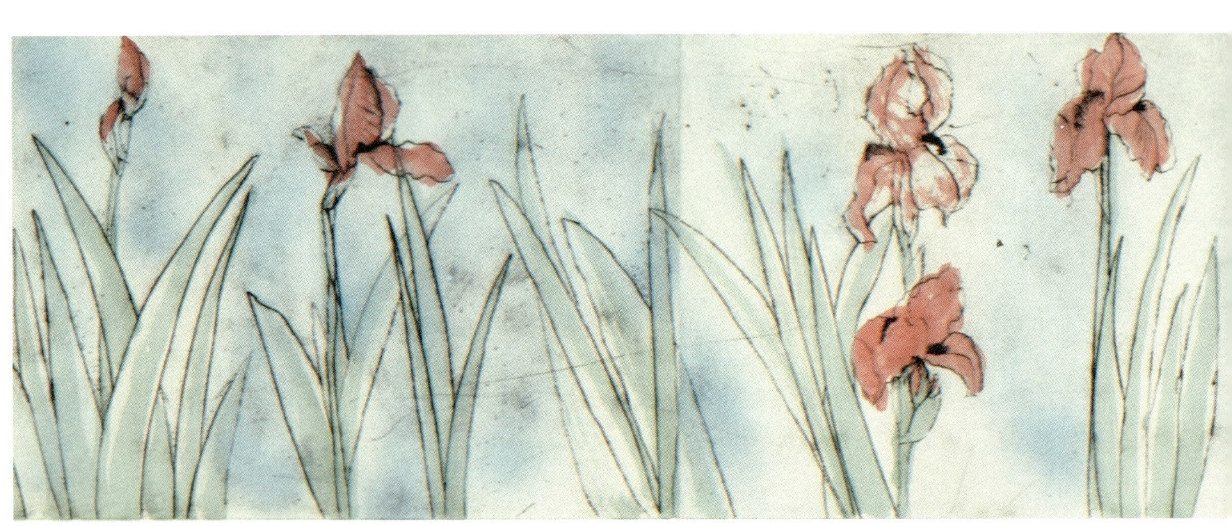

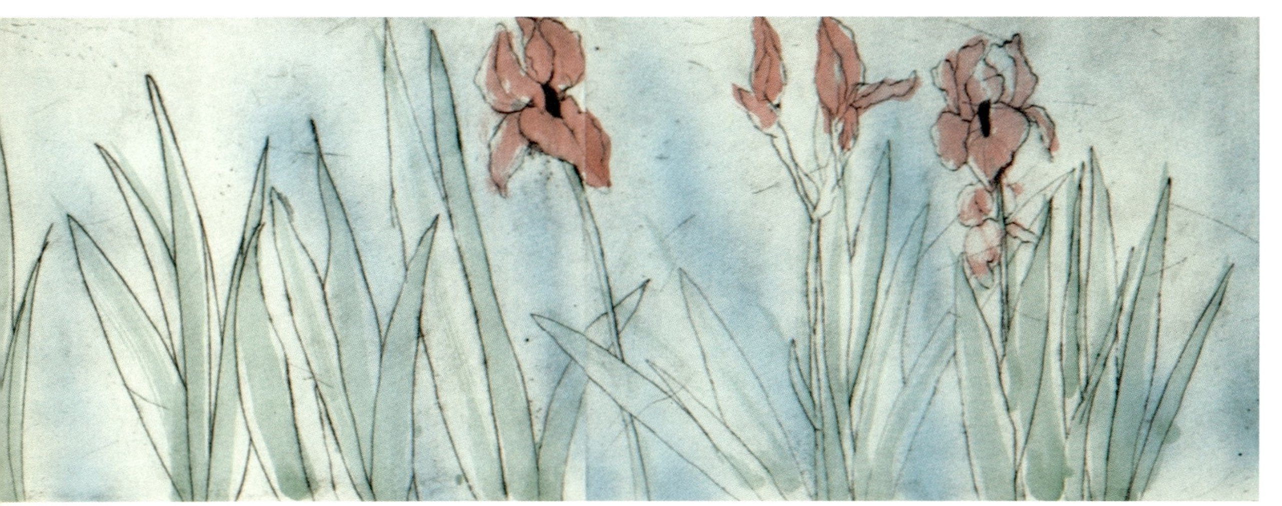

JIM DINE (American, b. 1935)
Rachel Cohen's Flags, State 1, 1979
Drypoint, with hand coloring
6 sheets, 17½ x 132½ (43.75 x 331.25) overall
Donald Saff
Pace Editions, New York, New York

Employing the long, narrow format of a traditional Japanese screen, this lyrical frieze is a tribute to Dine's grandmother. The drypoint technique creates the blurred texture characteristic of irises, also known as flags.

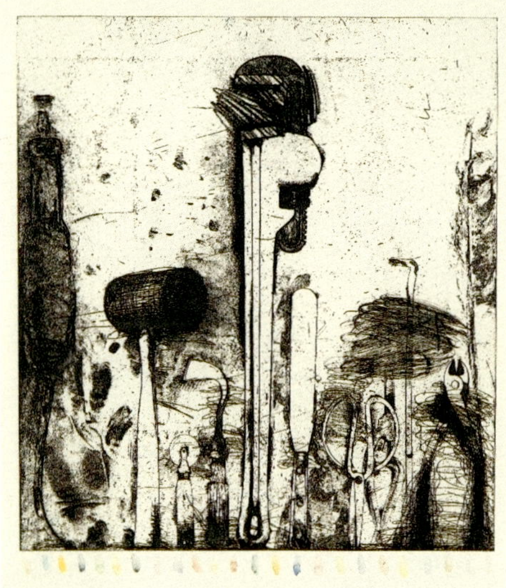

JIM DINE (American, b. 1935)
Piranesi's 24 Colored Marks, 1974-76
Etching, with hand coloring
39 x 27 (97.5 x 67.5)
Alan Uglow, Winston Roeth
Petersburg Press, New York, New York

The title refers to the 18th-century master engraver Piranesi, whose printmaking tradition Dine combines with today's freedom from strict media boundaries. Here, an impersonal lineup of tools is dramatized by the expressiveness of Dine's creative process.

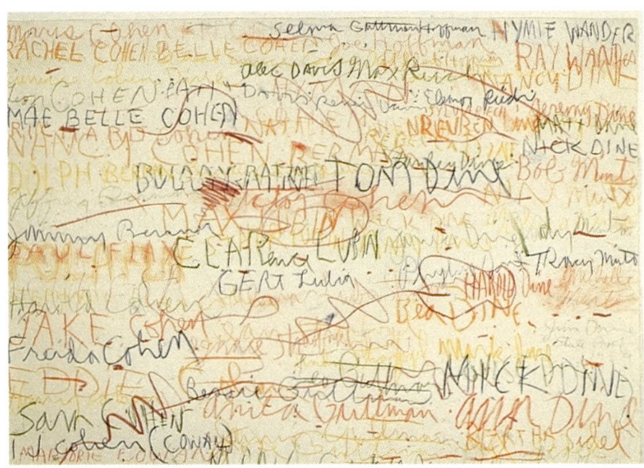

JIM DINE (American, b. 1935)
Cincinnati III, 1969
Lithograph
30 x 45 (75 x 112.50)
Petersburg Press Ltd., London, England

Once acclaimed as a Pop artist, Dine highlights art's relevance to human existence by using familiar images. In this print, the last of a series created while the artist was far from home, the scrawled and layered names of his Ohio family resemble a graffiti-covered wall.

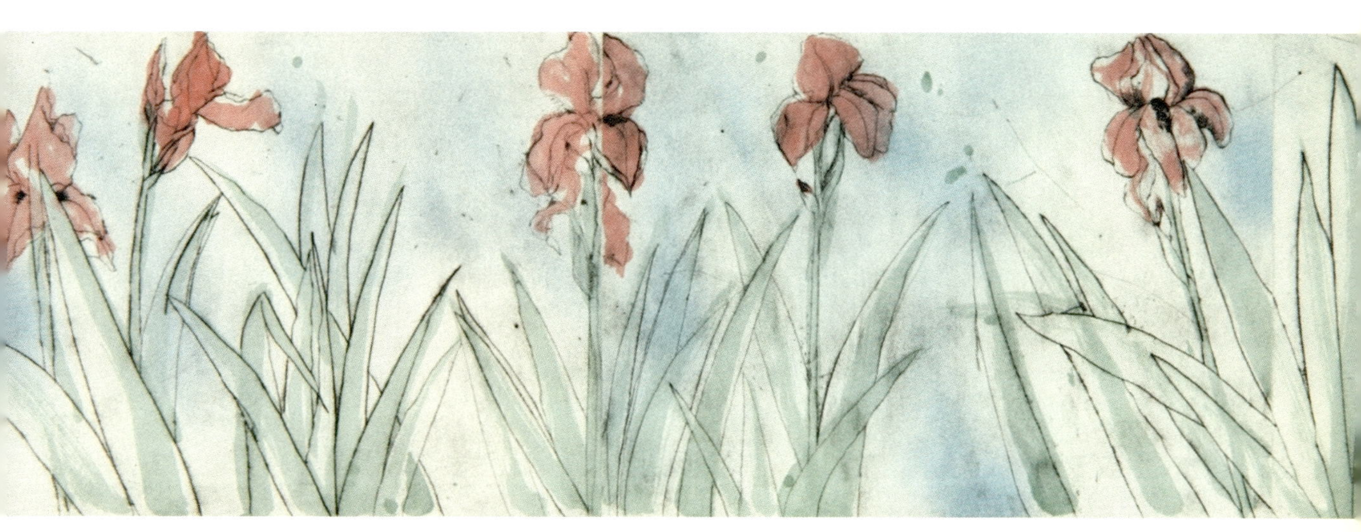

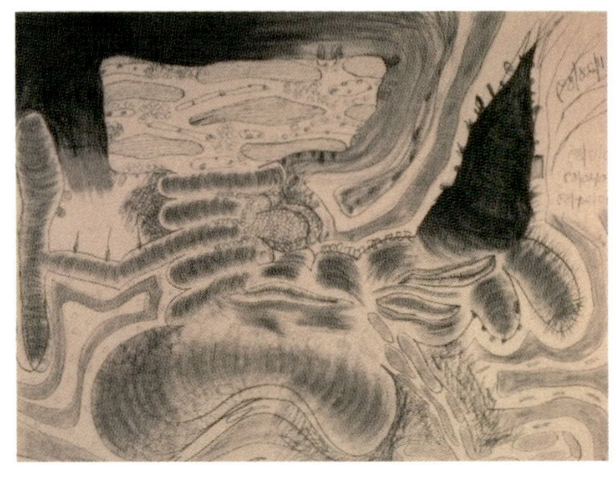

CARROLL DUNHAM (American, b. 1949)
Touching Two Sides, 1989
Drypoint, etching
20¼ x 26⅜ (50.25 x 65.75)
ULAE, West Islip, New York

Known as one of the bad-boy painters, Dunham has been described as working in a primordial baroque style: floating shapes, sharply outlined structure, a cartoon-like landscape. "I am not interested in looking back over my shoulder," he says, "or in any manifestation of nostalgia or irony vis-à-vis past styles. I am really interested in figuring out how to invent a new-looking artwork."

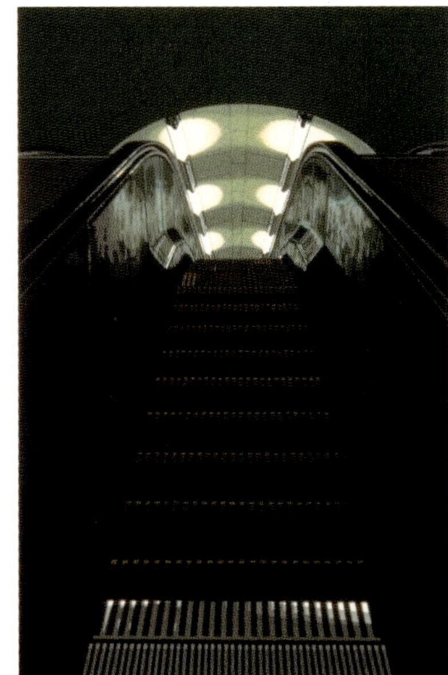

RICHARD ESTES (American, b. 1936)
Escalator, from the portfolio ***Urban Landscape II,*** 1979
Serigraph
27½ x 19½ (68.75 x 48.75)
Parasol Press, Ltd., New York, New York

Photo-realist Estes makes prints and paintings precisely delineating the contemporary urban environment. He often uses a photograph as a starting point, and this print is based on one he took in a London subway station. Serigraphy allows the artist to build up multiple layers of rich color and maintain crisp edges.

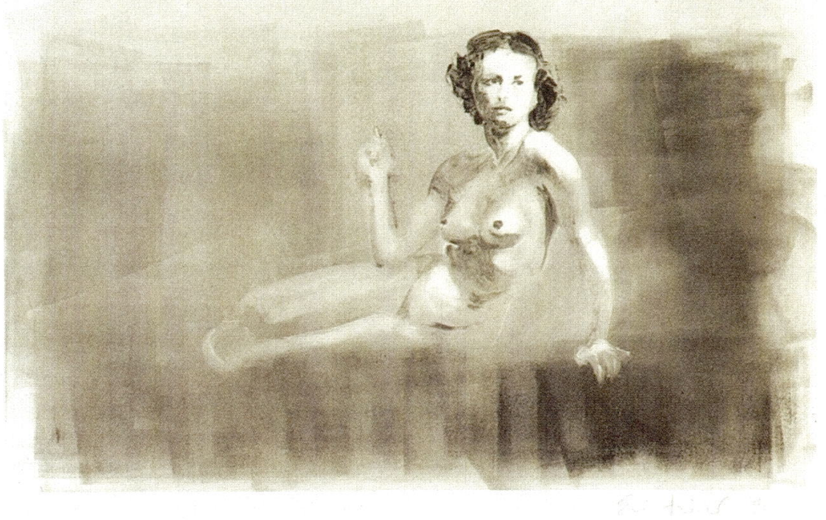

ERIC FISCHL (American, b. 1948)
Untitled, 1992
Monoprint
20½ X 30 (51.25 x 75)
Derrière l'Étoile Studios, New York, New York

Fischl's style of printmaking strongly reflects his painting style, incorporating delicate, brushy strokes and rich hues. He demands involvement from the viewer by depicting intensely private scenes of suburbia that intrigue, tempting you to become both a voyeur and participant.

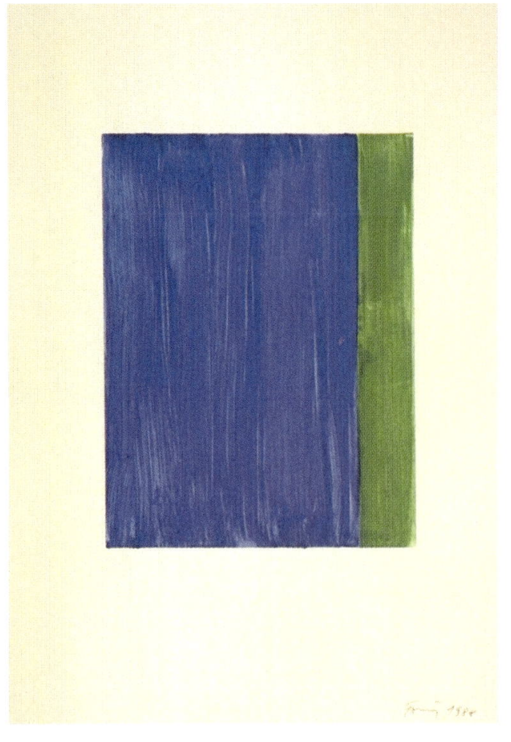

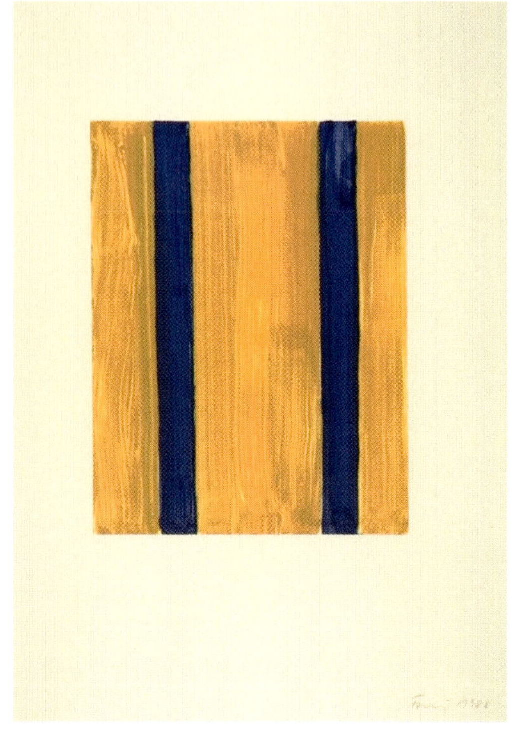

GÜNTER FÖRG (German, b. 1952)
Untitled, 1988
Monoprint
25½ x 19 (63.75 x 47.5)
Derrière l'Étoile, New York, New York

GÜNTER FÖRG (German, b. 1952)
Untitled, 1988
Monoprint
25½ x 19 (63.75 x 47.5)
Derrière l'Étoile, New York, New York

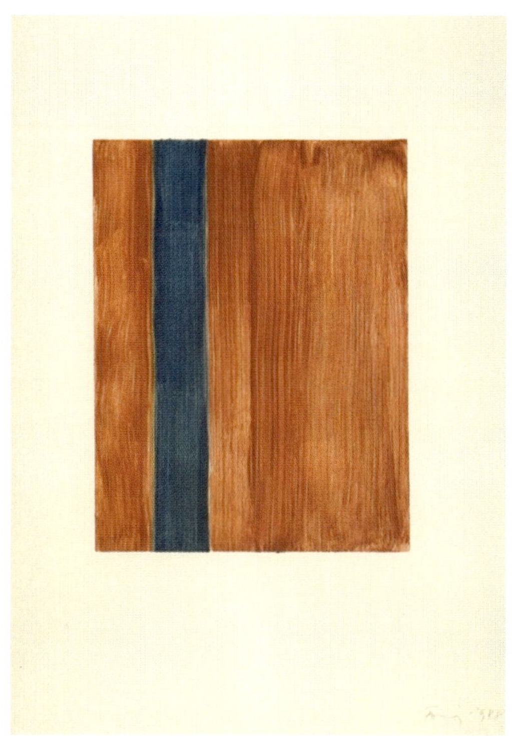

GÜNTER FÖRG (German, b. 1952)
Untitled, 1988
Monoprint
25½ x 19 (63.75 x 47.5)
Derrière l'Étoile, New York, New York

The reductive elegance of Förg's monoprints are typical of this Conceptual artist's geometric abstractions inspired by modern architecture. Like the effects of time and atmosphere on buildings, Förg's painterly washes and wavering edges mellow his starkly rectilinear compositions.

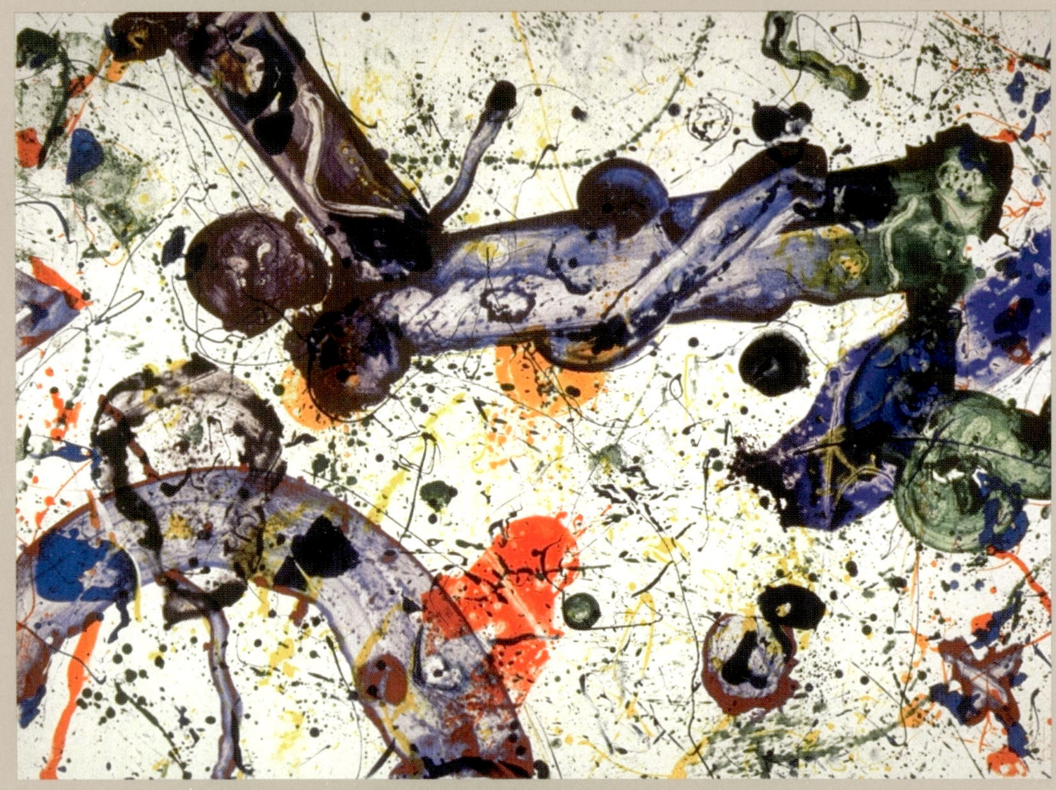

SAM FRANCIS (American, 1923-1994)
King Corpse, 1986
Serigraph
42 x 59 (105 x 147.5)
Gemini G.E.L., Los Angeles, California

Sam Francis began making prints in the 1950s. His work reflects an interest in Eastern and Western philosophies, and the concept of becoming rather than being is central to his work. In this piece, forms emerge and dissolve from the background, and contrasting areas of light and dark, density and openness, create a sense of tension and movement.

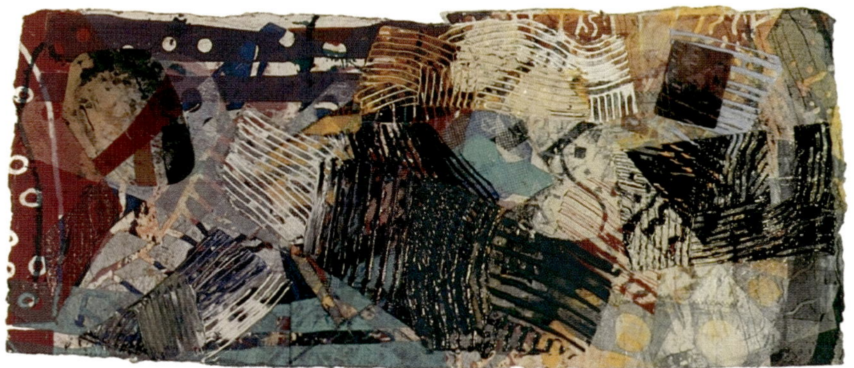

SAM GILLIAM (American, b. 1933)
Untitled #12, 1992
Monoprint
26 x 61 (65 x 152.5)
William Weege, Andrew Rubin
Tandem Press, Madison, Wisconsin

In this monoprint, Gilliam creates a foundation of relief elements for a variety of treatments, on handmade paper. He splashes ink onto the paper, cuts it apart, prints on it again, glues and sews the parts together, and rakes acrylic gel across the top. The result is an innovative and textural print.

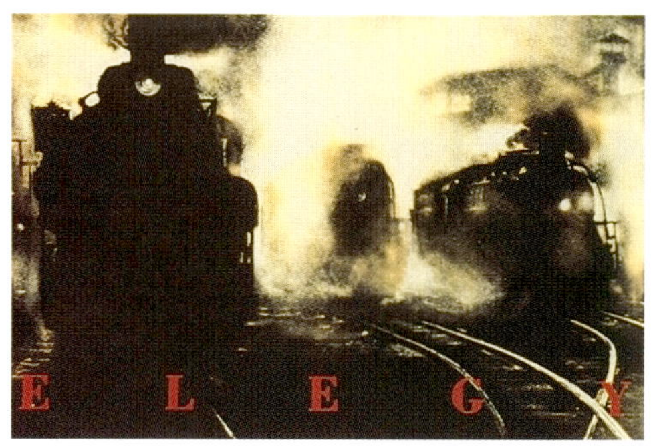

LAWRENCE GIPE (American, b. 1962)
Elegy, 1992
Etching, serigraph
22 x 30 (55 x 75)
Derrière l'Étoile Studios, New York, New York

Based on an old photograph of three steam engines at a train station, the word "elegy" reminds us that these trains are long gone. "I, like so many in my generation, grew up in a wash of media," explains Gipe, "it was the allure of old movies from the 30s and 40s rerun on television that dominates my memories."

NANCY GRAVES (American, 1940-1995)
Approaches the Limit of I, 1981
Lithograph
46 x 31¾ (116.8 x 80.6)
Kenneth Tyler, Lee Funderburg, Roger Campbell
Tyler Graphics Ltd., Mt. Kisco, New York

Graves used an abstract vocabulary to explore the sometimes elusive relationship between abstract and realistic art. By the 80s, Graves was especially interested in botany, and a very strong organic sense is typical of the forms in her work of that time.

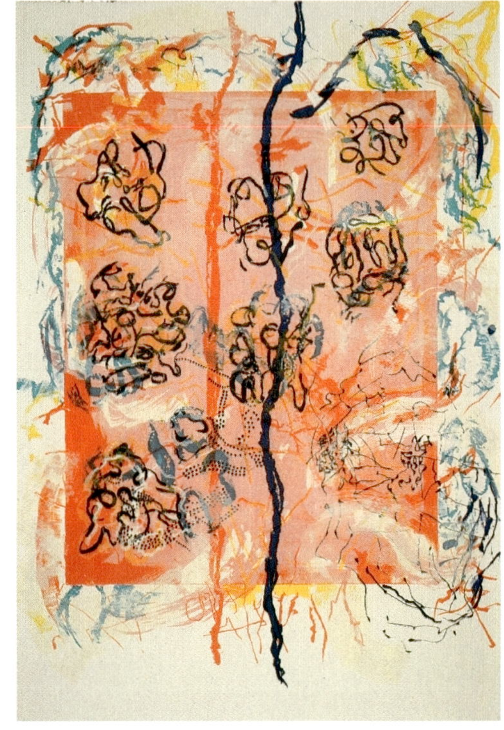

GRONK (American, b. 1954)
36th Street, 1994
Etching
22¾ x 22¾ (56.75 x 56.75)
Bruce Crownover, Andrew Rubin
Tandem Press, Madison, Wisconsin

Gronk, a Los Angeles artist, uses his immediate urban environment as his inspiration. In this etching, he offers a direct slice through the things that make up city life: cups, stones, garbage, a fork, a hand, faces, movement and energy.

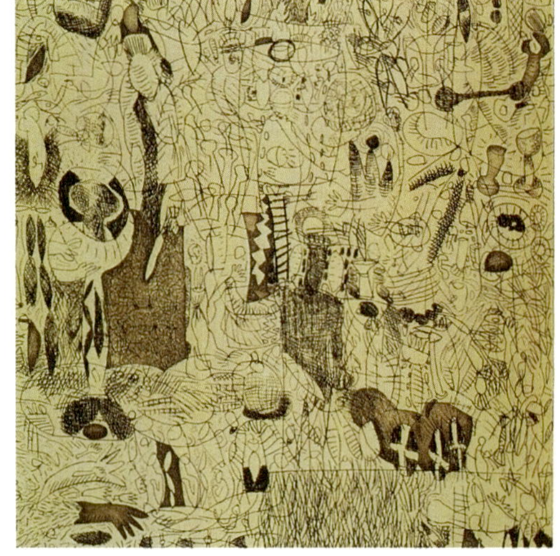

RED GROOMS (American, b. 1937)
Holy Hula, 1991
Lithograph
22 x 30 (55 x 75)
Shark's Inc., Boulder, Colorado

Grooms' sense of humor is evident in all his work. This print was made during his first trip to Hawaii and in it, he pokes fun at the Puritan modesty ethic. *Holy Hula* offers viewer participation in the form of two levers that move mountains and censor the dancers.

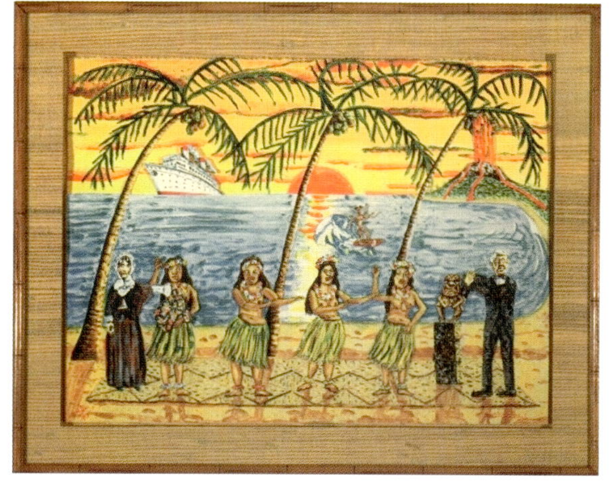

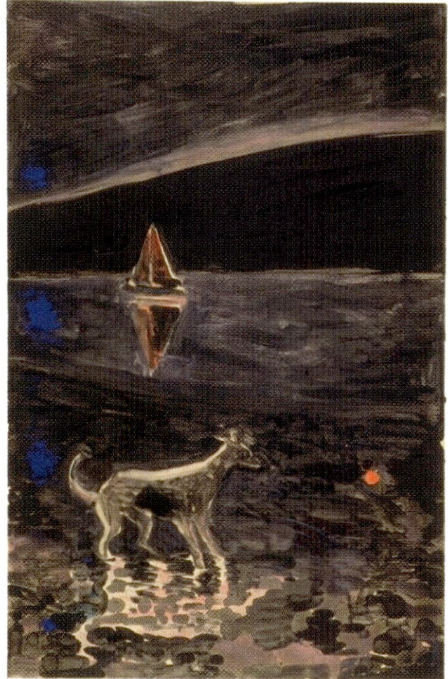

SUSAN HALL (American, b. 1943)
Orange Ball, 1990
Monoprint
30¾ x 22¼ (75.75 x 55.5)
Derrière l'Étoile Studios, New York, New York

Hall deftly extracts much poetry from minor, everyday incidents. She transforms a seemingly mundane occurrence – a dog chasing a ball – into a moment of drama. The relationship between the various elements in the composition is ambiguous enough to elude any specific interpretation.

DUNCAN HANNAH (American, b. 1952)
Northern Lights (Slate), 1990
Monoprint
41 x 31 (102.5 x 77.5)
Steve Andersen
Vermillion Editions Ltd., Minneapolis, Minnesota

Hannah's use of old-fashioned media imagery challenges the prevailing post-modern attitudes toward recycling past styles. A long-ago railway poster is the inspiration for this dreamlike image evoking the loneliness of hearing a distant train whistle in the night.

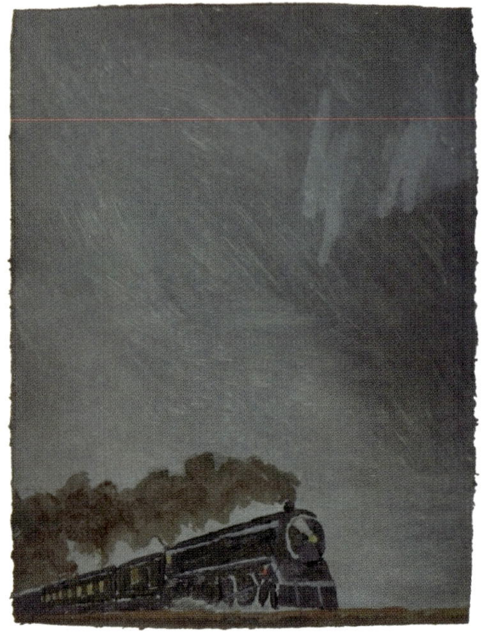

FREYA HANSELL (American, b. 1945)
Untitled, 1989
Monoprint
29 x 27 (72.5 x 67.5)
Derrière l'Étoile Studios, New York, New York

The sea is a common subject in Hansell's work, and she employs it as an effective carrier of emotion. In this monoprint, she investigates the forlorn, melancholy isolation experienced at the remote, often dangerous edges of the sea. The two lighthouses are as far apart from each other as possible, kept separate by a thick, white atmosphere.

AL HELD (American, b. 1928)
Pachinko, 1989
Woodcut
26¼ x 33¼ (65.5 x 83)
Tadashi Toda
Carved by Shunzo Matsuda
Crown Point Press, San Francisco, California

Held is known for his command of color, balance and design. In this print, the vivid colors and precise geometric forms are quintessential Held. The possibility of depicting space has always been of interest to him and he strives to create a tension between order and disorder. Here, two- and three-dimensional forms manifest themselves as infinite space, and the viewer is liberated from the force of gravity and carried to a world of eternally shifting geometry. The entire image seems to project toward the viewer.

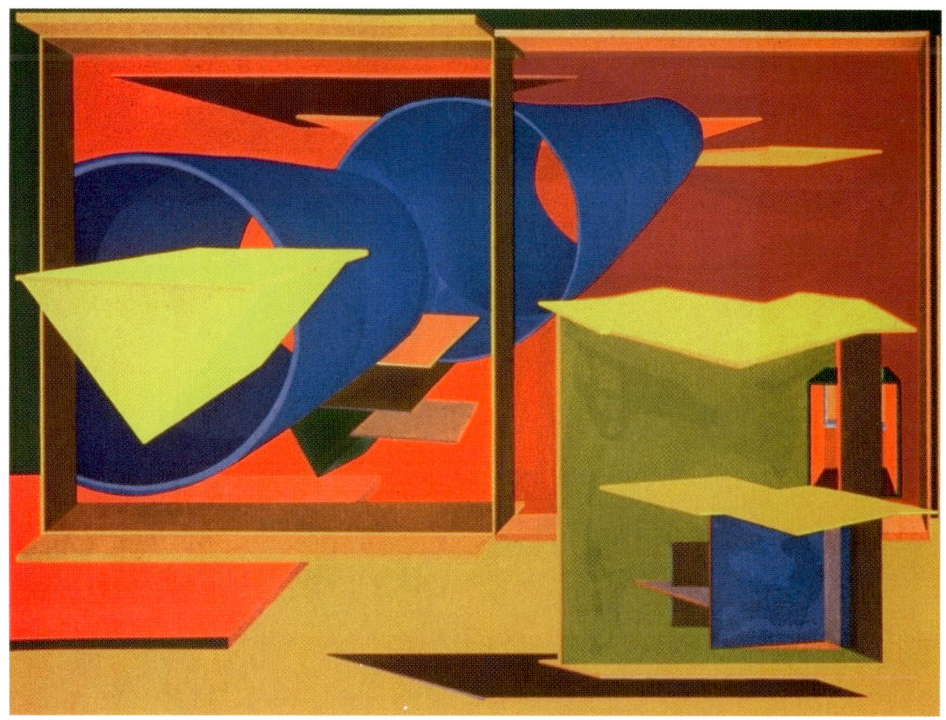

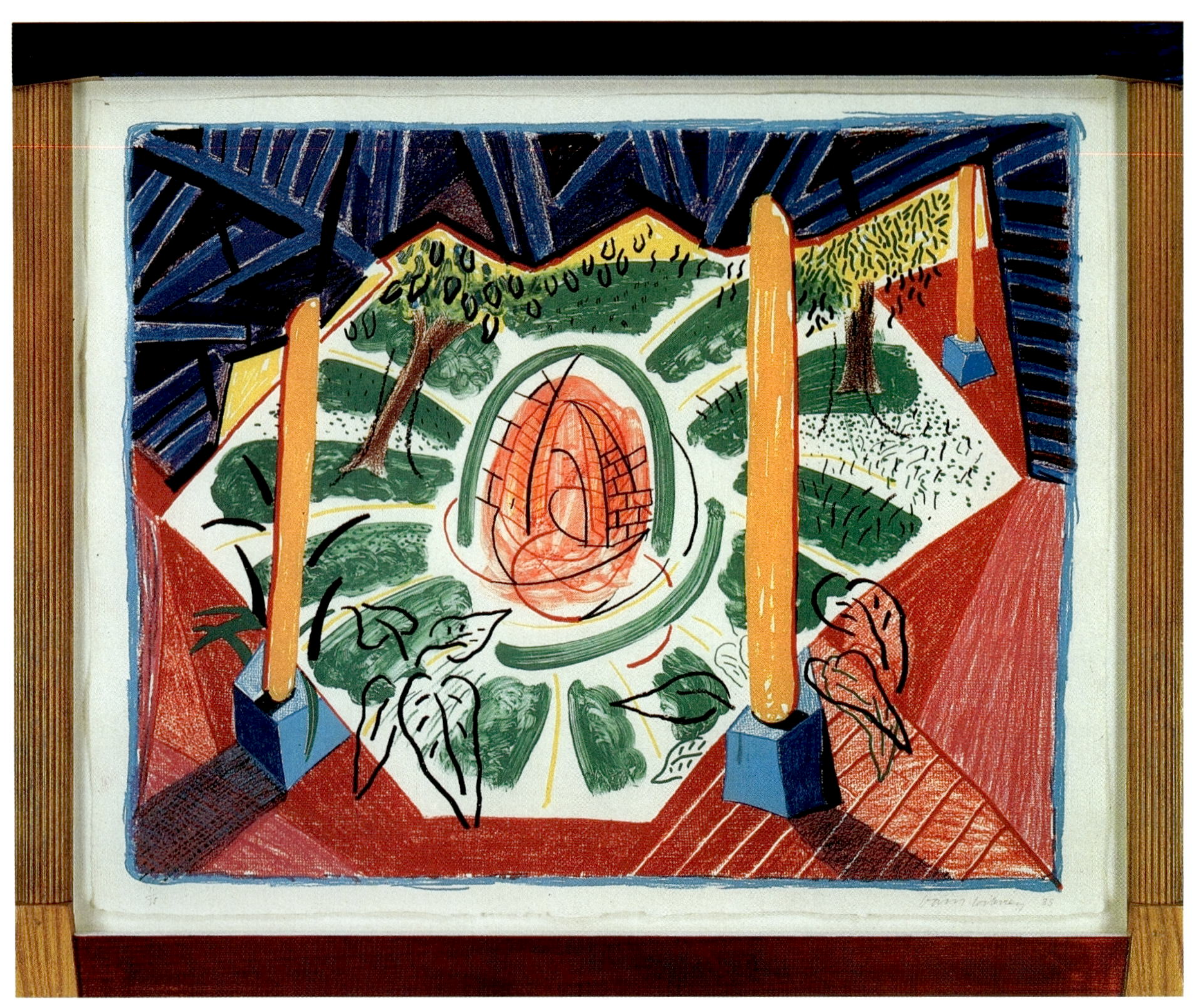

DAVID HOCKNEY (British, b. 1937)
***Views of Hotel Well II*, from the *Moving Focus Series*,** 1985
Lithograph
25 x 32 (63.5 x 81.3)
Kenneth Tyler, Lee Funderburg, Roger Campbell
Tyler Graphics Ltd., Mt. Kisco, New York

Hockney's vivid explorations of representational subject matter in Pop, Realist and Modernist idioms have endeared him to a wide public. This lithograph with its Matisse-like colors and hand-painted frame implies sun-drenched leisure. Inspired by Picasso and Chinese landscape painting, Hockney uses multiple viewpoints and reversed perspectives to abstract and compress into a panoramic circle the courtyard and covered terrace of a hotel in Mexico.

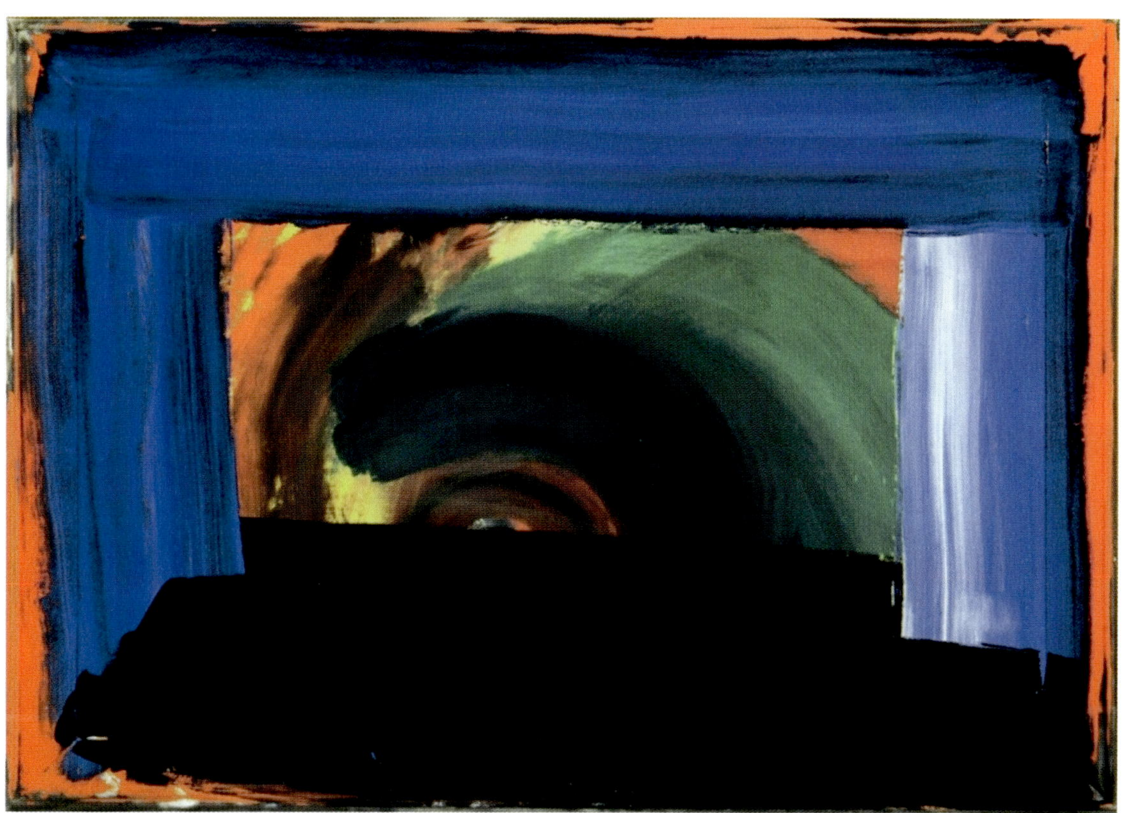

HOWARD HODGKIN (British, b. 1932)
Gossip, 1995
Serigraph
30 x 42 (75 x 105)
Lincoln Center, New York, New York

Howard Hodgkin is one of today's most celebrated British artists and is particularly noted for his handling of color. In this print, his technical finesse with surfaces and color is readily apparent. Although Hodgkin's work lies somewhere between abstraction and figural representation, there is a strongly private, almost autobiographical element in his work. The artist achieves a sense of intimacy with representational pictures of emotional situations.

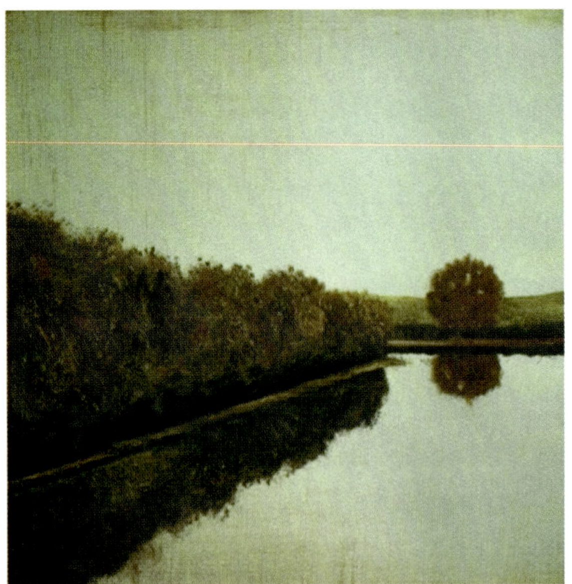

WADE HOEFER (American, b. 1948)
***Aestas I*,** 1993
Monoprint
28½ x 28 (71.25 x 70)
Experimental Workshop, San Francisco, California

Hoefer lives near the Russian River in northern California and his work centers on a very careful exploration of that serene and gentle landscape. He exploits the painterly effects possible with a monoprint to give a sense of the humid atmosphere along the river.

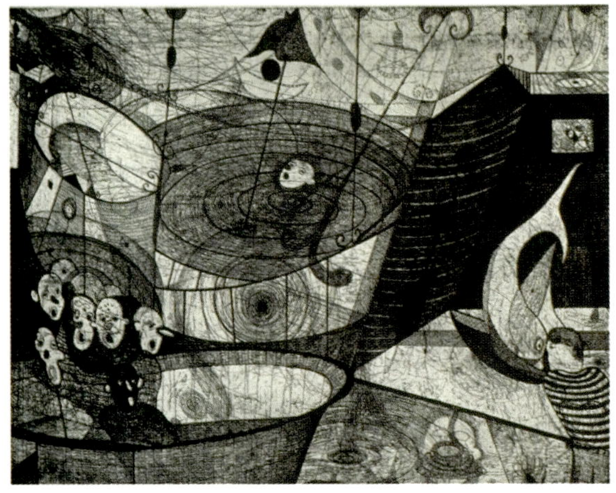

RICHARD HULL (American, b. 1955)
***Loamings*,** 1993
Hard-ground etching
18 x 24 (45 x 60)
Andrew Balkin
A.G.B.Graphics, Madison, Wisconsin

Hull typically constructs a stage for his characters to act in, full of changing, tilting pockets of space. He unites these various areas with a spiderweb formed by his whiplike, all-over lines.

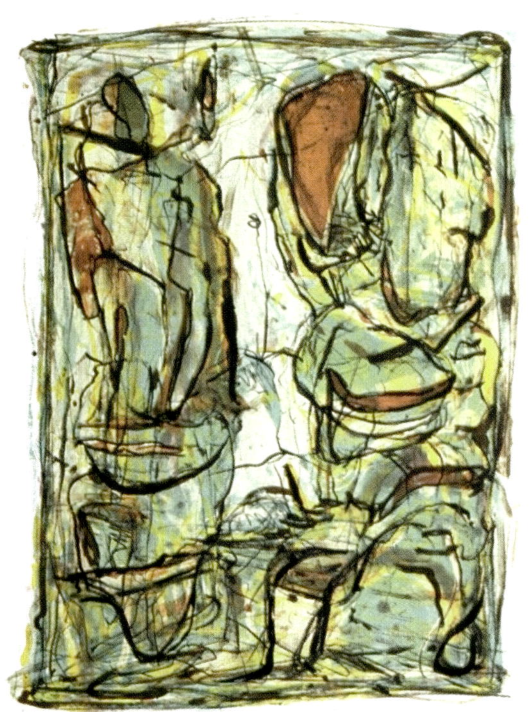

BRYAN HUNT (American, b. 1947)
Sedona Precipice, 1992
Soft-ground etching, with soap-ground etching, sugar-lift etching, spit-bite etching, aquatint, drypoint
41¾ X 31¾ (104.25 x 79.25)
Crown Point Press, San Francisco, California

Known for his rugged sculptures of waterfalls and lakes, Hunt also explores themes of nature and gravitational forces in various print media. In this etching, the precipitous fall of water is constricted by the boulders that contain it.

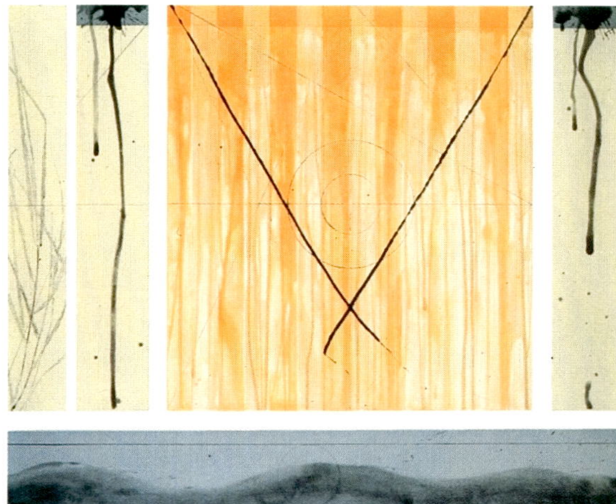

SHOICHI IDA (Japanese, b. 1941)
Between Air and Water No. 7, 1992
Aquatint, drypoint, with chine collé
41 x 45 (102.5 x 112.5)
Hidekatsu Takada
Crown Point Press, San Francisco, California

This etching is one of a series in which transparent, fluid washes traverse delicate fields of color. Colors are muted by the use of chine collé, a method of adhering thin paper onto a heavier one during printing.

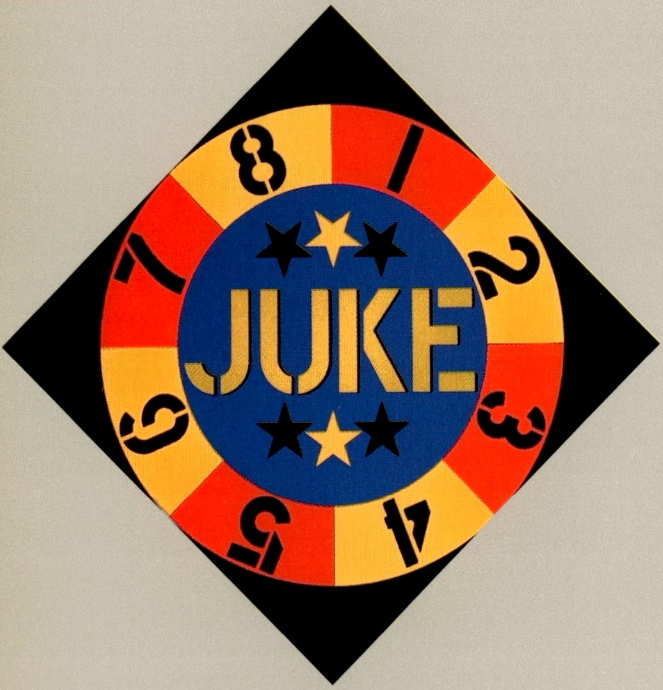

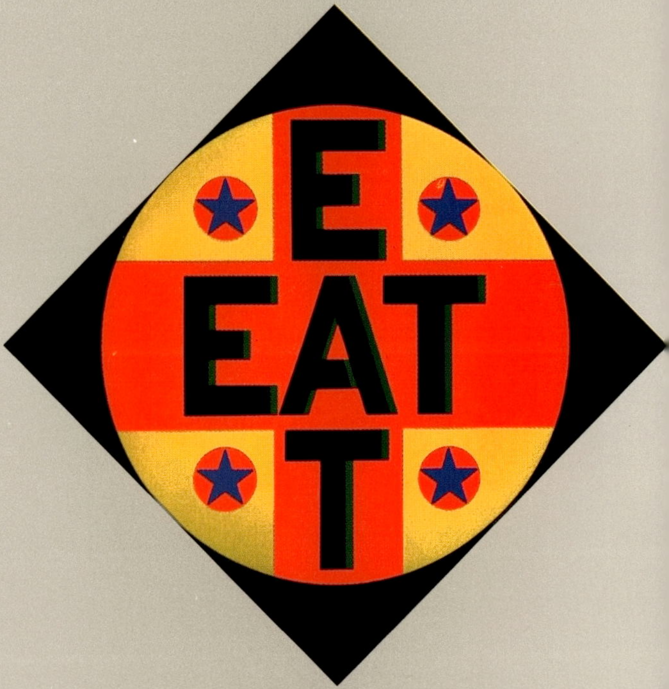

ROBERT INDIANA (American, b. 1928)
The American Dream #2, 1982
Serigraphs
4 sheets, 26 x 26 (65 x 65) each
Prestige Art Ltd., Mamaroneck, New York

Pop artist Robert Indiana is probably best known for his LOVE serigraphs and stamp commissioned by the U.S. Postal Service. Indiana's hard-edged graphic style and pop culture subject matter link two recurring approaches used by artists during the 1960s; he continues to use these methods in this set of works from 1982.

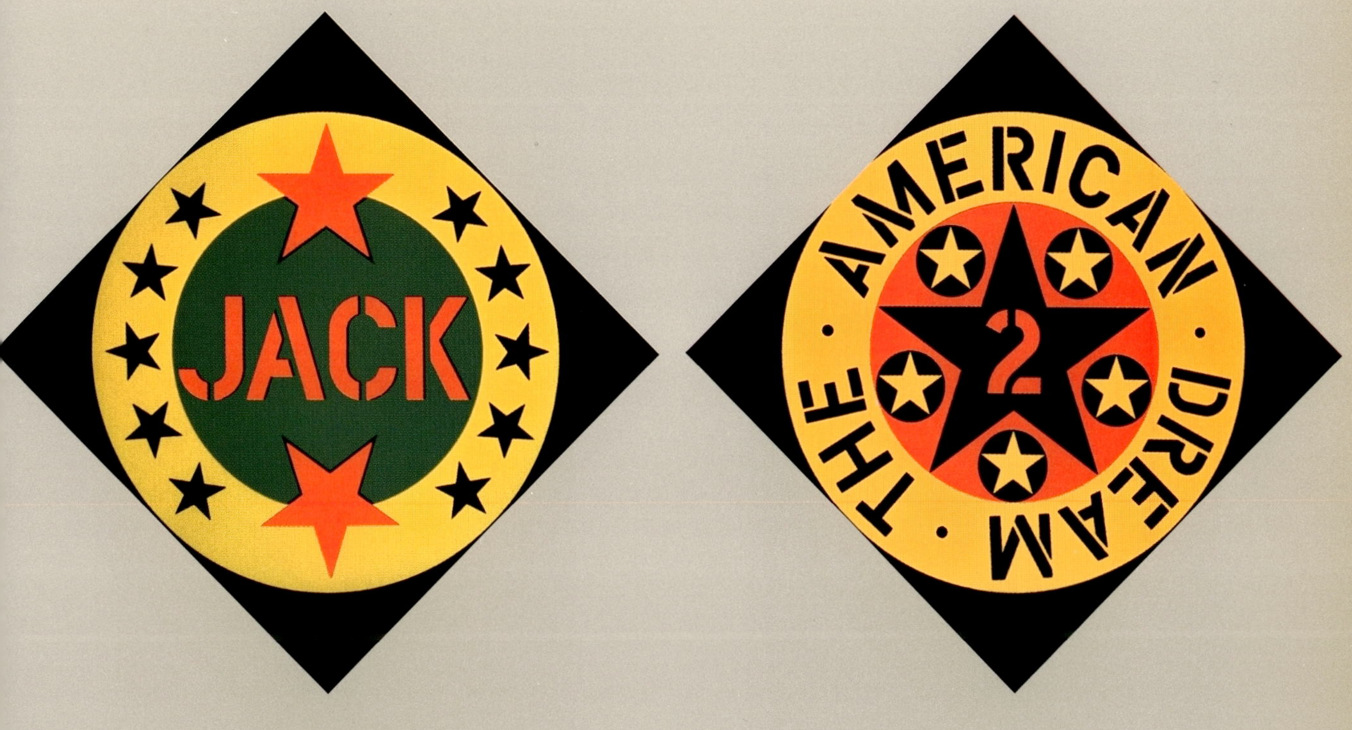
JACK
THE AMERICAN DREAM
2

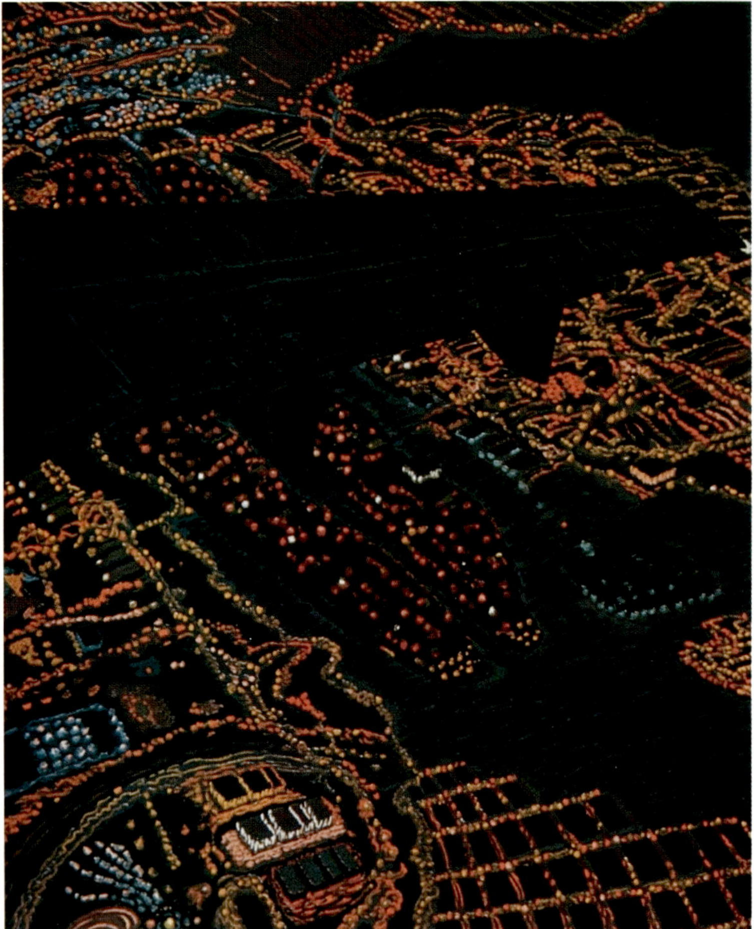

YVONNE JACQUETTE (American, b. 1934)
Night View Wing I**,** 1992
Serigraph
29¾ x 21¾ (74.25 x 54.25)
Norman Stewart
Stewart & Stewart, Bloomfield Hills, Michigan

Jacquette, specialist of the aerial view, frequently does her studies from an airplane. Her jetscapes often include the wing of the plant jutting across her strongly patterned, miniaturized city. She is a master at making color jump off the page. "It's always hard to get bright light to sing from a dark ground, but the white base provides the brilliance."

JASPER JOHNS (American, b. 1930)
Ale Cans III, 1975
Lithograph
12½ x 18⅛ (31.25 x 45.25)
Anthony Zepeda
Gemini G.E.L., Los Angeles, California

The master of flags, targets and numbers here renders another everyday object, ale cans. Famous for his re-working of images, Johns' investigation is all about exploring the way we see.

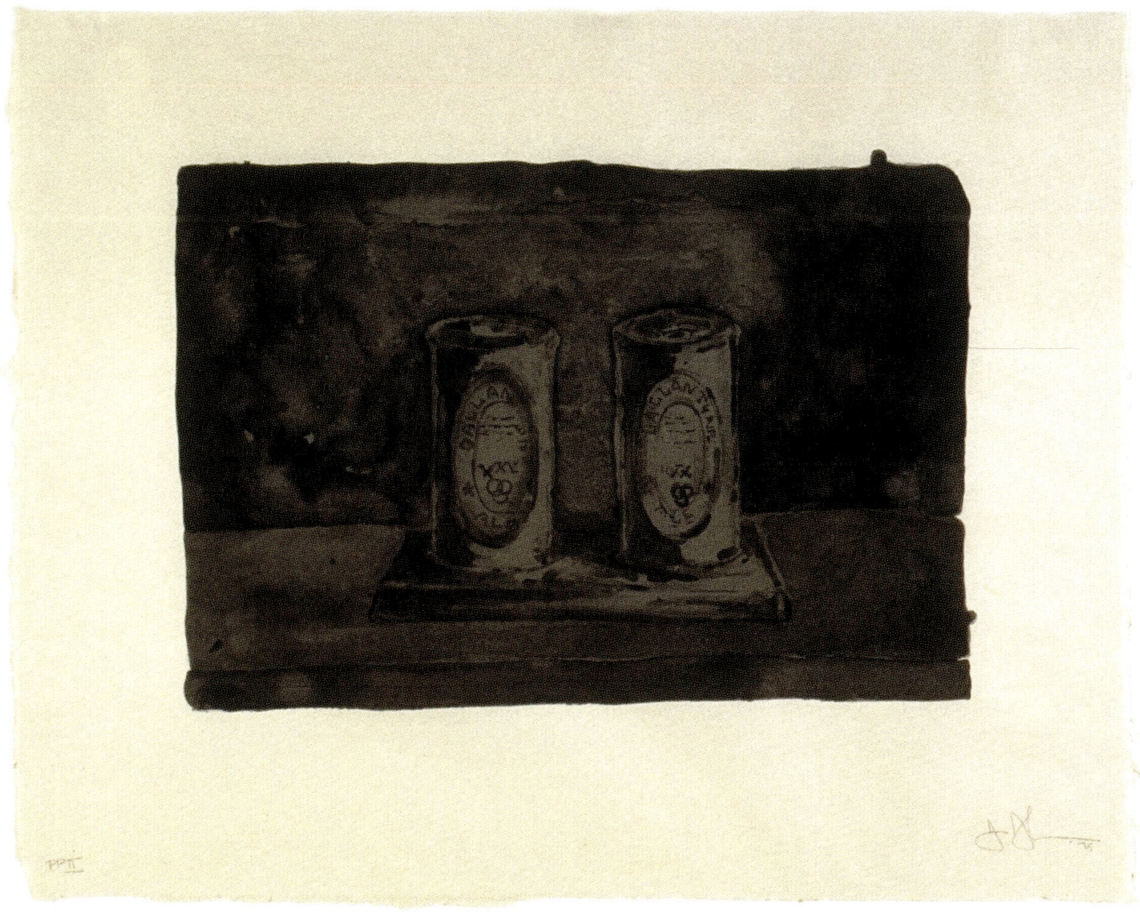

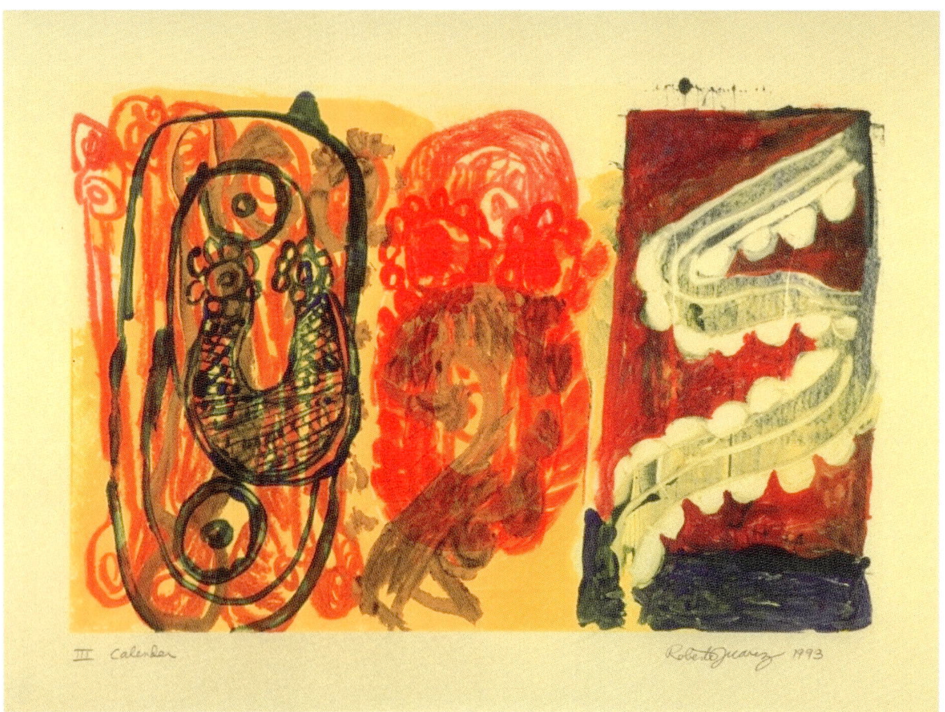

74 ROBERTO JUAREZ (American, b. 1952)
Calender, 1993
Monoprint
24 x 33 (60 x 82.5)
Derrière l'Étoile Studios, New York, New York

Using warm, vibrant colors and organic shapes, Juarez creates a luxurious environment. Many of the forms in his work are derived from underwater sea life. He lives part of the year in Miami Beach and derives much inspiration from his tropical surroundings.

DONALD JUDD (American, 1928-1994)
Red, 1989
Woodcuts
10 sheets, 23½ x 31½ (58.75 x 78.75) each
J. Miller, V. Lau, L. Gray, M. Sanchez
Brooke Alexander, Inc., New York, New York

Color always played an essential role in Judd's art. Known for his Minimalist sculpture, there is a strong correlation between his sculpture and prints. This is a series of 10, printed on Japanese paper of a very soft yellow color. Beginning with a simple rectangular field of color, he experimented with partitioning the color by inserting one or two lines of unprinted paper.

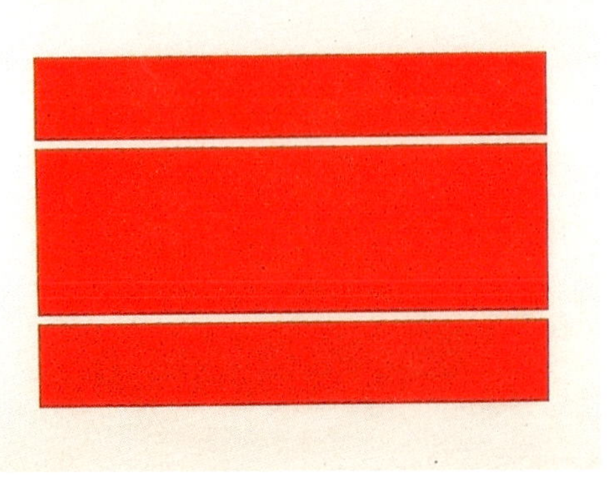

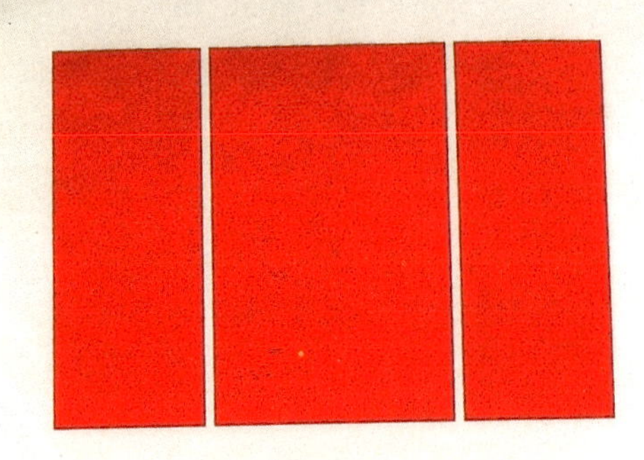

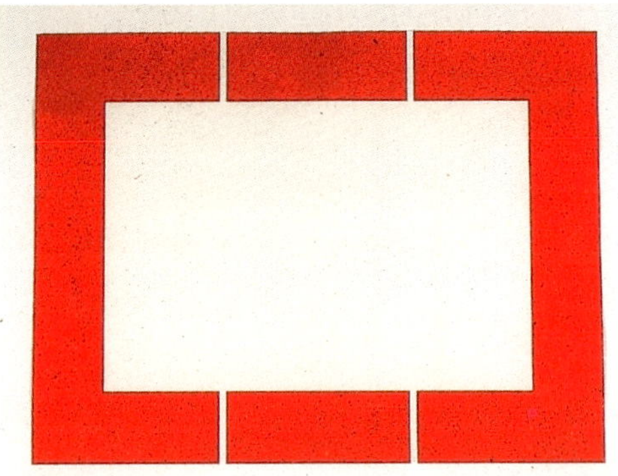

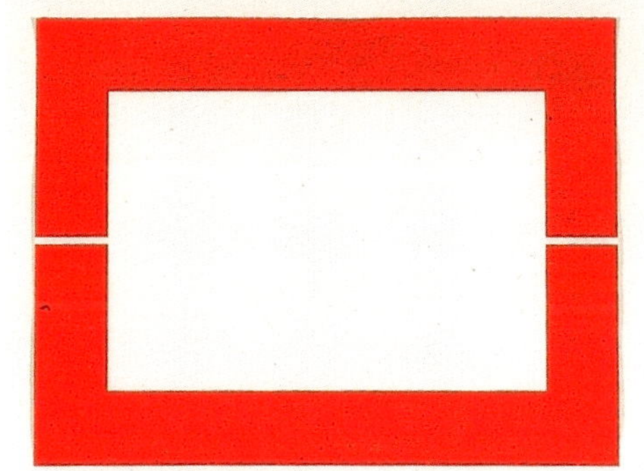

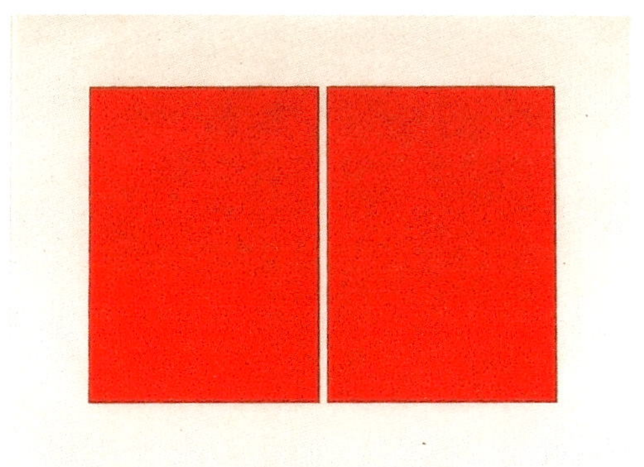

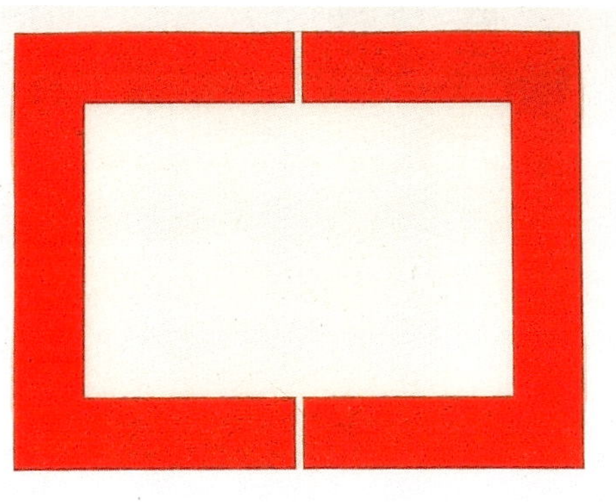

ANISH KAPOOR (Indian, b. 1954)
Untitled #11, 1990
Woodcut
22 x 24 (55 x 60)
Crown Point Press, San Francisco, California

Kapoor, master of luscious pigment, bears the influence of deep, saturated color indigenous to his native Indian culture. This quiet, intimate print is pure Kapoor, sensuous and mysterious. Like his sculpture, it suggests a living breathing organism. "I feel I have nothing to express. I am not here to express … I think the job is to allow a thing to give of its own."

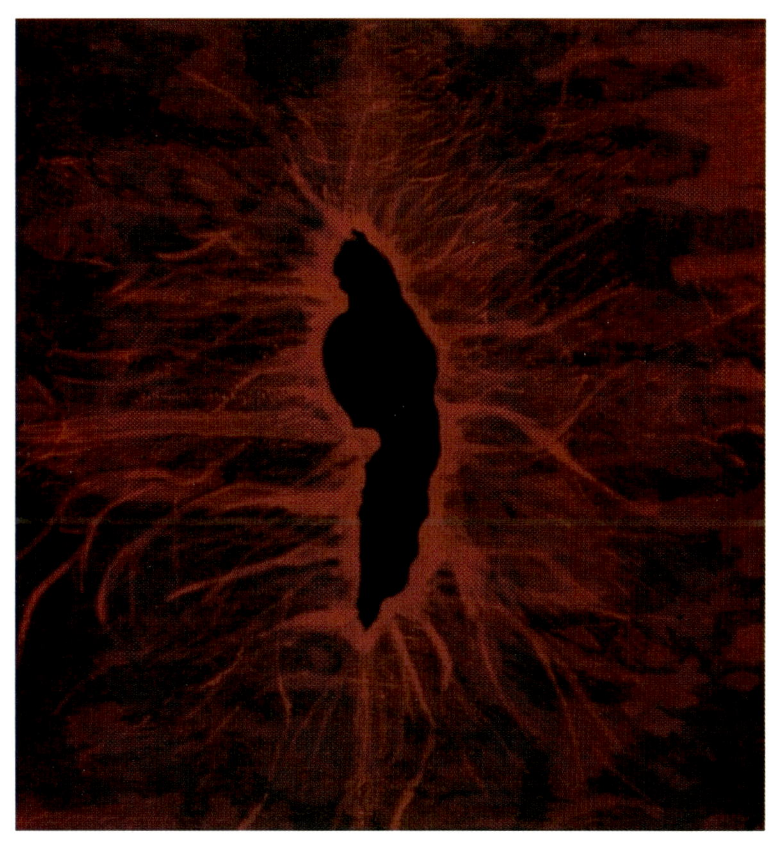

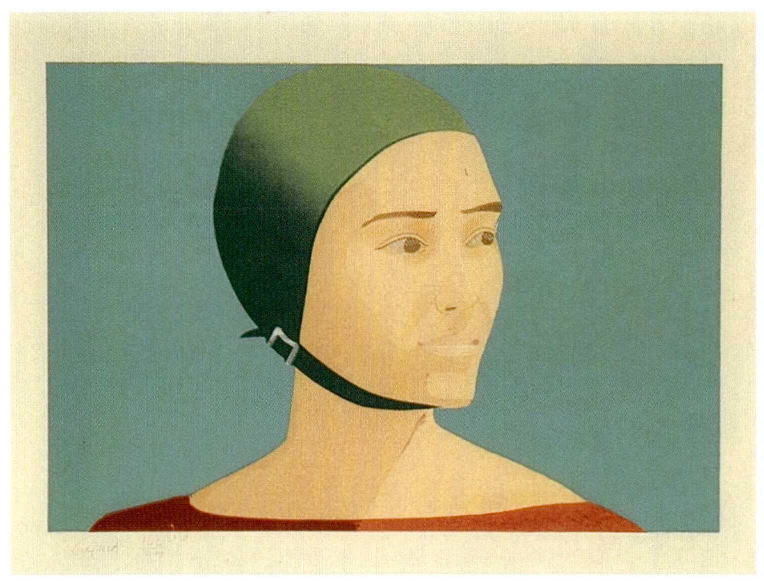

ALEX KATZ (American, b. 1927)
The Green Cap, 1985
Woodcut
17½ x 24 (43.75 x 60)
Tadashi Toda
Crown Point Press, San Francisco, California

Katz employs a minimalist style to capture family and friends in dispassionate, yet elegant, images. Simplified forms and flat planes of color fuse image and ground to give this woodcut of his wife the visual impact of a painting. It was printed in Japan using traditional woodcut methods.

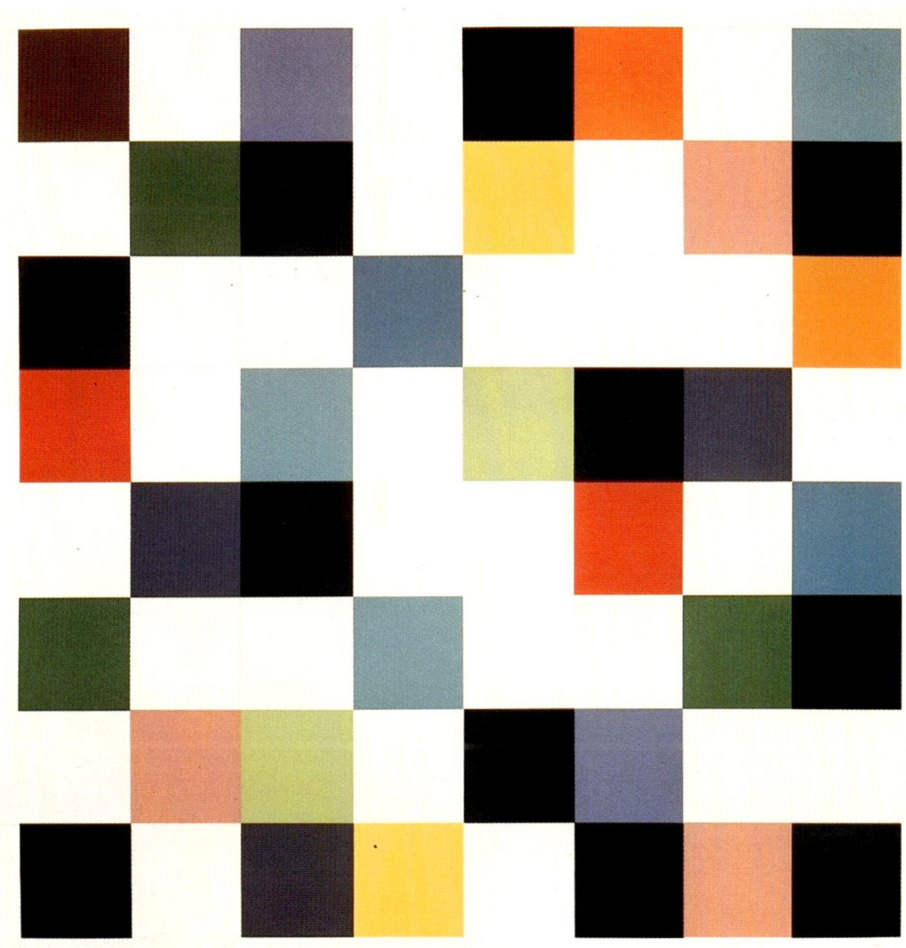

ELLSWORTH KELLY (American, b. 1923)
Colors on a Grid, Screenprint 1976, 1976
Serigraph, lithograph
48¼ x 48¼ (122.6 x 122.6)
John Hutcheson, Kim Halliday
Tyler Graphics Ltd., Mt. Kisco, New York

Abstract artist Kelly reduces art to its basic constituents, often presented in their most obvious form. In this screenprint, the colored squares are related by their common shape against a shared white background. The background simultaneously asserts the independent identity of the color it surrounds.

BARBARA KRUGER (American, b. 1945)
Savoir c'est pouvoir (Knowledge Is Power), 1989
Lithograph
36 x 35 (90 x 87.5 cm)
Derrière l'Étoile Studios, New York, New York

Kruger is known for her mechanically reproduced images accompanied by sparse, socially critical text. Kruger culls her images from the public domain. This print was done for the French government to commemorate their bicentennial.

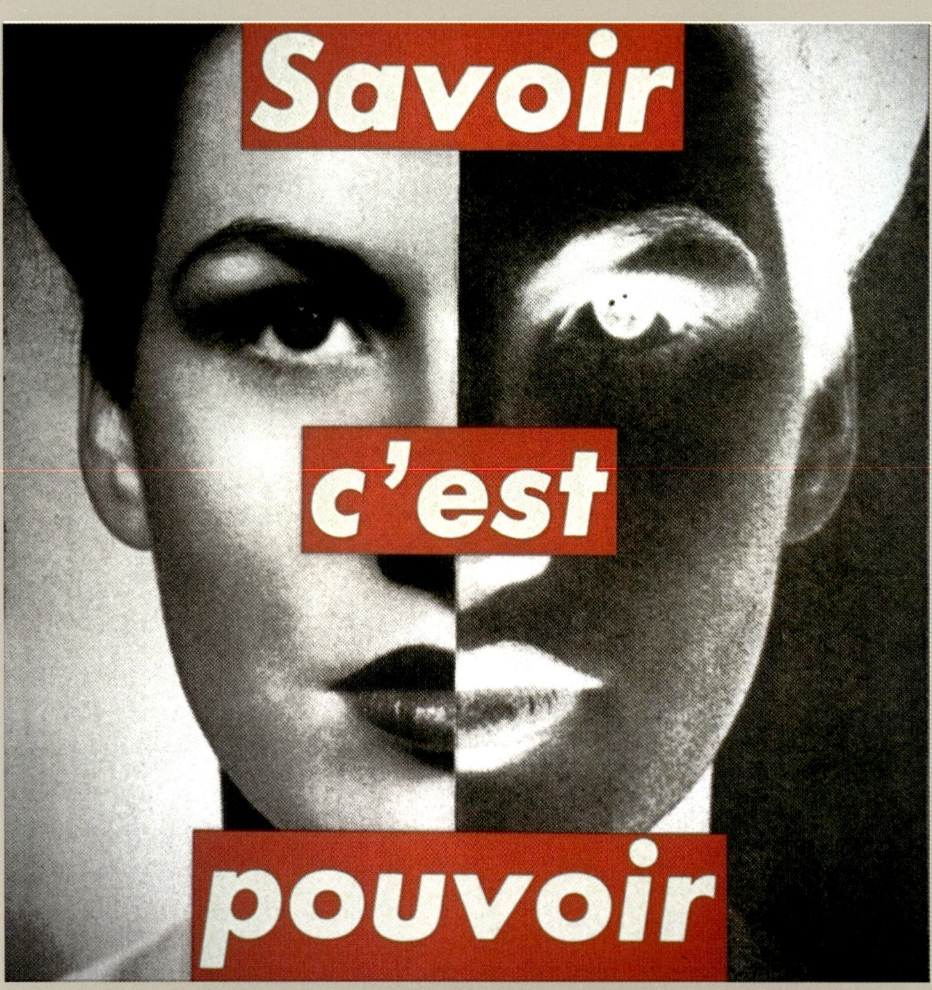

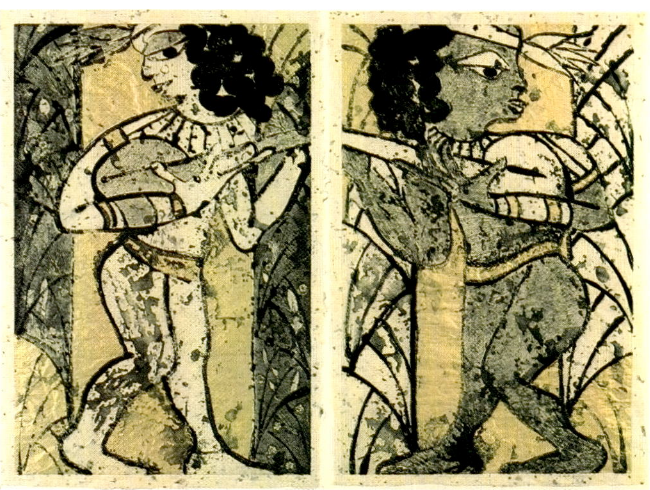

ROBERT KUSHNER (American, b. 1949)
Nubiana, 1982
Etching
Diptych, 36½ x 51 (91.25 x 127.5) overall
Peter Pettengill
Crown Point Press, San Francisco, California

Kushner's exuberant images draw on many traditions, from Matisse to ancient textiles and murals. In this symmetrical two-part print inspired by an Egyptian tomb painting, lights and darks and the direction of one of the Nubian dancing girls are reversed for decorative effect.

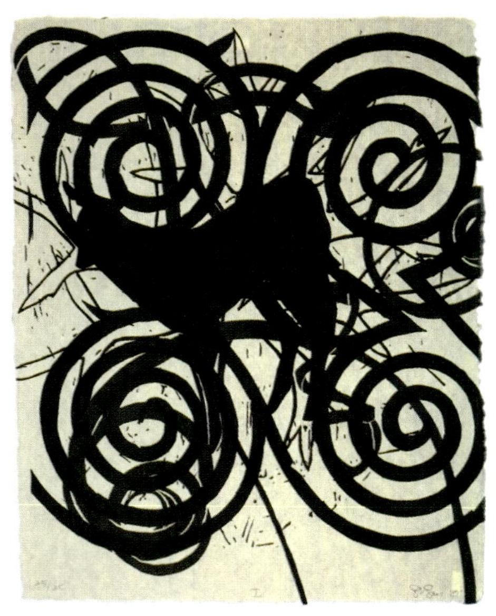

LOIS LANE (American, b. 1948)
Untitled, 1989
Linocut
21 x 17 (52.5 x 42.5)
Derrière l'Étoile Studios, New York, New York

Lane emerged in the 1980s as a key member of the New Image painters, who were interested in the differences between realistic and abstract art. In this print, Lane centers a floating black silhouette, then obscures it with a bold, swirling design.

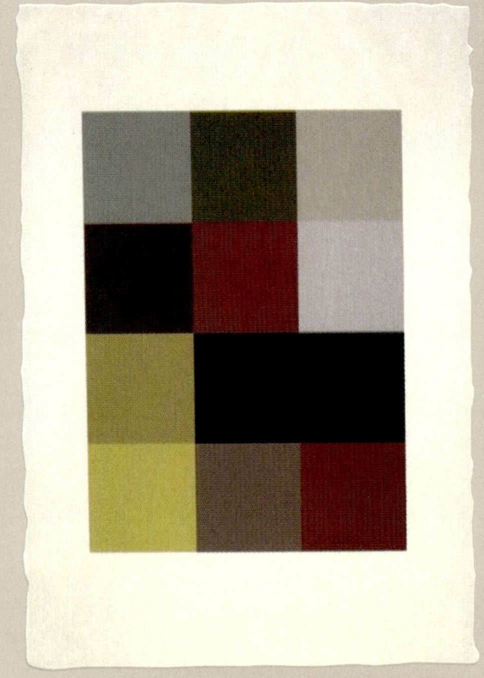

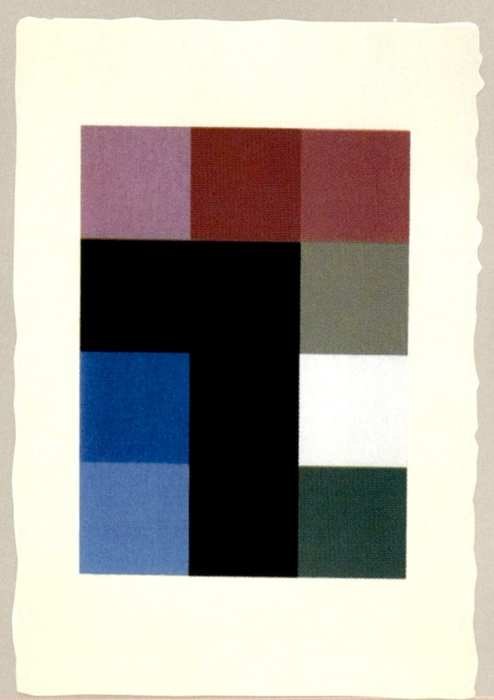

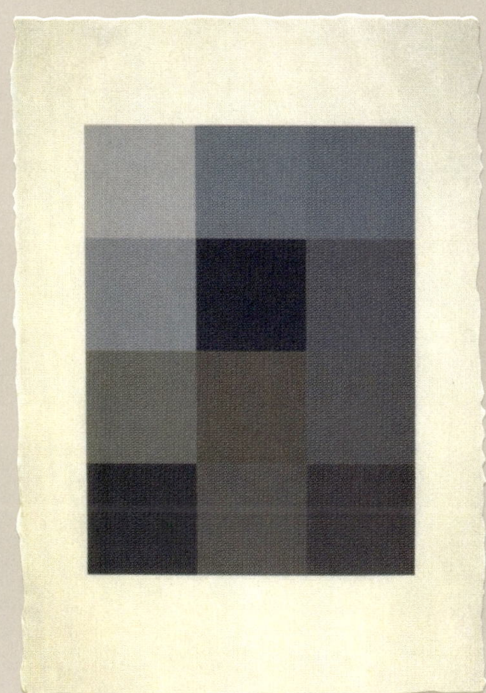

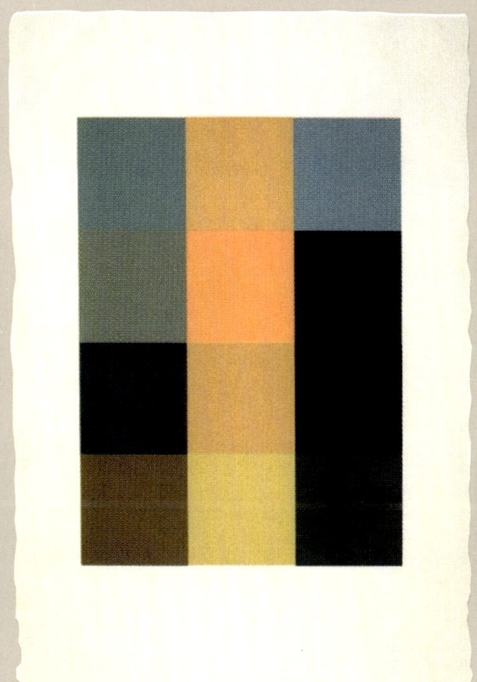

SHERRIE LEVINE (American, b. 1947)
Meltdown After Duchamp, Monet, Kirchner, Mondrian, 1989
Woodcuts
4 sheets, 37 x 26 (92.5 x 65) each
J. Miller, M. Sanchez, L. Gray
Peter Blum Editions, New York, New York

Levine has often borrowed images from art history for her work, often dealing with themes of artistic originality in a technological age. This series was made by scanning four famous art works. The scanner divided each work into 12 equivalent squares. The computer was asked to find the average color of each square. Levine matched the ink and printed via wood onto Japanese paper. These prints have been "melted down" from their renowned ancestors.

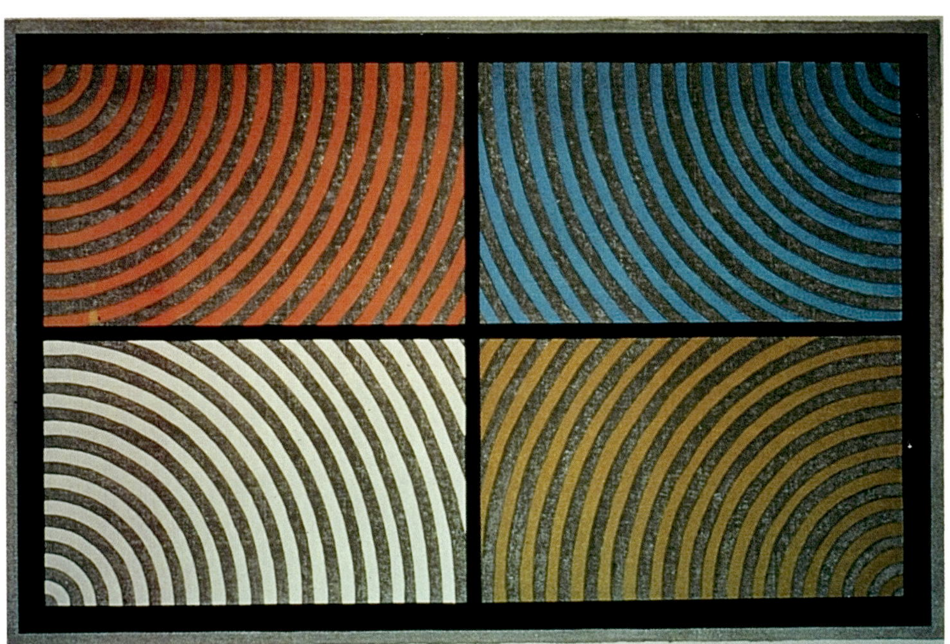

SOL LEWITT (American, b. 1928)
Arcs from Four Corners, 1986
Woodcut
21 x 33 (52.5 x 82.5)
Tadashi Toda
Carved by Shunzo Matsuda
Crown Point Press, San Francisco, California

In general, LeWitt uses only red, blue, yellow and black because these colors are basic to mechanical four-color printing. Master blockmakers in Japan cut the matrix according to a drawing provided by the artist.

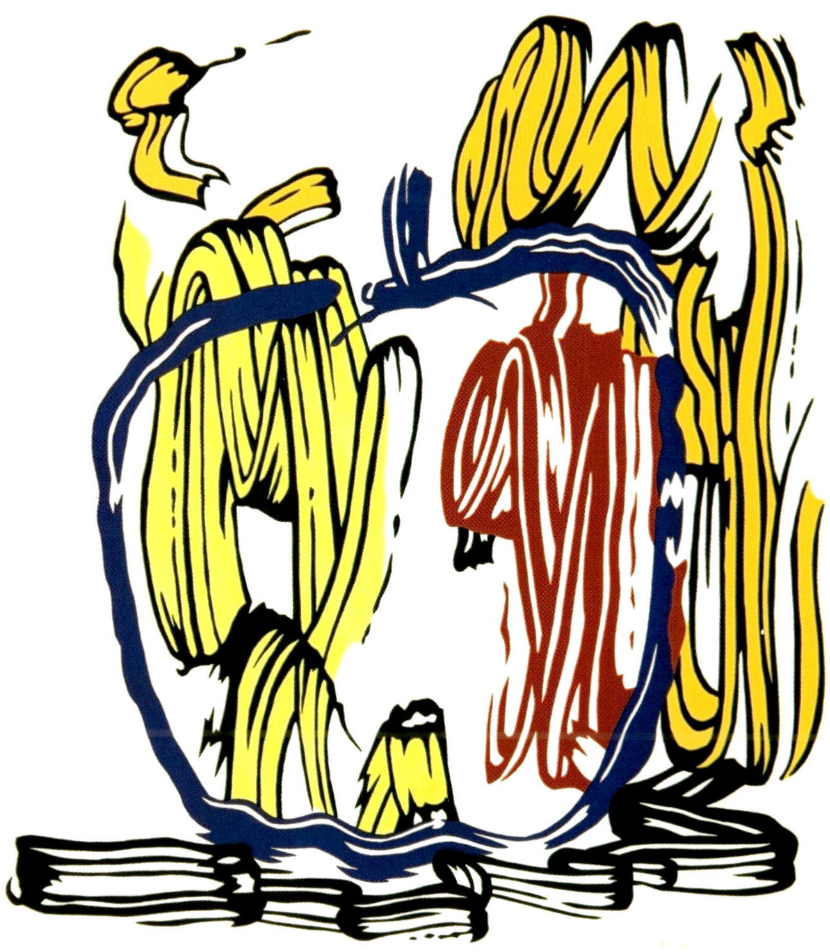

ROY LICHTENSTEIN (American, b. 1923)
Vertical Apple, from the series ***Seven Apple Woodcuts,*** 1983
Woodcut
37¼ x 32¾ (94.5 x 83)
Diane Hunt, Shigemitsu Tsukaguchi
Petersburg Press, New York, New York

In this Pop art approach to the traditional still-life, Lichtenstein abandons the Benday dots of his well-known comic-strip blow-ups for what seems to be a take-off on the "primal gesture" style of his Dutch contemporary, Karel Appel.

ROY LICHTENSTEIN (American, b. 1923)
I Love Liberty, 1982
Serigraph
39 x 27 (97.5 x 67.5)
Barbara Dunham, Julie McPherson, Ron McPherson
People for the American Way, Washington, D.C., and the artist

A founder of the Pop art movement, Lichtenstein subjects an emotionally charged American icon, the Statue of Liberty, to the formal concerns of composition and graphic impact. Dramatically fragmented and foreshortened, this serigraph reproduces the bold lines and contrasts associated with woodcuts, the first mass print medium.

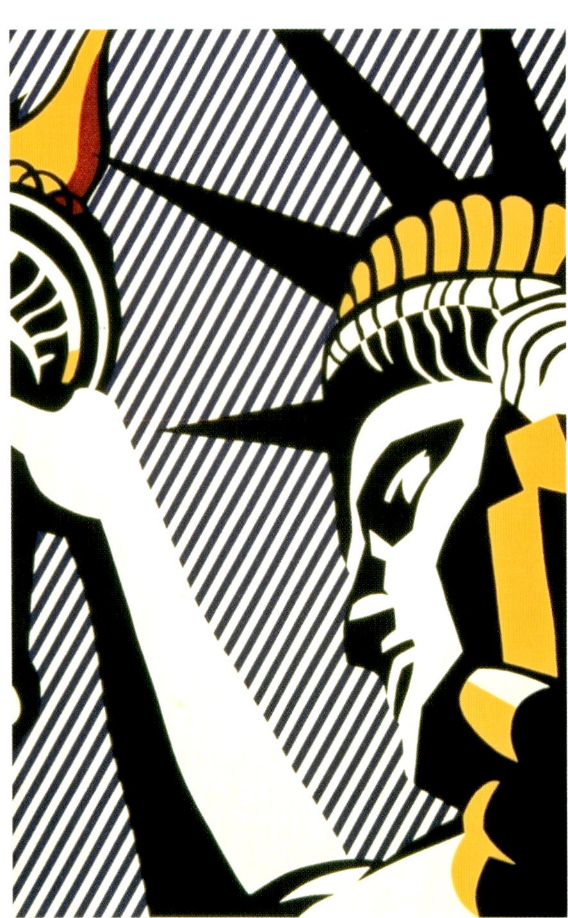

ROBERT LONGO (American, b. 1953)
Larry, Joanna from the suite ***Men in the Cities,*** 1983
Lithographs
Diptych, 72 x 36 (180 x 90) each
Editions Schellmann, Munich, Germany

In this dramatic series, photo-derived images are cropped, enlarged, isolated and stylized until they transcend their snapshot and tabloid sources. Are these anonymous figures dancing, recoiling or falling? The silhouettes are printed in three shades of black against stark white.

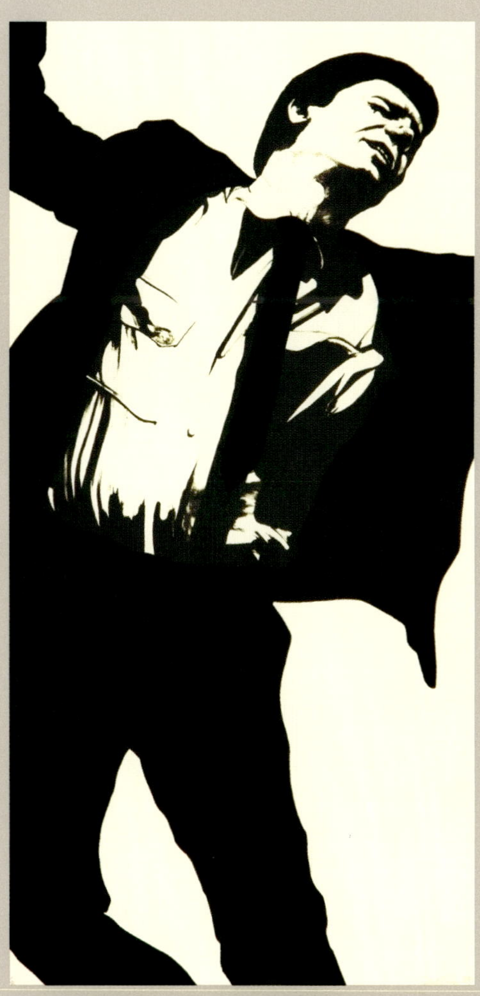

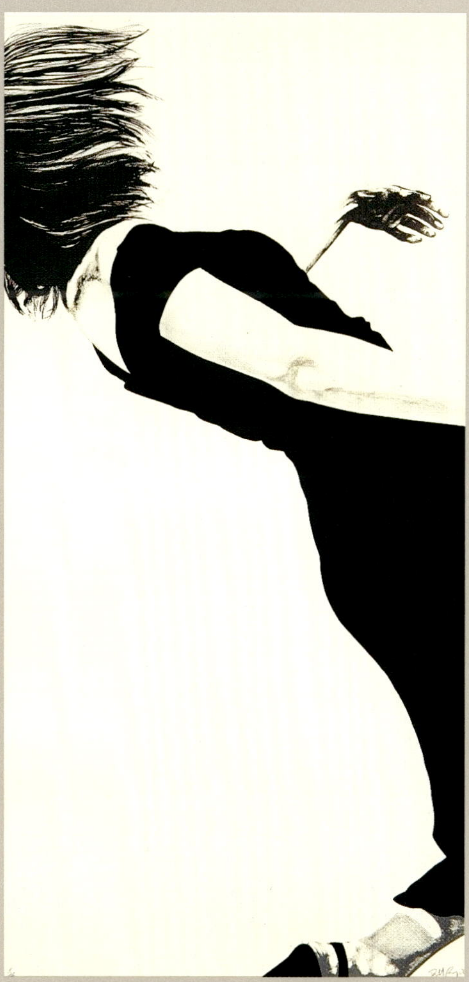

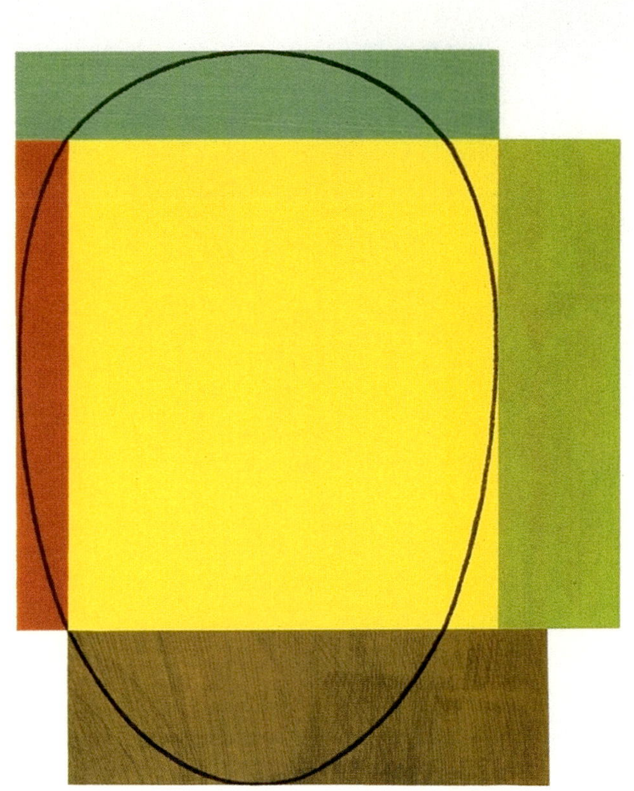

ROBERT MANGOLD (American, b. 1937)
Five Color Frame, 1985
Woodcut
25 x 21 (62.5 x 52.5)
Tadashi Toda
Carved by Shunzo Matsuda
Crown Point Press, San Francisco, California

The idea of an instinctive balance between color, line and shape has been at the center of Mangold's work since the early 60s. His *Frame Paintings* of 1984 were the culmination of his wish to work out this balance. In each work from this series, four rectangular canvases surround an area of blank wall space. Through each four-sided frame, a slightly askew oval is drawn. In this woodcut, Mangold's challenge was to achieve the same effect of these paintings on a single sheet of paper. This work is a study in asymmetry with each form slightly different from what we expect it to be.

GEORGIA MARSH (b. 1950)
Science of the Night, 1992
Monoprint
3 sheets, 18 x 22 (45 x 55) each
Derrière l'Étoile, New York, New York

Marsh is known for her close views of nature. Influenced by Taoist philosophy, her pictoral views have a gentle, serene, abstract quality. This beautiful monoprint draws one into tranquility.

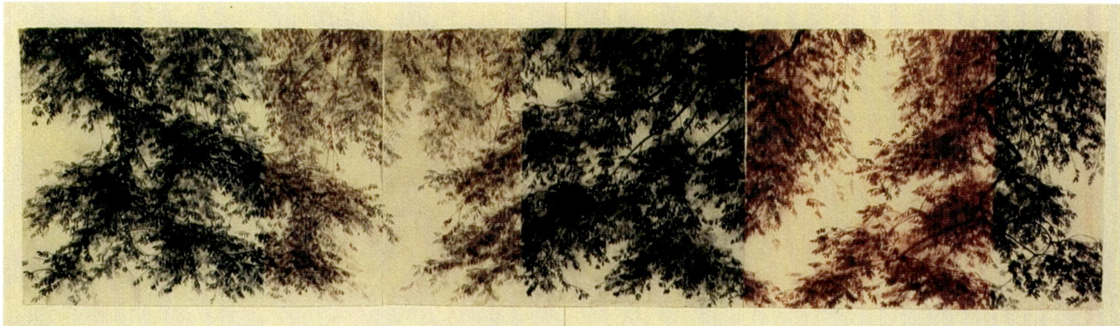

ANN MCCOY (American, b. 1946)
Night Sea, 1978
Lithograph
Diptych, 65½ x 34 (163.75 x 85) each
Derrière l'Étoile Studios, New York, New York

This mysterious diptych combines two worlds, in a rare view of the wonders of the ocean and cosmos. "My recurring childhood fantasy was from Jules Verne's *20,000 Leagues Under the Sea.* I dreamed I lived in a large house with a window that opened like an aperture of a camera ..." Here her ocean view includes the cosmos.

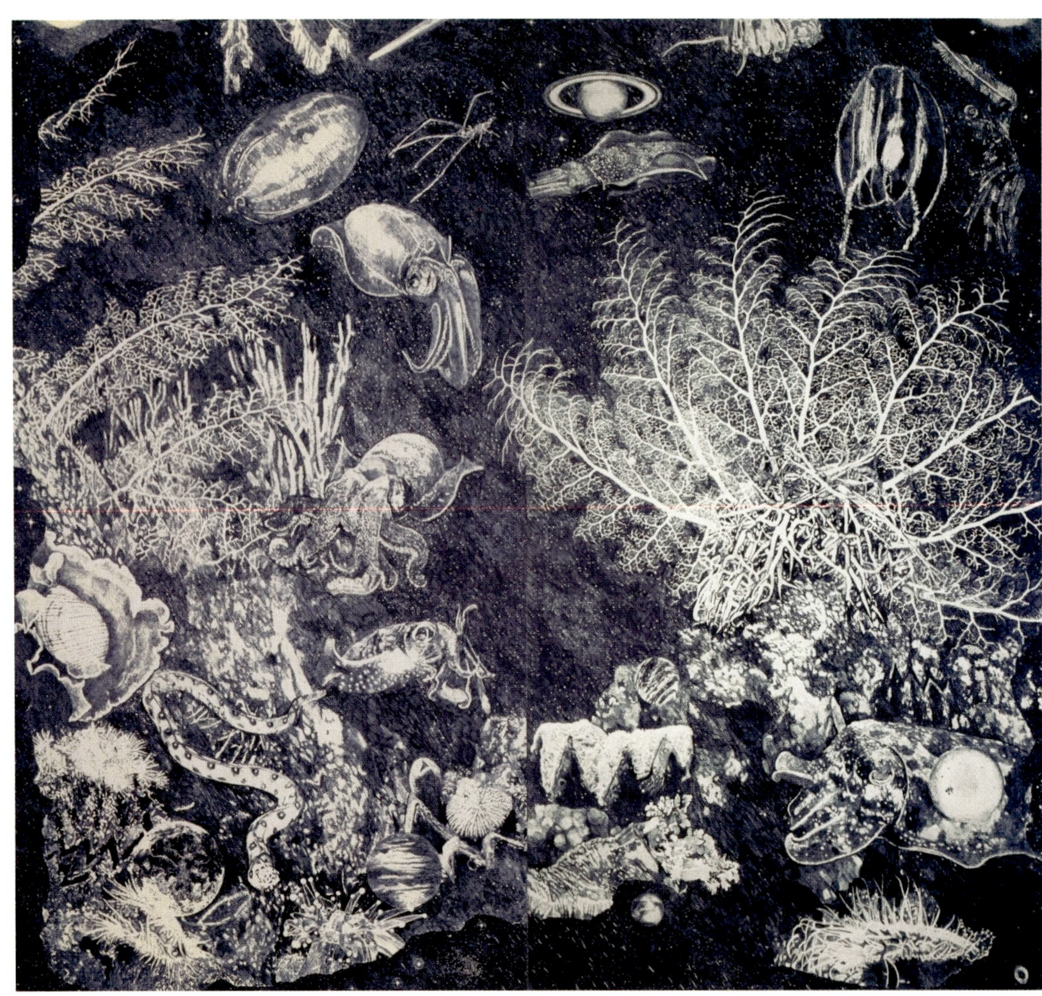

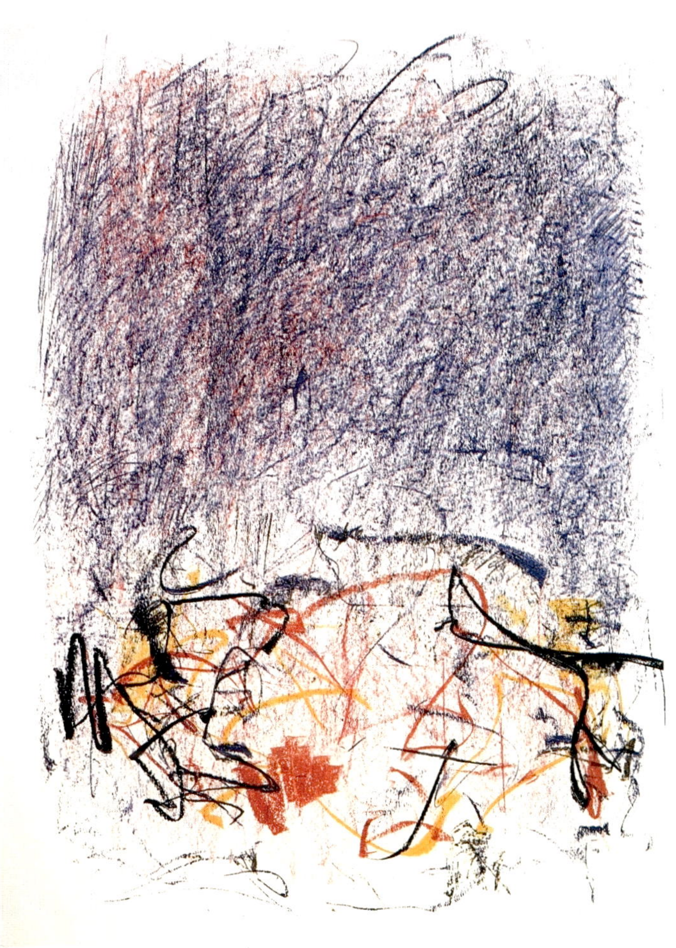

JOAN MITCHELL (American, 1926-1992)
Bedford I, from the ***Bedford Series,*** 1981
Lithograph
45½ x 32½ (115.6 x 82.6)
Kenneth Tyler, Lee Funderburg, Roger Campbell
Tyler Graphics Ltd., Mt. Kisco, New York

This print is from a series of 11 lithographs that Mitchell created at the workshop of Kenneth Tyler in Bedford Village, New York. The prints explore the relationship between land, horizon and sky in a landscape. The artist commented, "They're about a feeling that comes to me from the outside, from landscape."

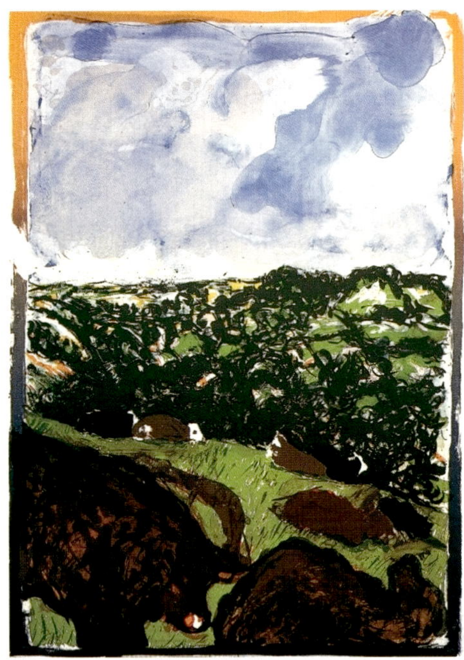

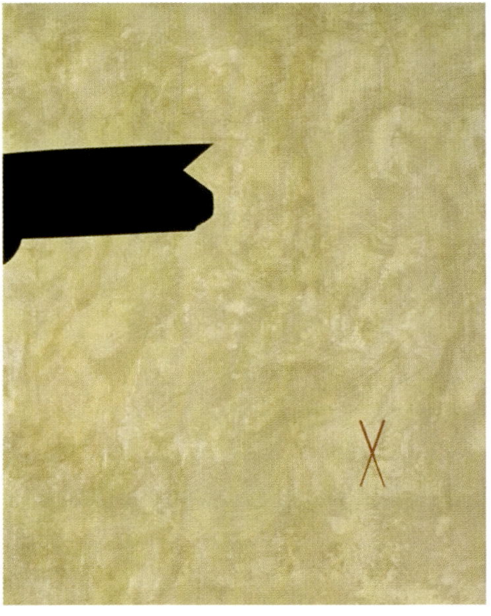

MALCOLM MORLEY (British, b. 1931)
Devonshire Bullocks, 1982
Lithograph
47¾ x 35 (121.3 x 88.9)
Kenneth Tyler, Lee Funderburg, Roger Campbell
Tyler Graphics Ltd., Mt. Kisco, New York

Inspired by an exhibition of American Abstract Expressionist paintings at London's Tate Gallery, Morley emigrated to New York to paint. A trip to Greece and his childhood spent in rural Devonshire inspired this work.

ROBERT MOSKOWITZ (American, b. 1935)
Cadillac Chopsticks, 1985
Lithograph
36 x 30 (90 x 75)
Vermillion Press, Minneapolis, Minnesota

Moskowitz first gained critical attention in the late 1960s when he produced pale, monochromatic paintings depicting the ambiguous geometry of a corner. Later, he began a deliberate investigation of the symbolic use of color and more recognizable subject matter. He often combines abstraction and representation in one work, allowing the viewer to explore the relationship between the two.

ROBERT MOTHERWELL (American, 1915-1991)
Rite of Passage III, 1980
Lithograph, with chine appliqué
24¾ x 34 (62.9 x 86.14)
Steve Reeves, Rodney Konopaki, Lindsay Green, Kenneth Tyler, Lee Funderburg
Tyler Graphics Ltd., Mt. Kisco, New York

Motherwell was one of the originators of the Abstract Expressionist movement. With little formal training, he became an art world icon. This print typifies the gestural, automatic style that became the movement's emblem. To break the ice, he practiced "automatic drawing." One mark led to the next and the next. In this way, he delved into his subconscious, often editing as he went. "Mainly, I use black and white as the protagonists, representing being and non-being, life and death."

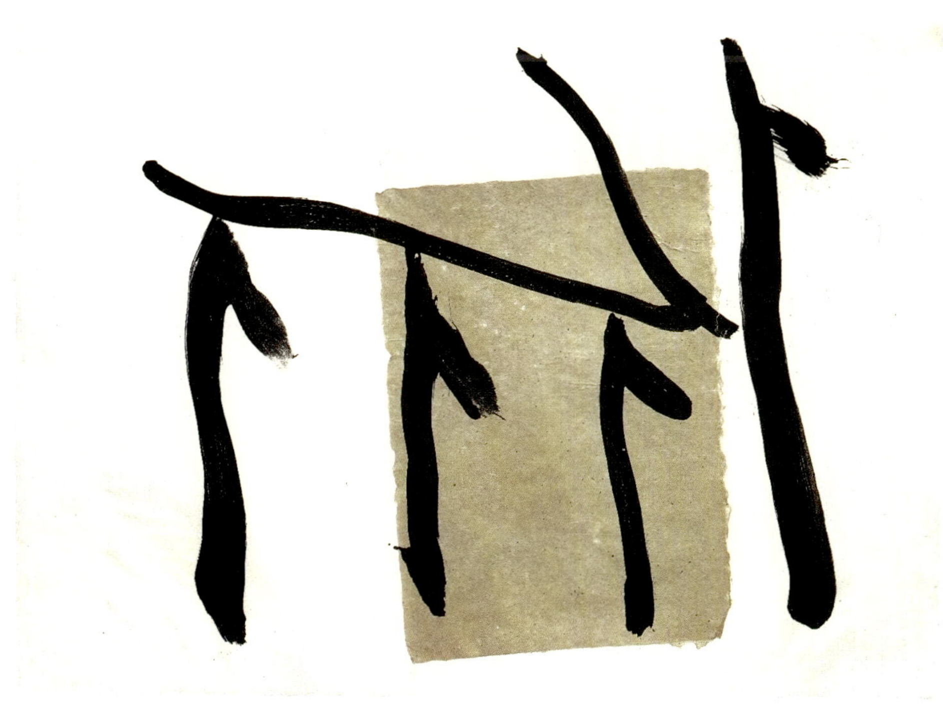

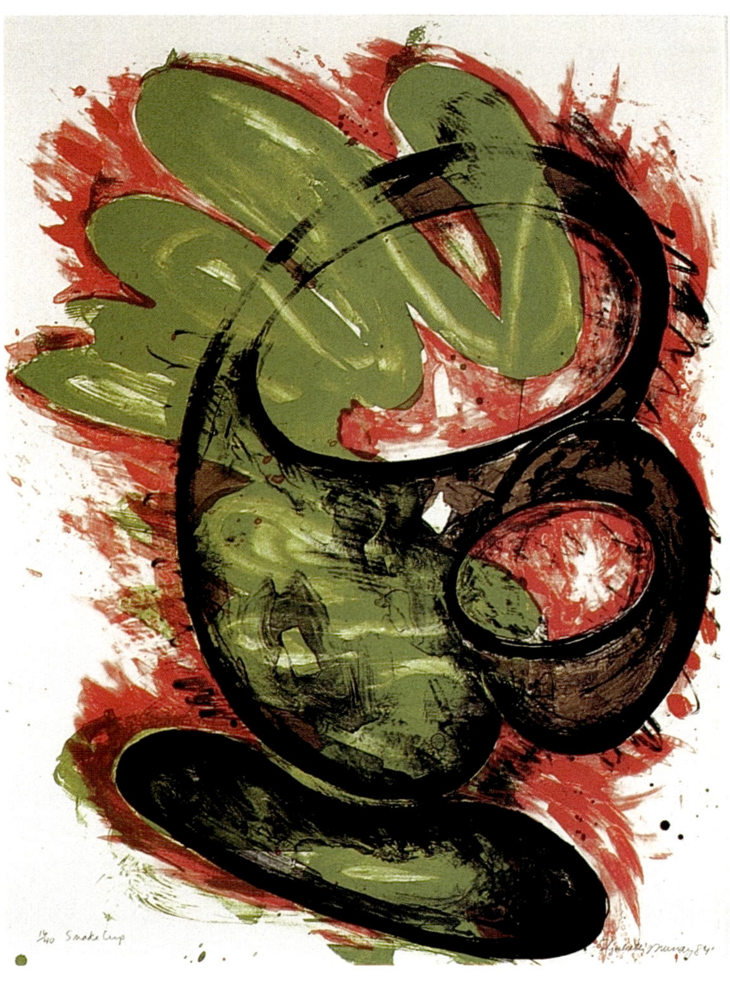

94 ELIZABETH MURRAY (American, b. 1940)
Snake Cup, 1984
Lithograph
32 x 25 (80 x 62.5)
Brooke Alexander Inc., New York, New York, and
Paula Cooper Editions, New York, New York

The coffee cup, with its repeated circular shapes and domestic associations, is a favorite motif of Murray's. The image's off-beat exuberance, risky tilt and dynamic tension between impulse and control add to its emotional and visual impact.

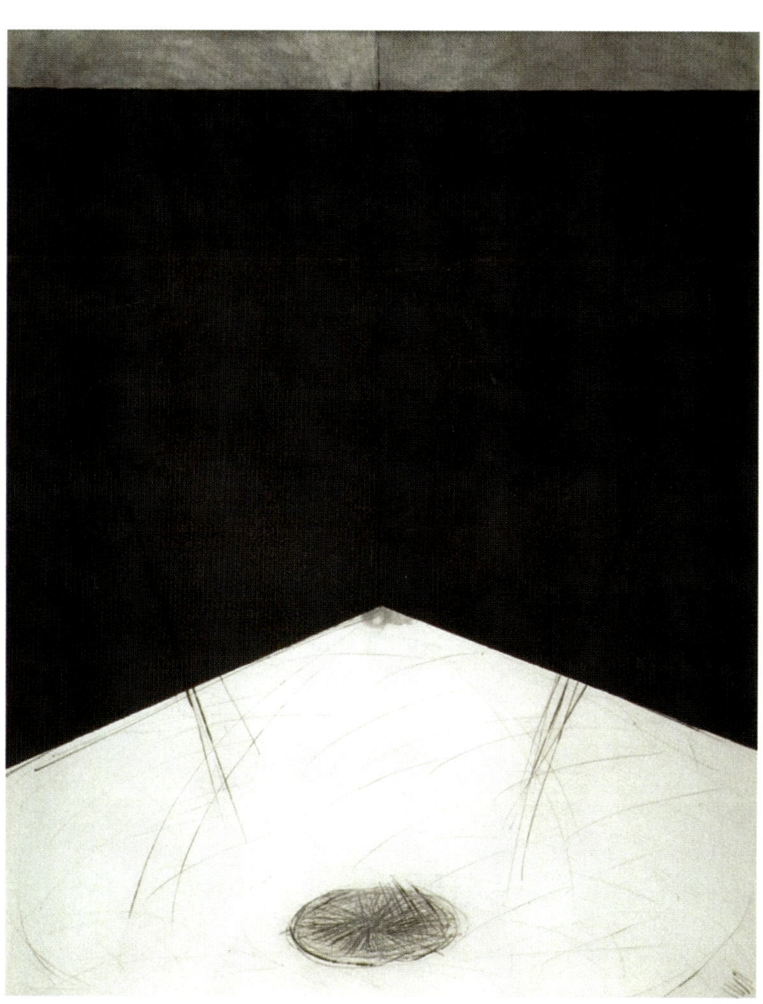

BRUCE NAUMAN (American, b. 1941)
Floor Drain, 1985
Etching, with drypoint and aquatint
39 x 28 (97.5 x 70)
Gemini G.E.L., Los Angeles, California

Nauman has lent his style to works of sculpture, drawing and printmaking, holography, video and performance art. The subject that most fascinates Nauman is the ever-changing complexities of the human condition. He is constantly exploring language, philosophy and psychology in startling, disturbing ways. Many of his works are confrontational, causing the viewer a wide range of emotions, from surprise to embarrassment.

BARNETT NEWMAN (American, 1905-1970)
Untitled, 1969
Etching, aquatint
15 x 24 (37.5 x 60)
Universal Limited Art Editions (ULAE), West Islip, New York

Newman was a major force in painting in the New York school of Abstract Expressionism. His approach was simplification of elements. His famous "zip" came to be on his birthday in 1948. The "zip" charges through flat, static color fields in his works. He extolled, "It does not cut in half, but unites, creates a totality." Here the "zip" unites two unequal white fields bounded by narrow etched lines along the vertical margins. This print was one of Newman's rare experiments with printmaking.

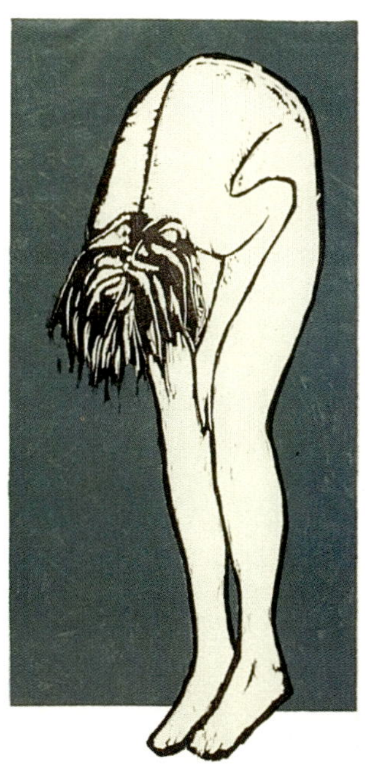

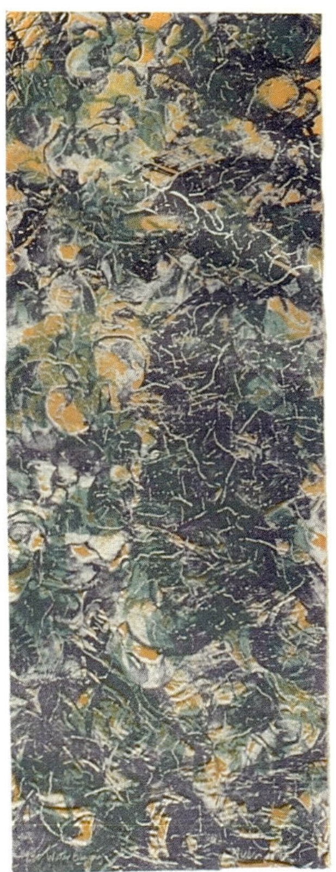

STUART NIELSEN (American, b. 1947)
Untitled, 1983
Woodcut, serigraph
62 x 13 (155 x 32.5)
Vermillion Press, Minneapolis, Minnesota

Nielsen is a Minnesota artist known for his murals. More than five feet high and in a striking vertical format, *Untitled* has an interesting mix of print mediums. The stark figure is boldly defined by woodblock, and is dramatically perched over a richly colored pool made possible by screen printing.

CLAES OLDENBURG (American, b. in Sweden, 1929)
The Letter Q as Beach House, with Sailboat, 1972
Lithograph
39 x 29½ (97.5 x 73.75)
Kenneth Tyler, George Page
Gemini G.E.L., Los Angeles, California

Oldenburg takes everyday objects and transforms them in scale and context, injecting his compositions with humor and irony. From the late 60s to the mid-70s, letters of the alphabet figured prominently in his work, and the Q was particularly important, being the subject of more than forty works. In this print, the colossal Q assumes the improbable function of a vacation home that dominates its watery setting. He turned the letter upside down since "an inverted position seemed necessary because a Q with its tail buried wouldn't be a Q at all."

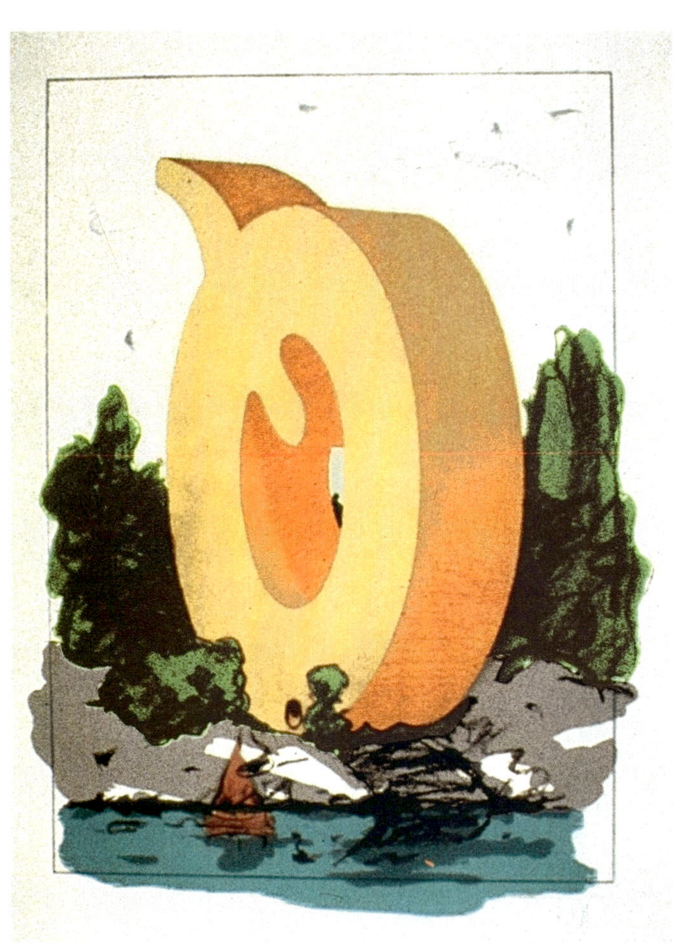

ROBERT PETERSEN (American, b. 1945)
September 1976, 1977
Lithograph, with chine collé
43 x 30 (107.5 x 75)
Styria Studio, New York, New York

Although Peterson's Minimal art emphasizes the purely visual experience of basic shapes, in this lithograph the planklike surfaces of the two divided squares may also be associated with the world of ordinary objects. Variations of tone and texture, and contrasts of delicate line with rough plane, relieve the austerity of the work.

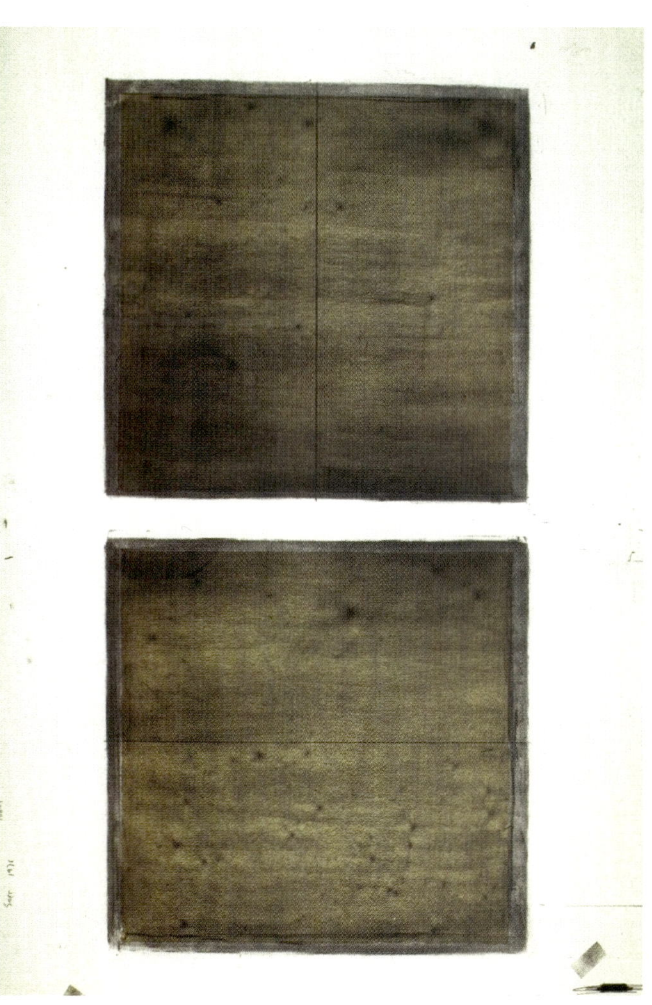

JUDY PFAFF (English, b. 1946)
Half a Dozen of the Other: Che Cosa É Acqua, 1992
Etching, drypoint, spit-bite aquatint, soft-ground etching, sugar-lift aquatint
42⅞ x 50⅝ (107.25 x 126.75)
Lawrence Hamlin
Crown Point Press, San Francisco, California

Pfaff populates her compositions with biomorphic shapes that ebb and flow across the print. The clear linear strength and the rich, deep colors are the result of her skill at combining several printing techniques.

JAUNE QUICK-TO-SEE SMITH (Native American, b. 1940)
Fish for a Lifetime (State IV), 1994
Lithograph
11¼ x 15 (28 x 37.5)
Tamarind Institute, Albuquerque, New Mexico

Quick-To-See Smith, of French, Cree and Shoshone heritage, is internationally known for her painting and printmaking. This print illustrates the adage about teaching a man to fish, rather than giving him a fish; an old lesson from Native American culture.

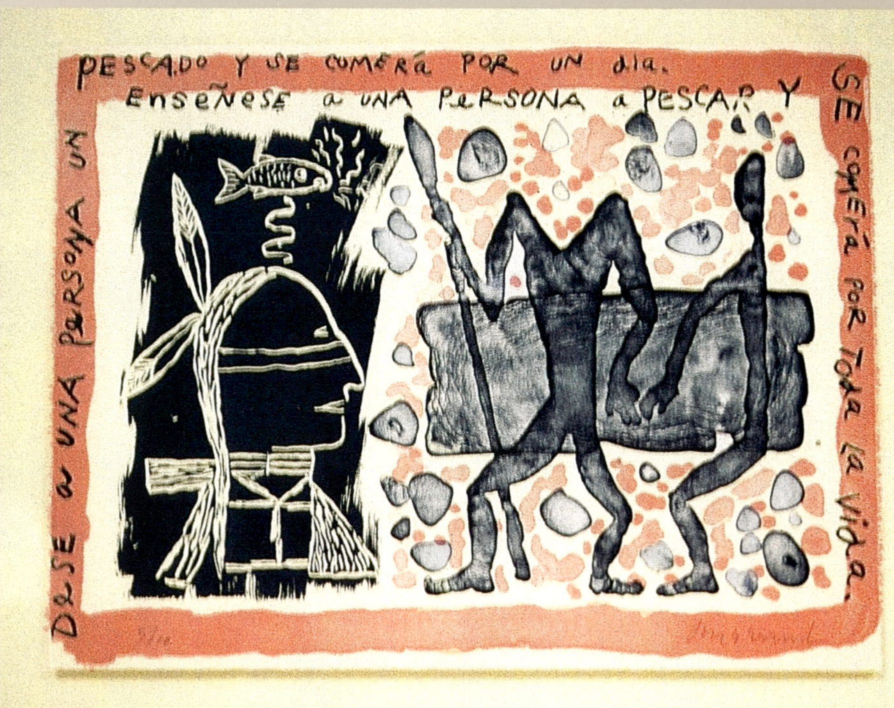

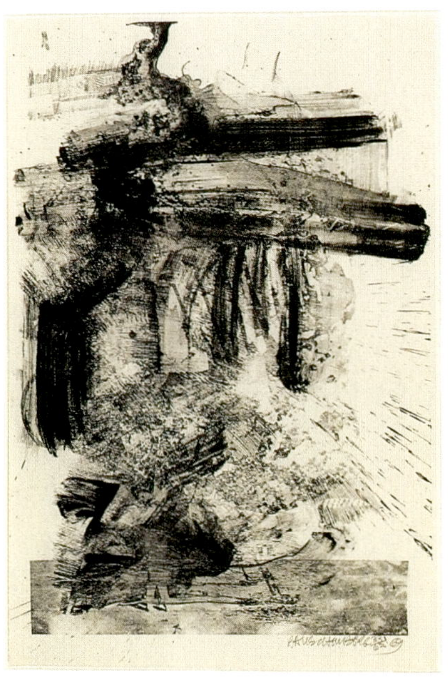

ROBERT RAUSCHENBERG (American, b. 1925)
Earth Crust, from the ***Stoned Moon Series,*** 1969
Lithograph
34 x 25 (85 x 62.5)
Kenneth Tyler, Charly Ritt, Ron Adams,
Ron McPherson, Robert Petersen, Andrew Vlady,
Timothy Isham, Stuart Henderson
Gemini G.E.L., Los Angeles, California

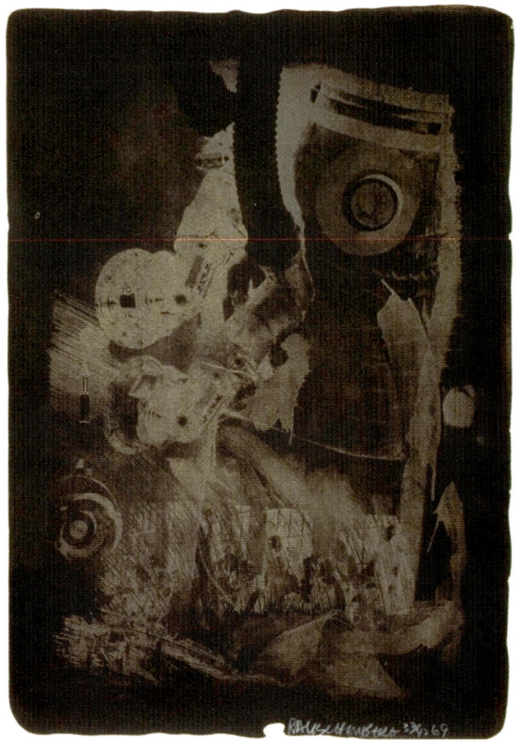

ROBERT RAUSCHENBERG (American, b. 1925)
Fuse, from the ***Stoned Moon Series,*** 1969
Lithograph
38 x 26 (95 x 65)
Kenneth Tyler, Charly Ritt, Ron Adams,
Ron McPherson, Robert Petersen, Andrew Vlady,
Timothy Isham, Stuart Henderson
Gemini G.E.L., Los Angeles, California

Rauschenberg has been a major figure in American Pop art since the 60s and ranks among the most innovative artists to work in printmaking in the past two decades. The images in his *Stoned Moon Series* were derived from official photographs provided by NASA shortly after Rauschenberg's visit to the Kennedy Space Center.

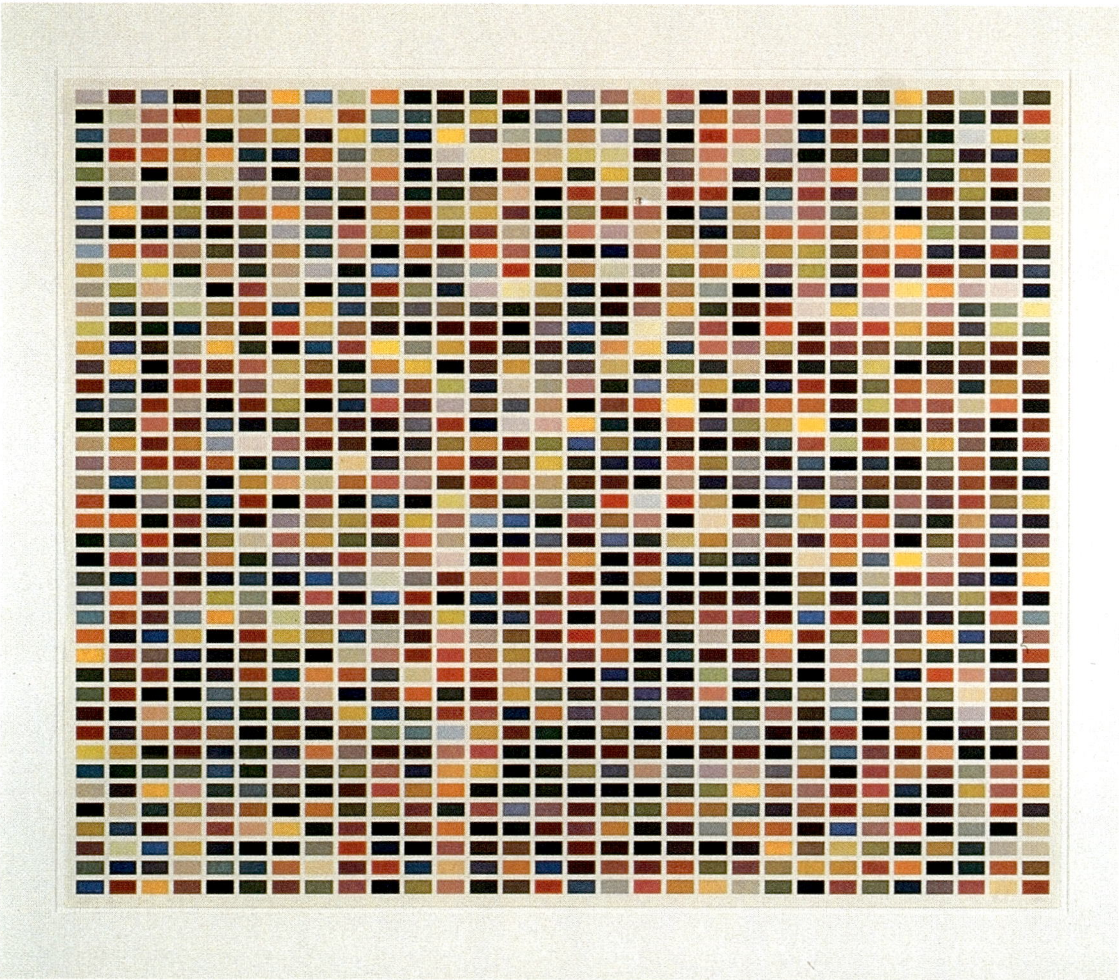

GERHARD RICHTER (German, b. 1932)
Farbfelder (Color Fields: Six Arrangements of 1260 Colors), 1974
Lithograph
25½ x 31¼ (63.75 x 78 cm)

Richter made a series of paintings and prints dealing with color charts. He explained, "In order to present all the existent color tones in one picture, I developed a system which – based on the three primary colors plus gray – permitted a progressive differentiation in constantly uniform steps.... The arrangement of the color tones in the fields was coincidental, so as to achieve a diffuse, indifferent effect and thus permit exciting details."

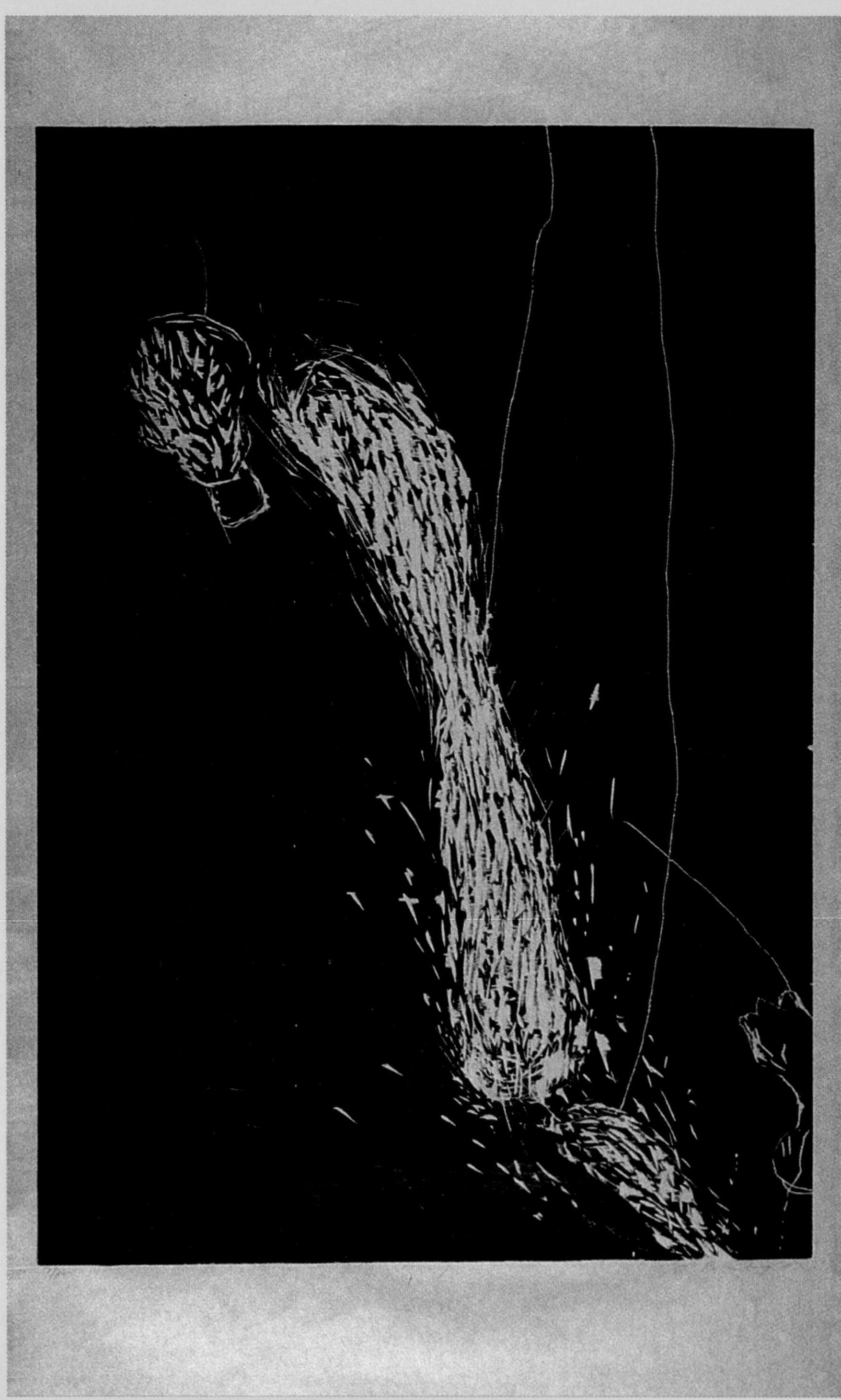

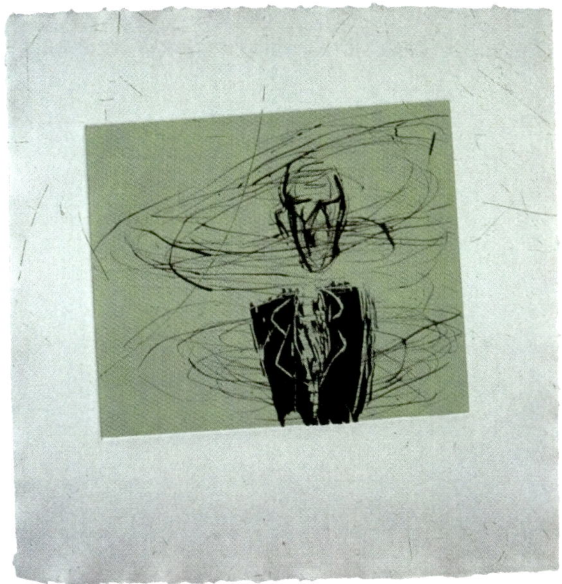

SUSAN ROTHENBERG (American, b. 1945)
Breath-Man, 1986
Drypoint, woodcut, engraving
21 x 21 (52.5 x 52.5)
Ken Farley, Diana Kingsley, William Padien, Anthony Zepeda
Gemini G.E.L., Los Angeles, California

In her shift from her favorite horse motif to human figure in the 1980s, she began to study the portrayal of motion. Although the figure is static, there is a frantic sense of movement in this print of a man who seems to struggle with the swirls of air, mist or smoke enveloping him.

SUSAN ROTHENBERG (American, b. 1945)
Puppet, 1983
Woodcut
47½ x 33½ (119 x 83.75)
Multiples Inc., New York

Rothenberg creates psychologically charged, more or less figural images. The flickering broken marks which simultaneously assault and merge with the black ground of this woodcut are typical of Rothenberg's style. The disquieting form with its snarling mouth dangles from fragile strings, seeming to emerge from a ghostly cocoon.

ED RUSCHA (American, b. 1937)
Home with Complete Electronic Security System, 1982
Serigraph
19 x 48 (47.5 x 120 cm)
Printed by the artist

Ruscha, a West Coast Pop artist, has made the everyday world of Los Angeles his inspiration. Here we see his familiar landscape found in Standard station and Hollywood, visual icons of the 60s.

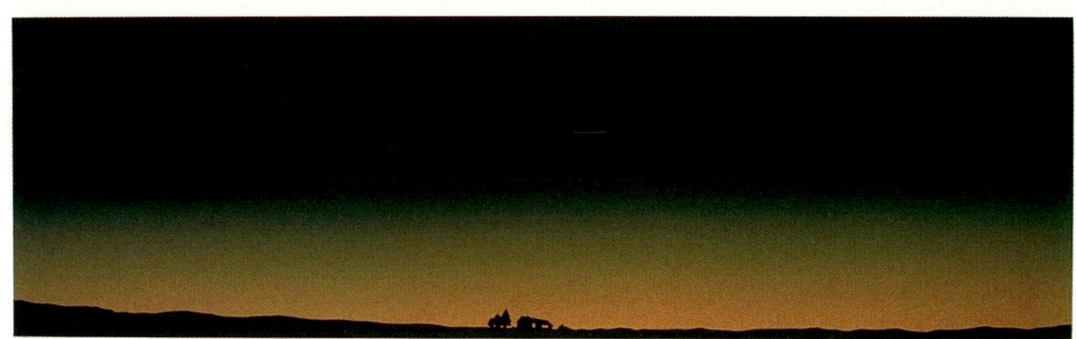

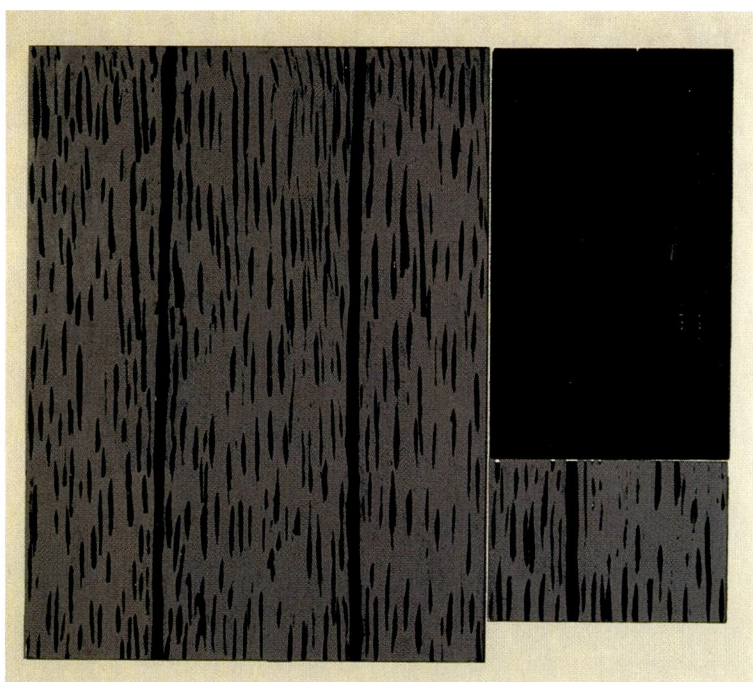

SEAN SCULLY (American, b. in Ireland, 1945)
Block, 1986
Woodcut
29⅞ X 35 (74.25 x 87.5)
Diane Villani Editions, New York, New York

Scully's work comprises vertical and horizontal stripes of varying width and breadth, occasionally mixed with diagonal lines. A viewer may first be struck by the cold, geometric shapes of Scully's works, but the complex surfaces and irregular borders often spark an emotional reaction to his work. "I don't want to make things just to look at; I want to make things that make people react," Scully says.

108 RICHARD SERRA (American, b. 1939)
Spoleto Circle, 1972
Lithograph
35 x 51 (87.5 x 127.5)
Serge Lozingot
Gemini G.E.L., Los Angeles, California

Serra has established himself as a leading sculptor and printmaker. This lithograph is from a series of prints based on sculptural installations of the early 1970s. The deep, rich black is analogous to the dark, heavy industrial material, such as lead or steel, that he uses in his sculpture.

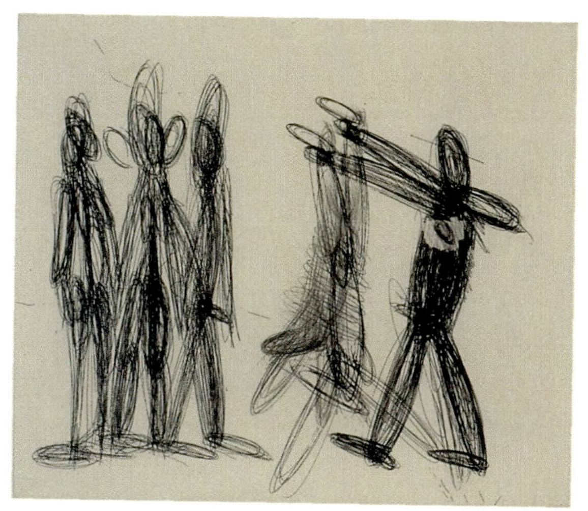

JOEL SHAPIRO (American, b. 1941)
untitled (O), 1995
Hard-ground etching, drypoint
20½ x 17 (51.25 x 42.5)
Joel Shapiro
Maurice Payne, New York, New York

Shapiro has modified the Minimalism of his early sculptures with increasingly figurative, emotive associations. The rough figures in these etchings (from a series of 18) are composed of primal stick or blocklike parts, recalling the joined cylinders and cubes of his sculpture. The tilting, shifting shapes and scribbled gestures suggest the dynamics of transformation, confrontation and conflict.

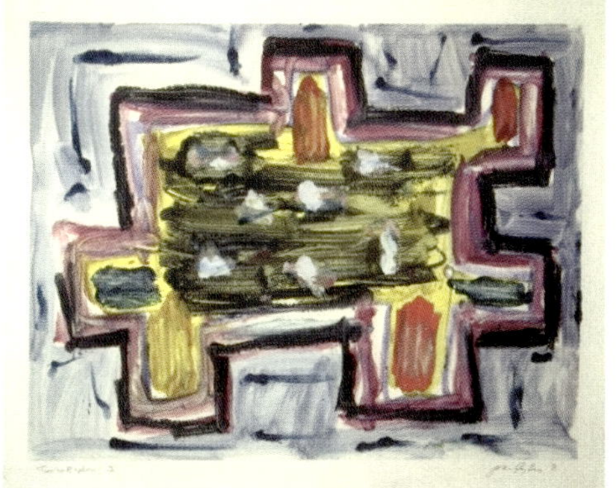

JOAN SNYDER (American, b. 1940)
Free to Explore, 1982
Monoprint
22 x 30 (55 x 75)
Derrière l'Étoile, New York, New York

Snyder is an artist whose feminist concerns are the driving force in her work. An Expressionist, Snyder deals with the difficult issues women face, making order out of pain. "When I started painting it was like I was speaking for the first time."

ROBERT STACKHOUSE (American, b. 1942)
Soundless, 1992
Spit-bite etching
38 x 58 (95 x 145)
Andrew Rubin
Tandem Press, Madison, Wisconsin

Stackhouse chose the intaglio processes of spit-bite etching to create a mystical image of a ship hull and its reflection. He is fascinated with the mystique of Viking transatlantic voyages and feels that the image of a boat symbolizes his own journey through life.

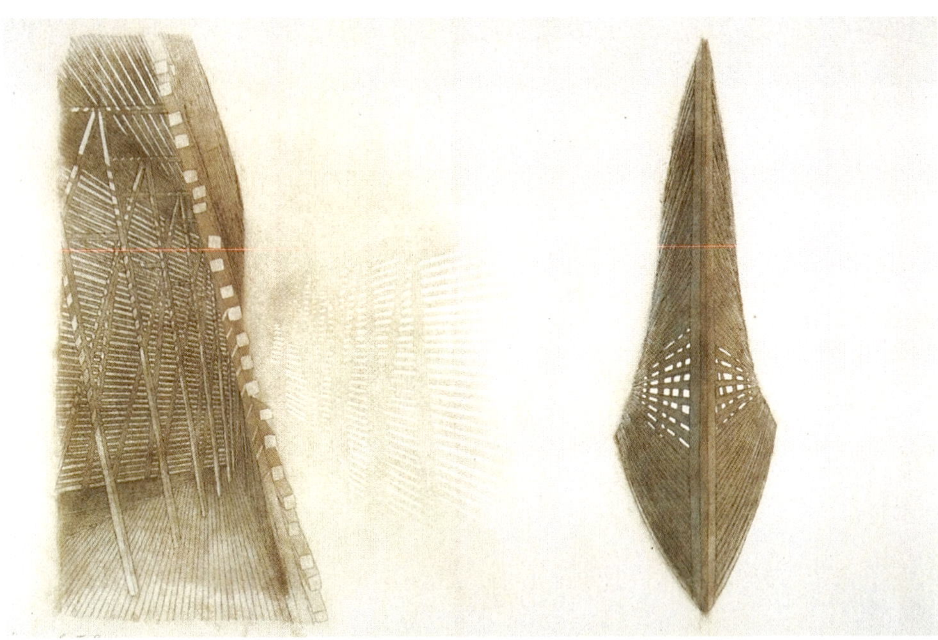

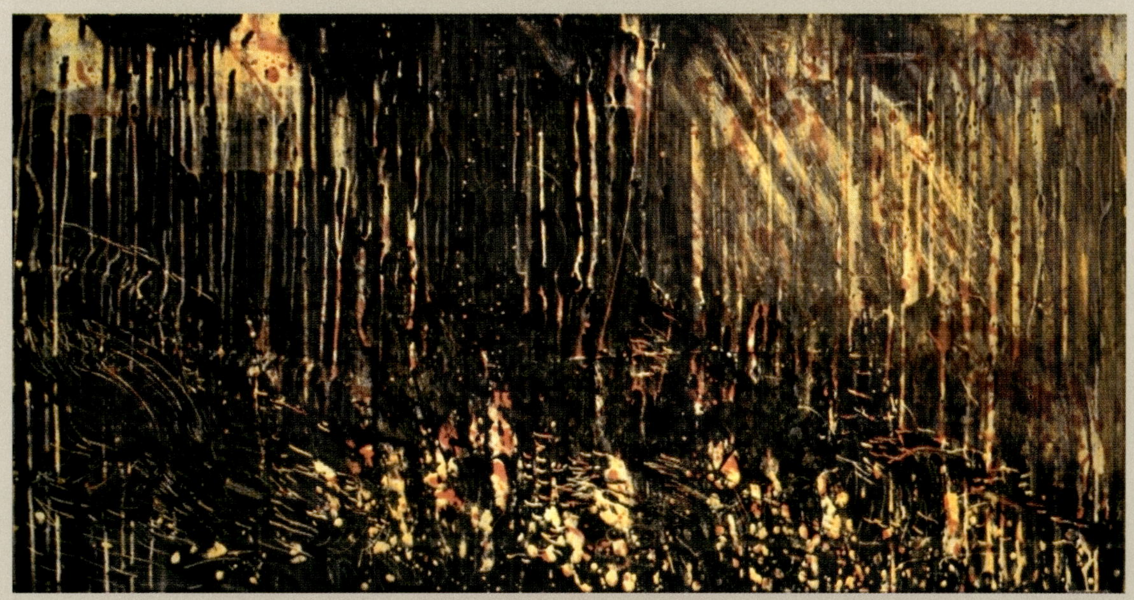

PAT STEIR (American, b. 1940)
Long Horizontal, 1991
Aquatint, spit-bite aquatint, aquatint rosin reversal, with drypoint, burnishing, sanding
30 x 51 (75 x 127.5)
Brian Shure
Crown Point Press, San Francisco, California

Since the mid-1980s, Steir has been exploring waterfalls, bringing the downward plunge of water up close to eliminate any boundaries. In this work, the water rushes down amid warm reds and yellows, imparting a sense of movement and shimmering light. Steir's waterfalls deal with the relationship between abstract and representational art.

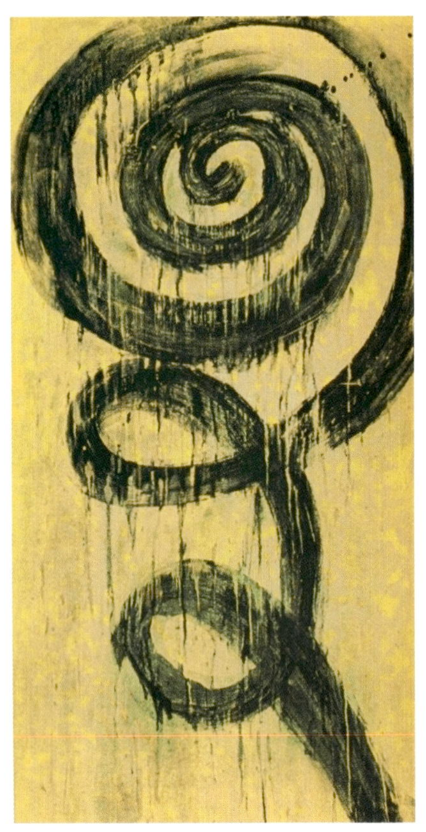

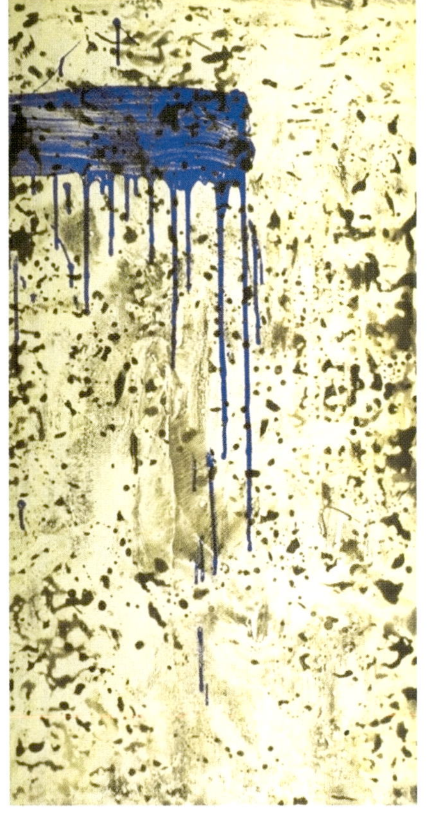

PAT STEIR (American, b. 1940)
Fern, 1993
Etching, soap-ground reversal, with aquatint, spit-bite aquatint
54 x 29⅞ (135 x 74.25)
Daria Sywulak
Crown Point Press, San Francisco, California

PAT STEIR (American, b. 1940)
Evening, 1993
Etching, soap-ground reversal, with aquatint, spit-bite aquatint
54 x 29⅞ (135 x 74.25)
Daria Sywulak
Crown Point Press, San Francisco, California

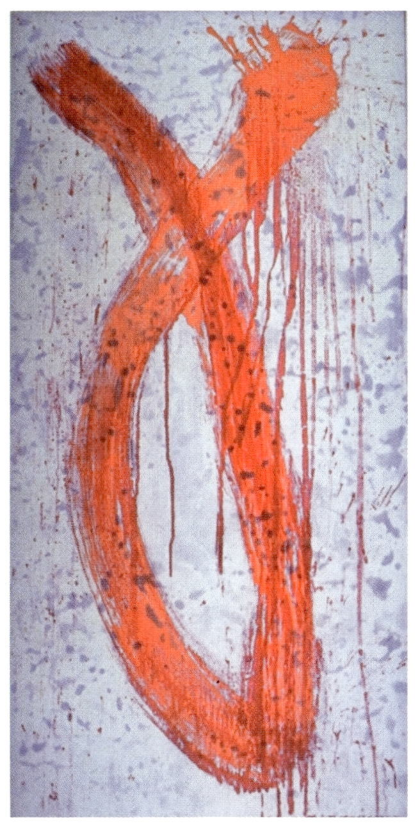

Throughout her career, Steir has been a dedicated printmaker, commonly making multi-piece series. In each of these three prints, she explores the relationship of a single figure against a background within an unusual vertical format.

PAT STEIR (American, b. 1940)
Peony, 1993
Etching, soap-ground reversal, with aquatint, spit-bite aquatint
54 x 29⅞ (135 x 74.25)
Daria Sywulak
Crown Point Press, San Francisco, California

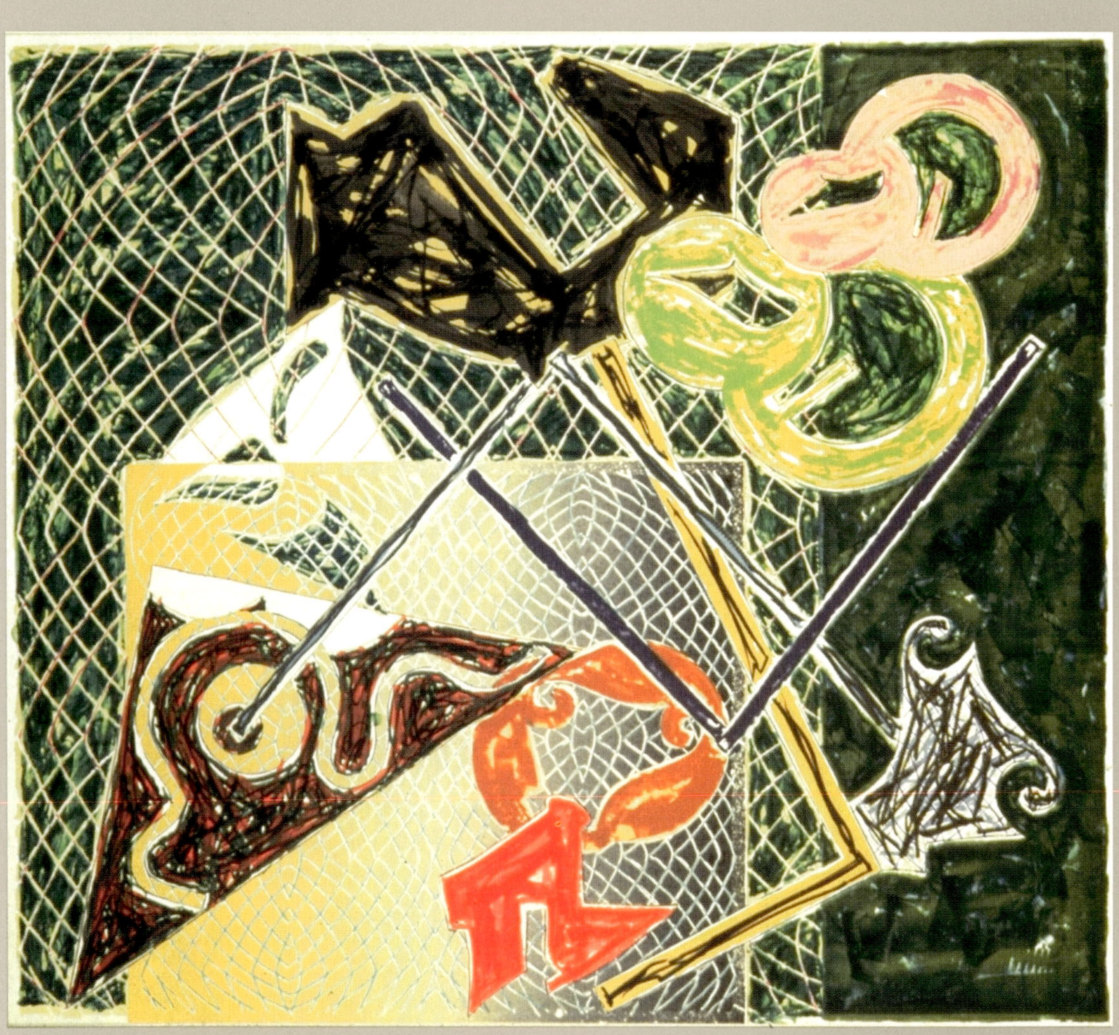

CAROL SUMMERS (American, b. 1925)
Kali Gandaki, 1983
Woodcut
37 x 37 (92.5 x 92.5)
Printed by the artist

Summers works almost exclusively with woodcuts to show imaginary landscapes. According to the artist, the work is "an expression of feelings and states of mind, often vague and illusive, perhaps completely unconscious, but still strong and pervasive. In that sense, these prints are all self-portraits."

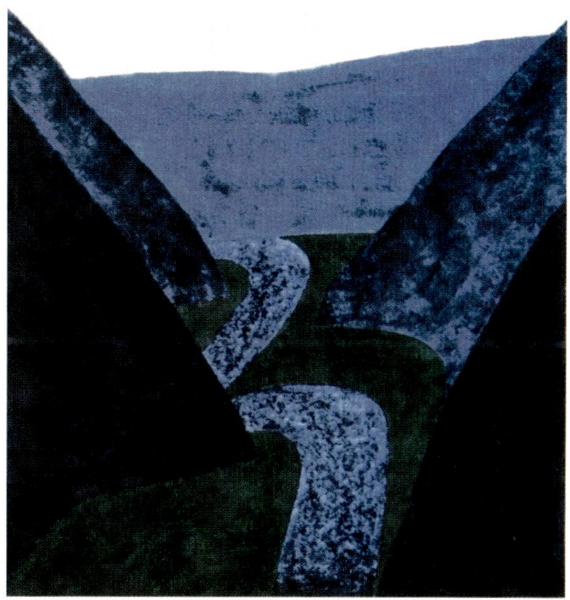

FRANK STELLA (American, b. 1936)
Shards V, 1982
Lithograph, serigraph
39⅞ x 45 (99.25 x 112.5)
Petersburg Press, London, England

The recognizable tools of draftsman and architect are integrated in this print, one of a series inspired by bits and pieces discarded during the printmaking process. Complicated linear patterns combined with spontaneous brushwork and color variations create a sense of deeply layered space.

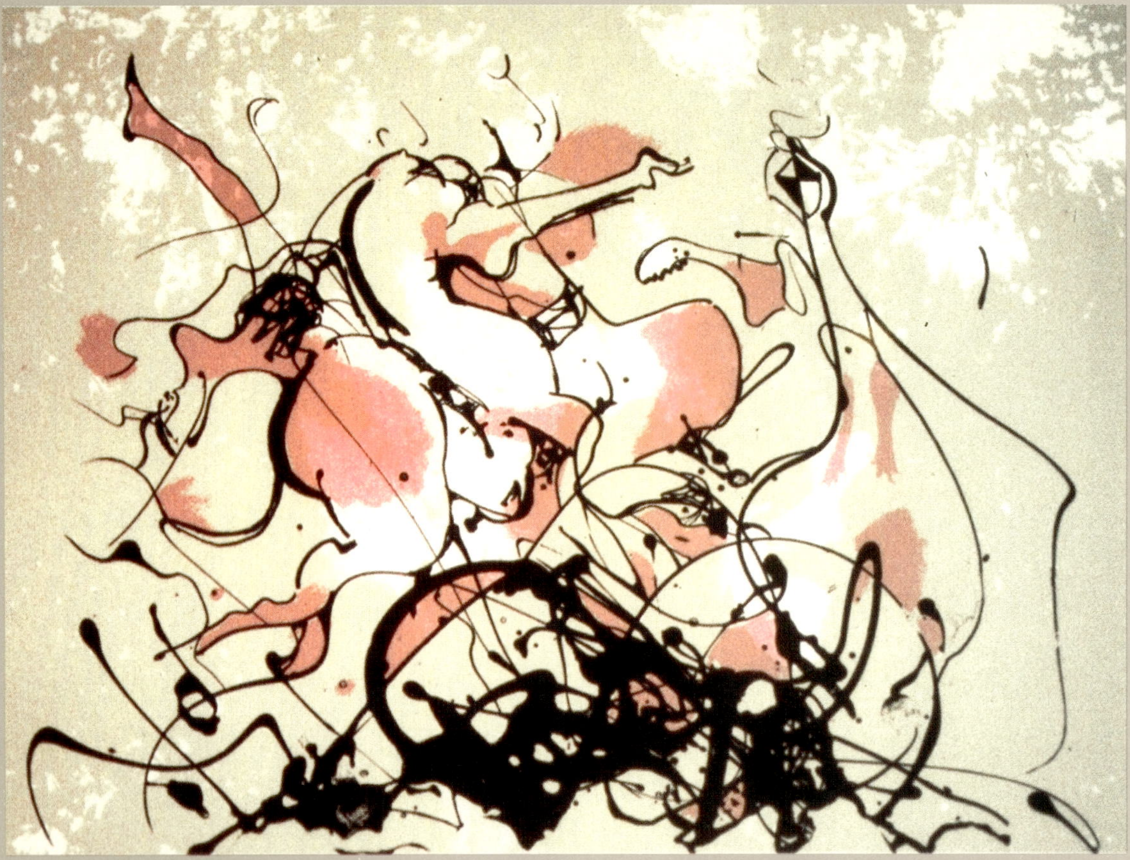

DOROTHEA TANNING (American, b. 1911)
Untitled, 1992
Lithograph
19 x 21¼ (47.5 x 53)
Derrière l'Étoile Studios, New York, New York

Tanning has been a major figure in the surrealist movement since the 1940s. She married the artist Max Ernst in 1946 and has worked in the U.S. and France. Tanning is known for her command of graphic expression, sureness of touch and very personal iconography.

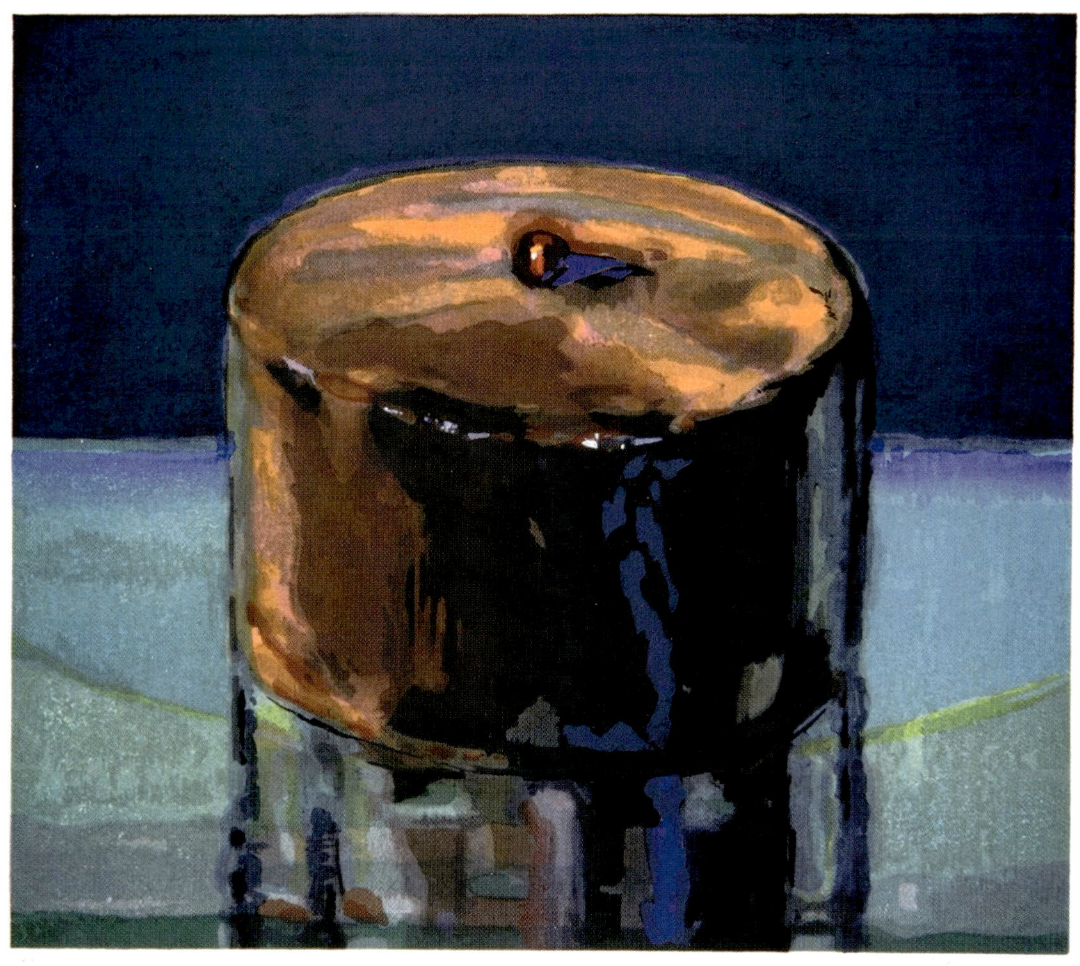

WAYNE THIEBAUD (American, b. 1920)
Dark Cake, 1983
Woodcut
17½ x 20 (43.75 x 53)
Crown Point Press, San Francisco, California

Thiebaud worked at the Disney studios and in advertising. His bright pictures of mass-produced food displays first attracted attention in the Pop art context of the 1960s. Thiebaud has likened cakes to "glorious toys," and reproduces the luscious quality of his painting in this spot-lit confection.

RICHARD TUTTLE (American, b. 1941)
Perceived Obstacles, 1991
Lithographs, printed in color
5 sheets, 12 x 36 (30 x 90 cm) each
M. Sanchez, J. Miller, J. Petruzzelli, L. Gray
Brooke Alexander Editions, New York, New York

In this suite of five lithographs, tiny images force the viewer to zero in on the subject. In an essay on Tuttle's 1975 exhibition at the Whitney Museum of American Art, Marcia Tucker comments: "Tuttle's work, in order to be seen at all, focuses on the viewer's attention in a particular way, forcing a concentration that alters one's vision…"

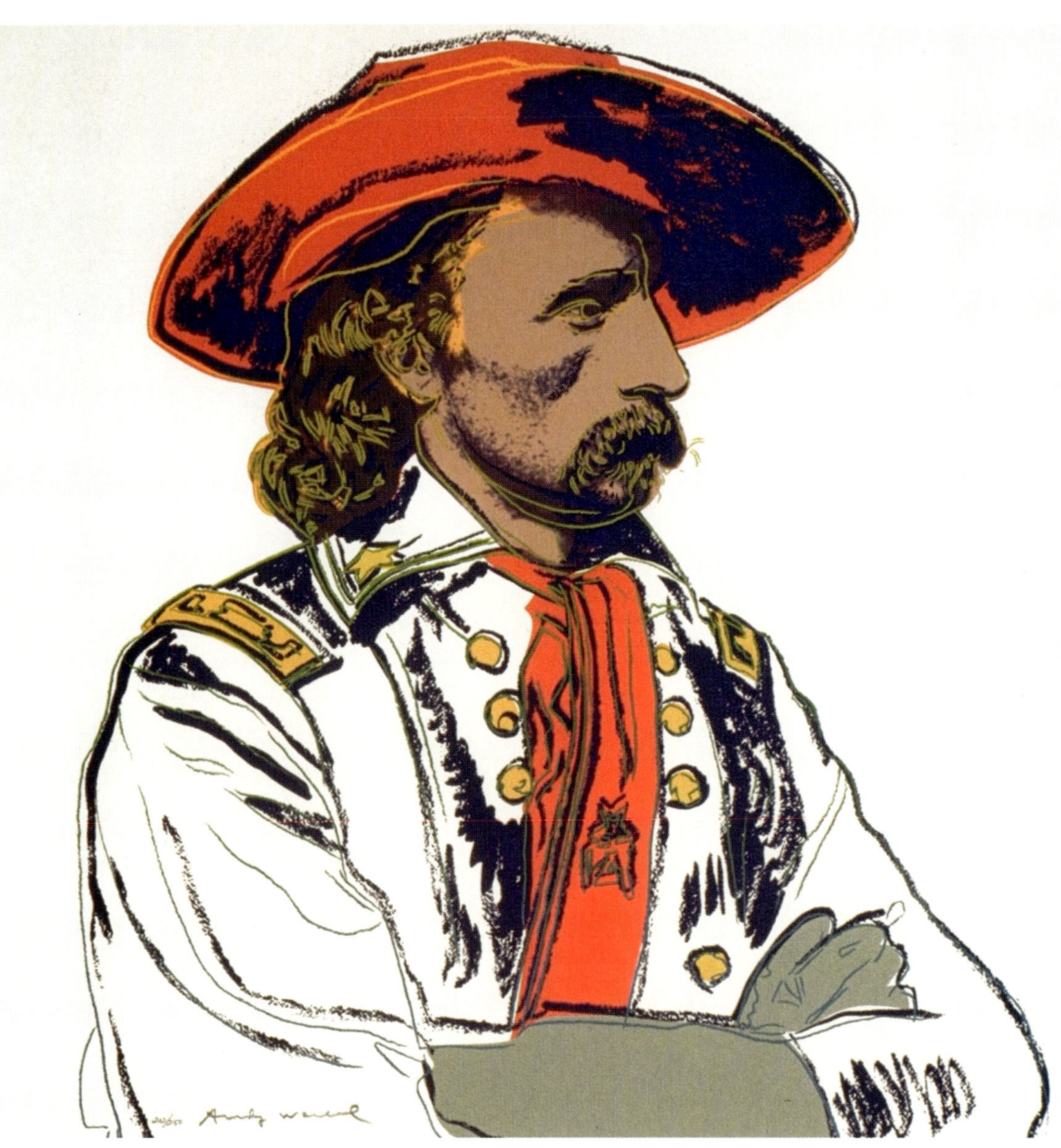

ANDY WARHOL (American, 1928-1987)
General Custer, 1986
Serigraph
36 x 36 (90 x 90)
Gaultney-Klineman Art, Inc., New York, New York

Warhol, the quintessential Pop artist, began his career in commercial art. He was always fascinated by American culture, and early on he recognized the power of mass media. In the 1960s, Warhol began incorporating magazine and newspaper ads, comics, movies and television into his art. His works depicting pervasive images of American culture such as money, Elvis Presley and soup cans made him one of the most famous American artists of this century. In this print, unexpected color has been added to a well-known image of the doomed Custer, creating a classic Warhol look.

TOM WESSELMANN (American, b. 1943)
Study for Nude Painting, 1988
Lithograph, printed in color
35 x 24 (87.5 x 60)
Aeropress

In 1961, the Pop artist Tom Wesselmann began painting a series titled *The Great American Nude*. These paintings and related prints of cropped bodies with almost featureless faces are treated in a flat, bright billboard style, calling attention to American popular culture's view of the female as a sex object. Wesselmann both appropriates and subverts the traditional nude of Western art from Titian to Matisse. The visual impact of this print as elegantly stylized form and color is pitted against its associations with Hugh Heffner's *Playboy* centerfolds.

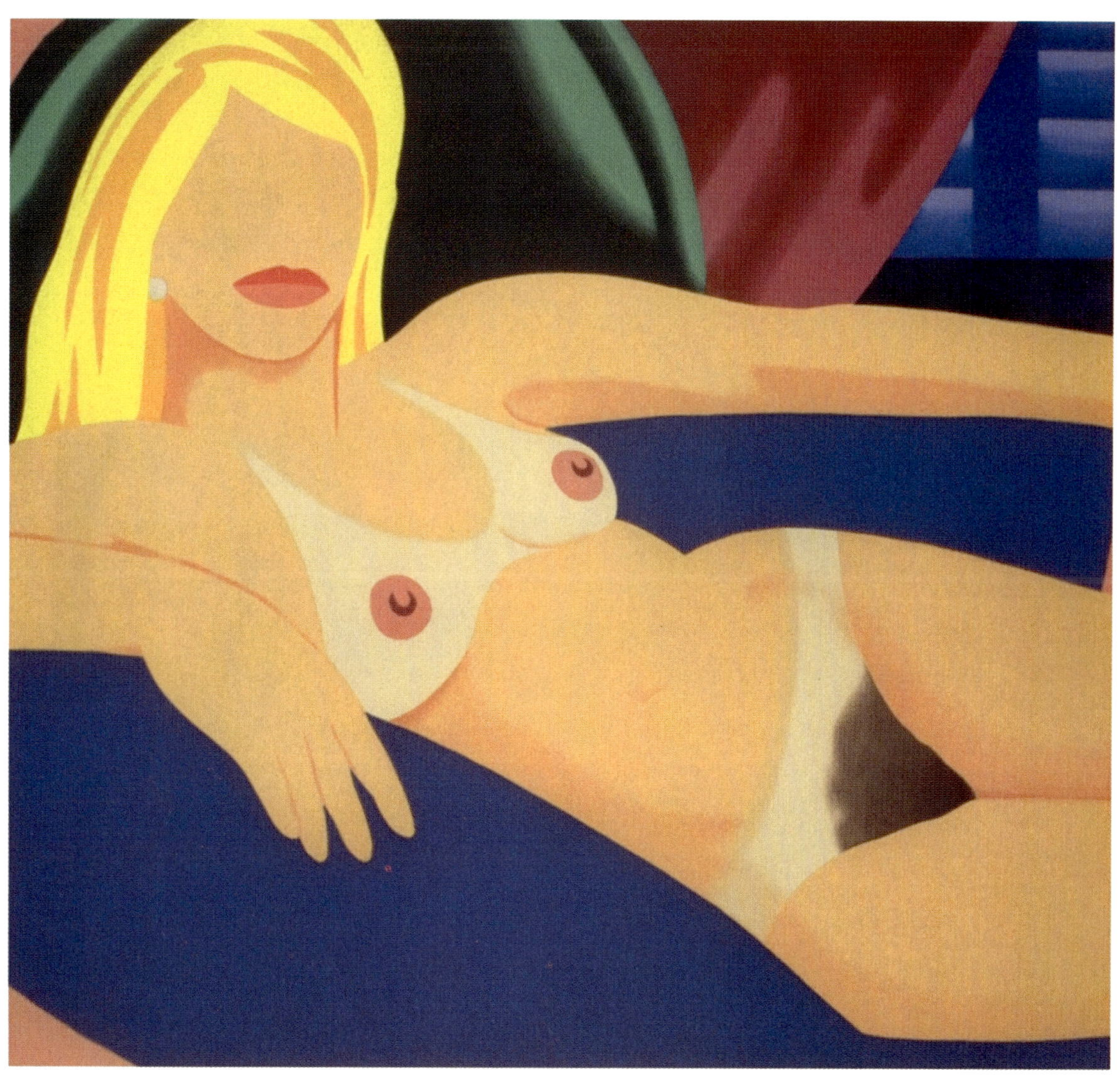

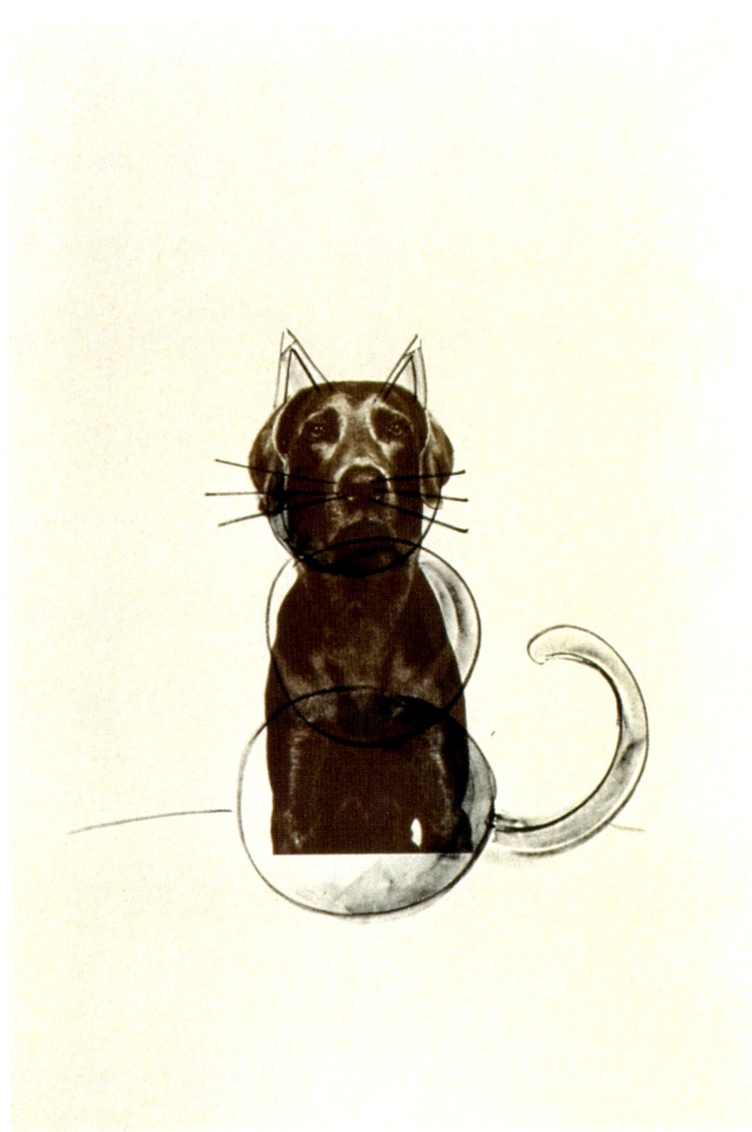

WILLIAM WEGMAN (American, b. 1943)
Ray Cat, 1988
Lithograph
35 x 24 (87.5 x 60)
Judith Solodkin
Solo Impression Inc., New York, New York

Wegman has made a career of photographing his beloved dogs Man Ray and Fay Ray. Wegman tests his dogs' loyalty by imposing curious costumes on them. Here, he makes one wear its alter ego, the age-old foe, just for the fun of it.

WILLIAM T. WILEY (American, b. 1927)
#4, 1976
Monoprint
22 x 30 (55 x 75)
Landfall Press, Chicago, Illinois

An originator of the California Funk movement, Wiley is known for zany, mixed-media narratives. This clownlike character is typical of the artist, who often depicts himself as a dunce-capped "Mr. Unnatural." The painterly immediacy of this monoprint is a departure from the tighter linear style of most of his work.

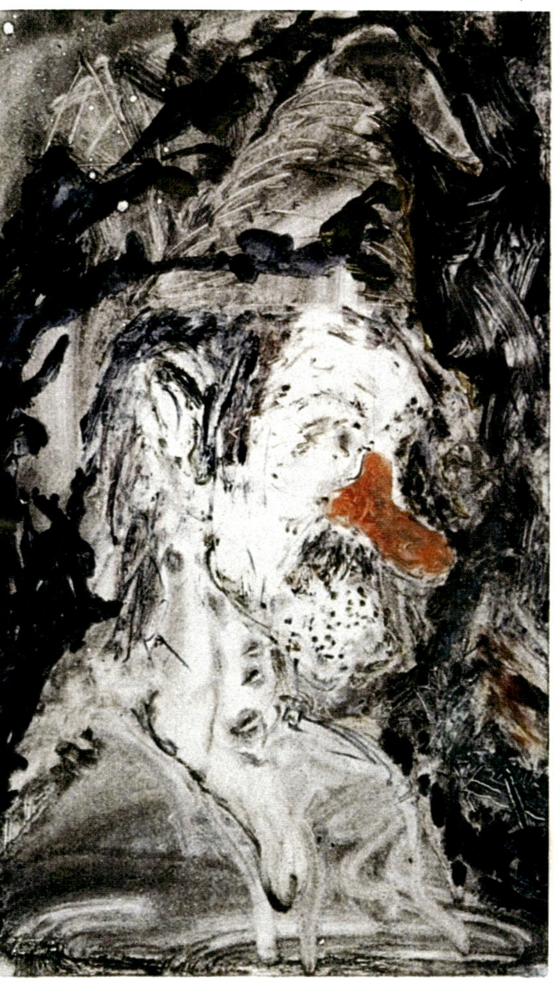

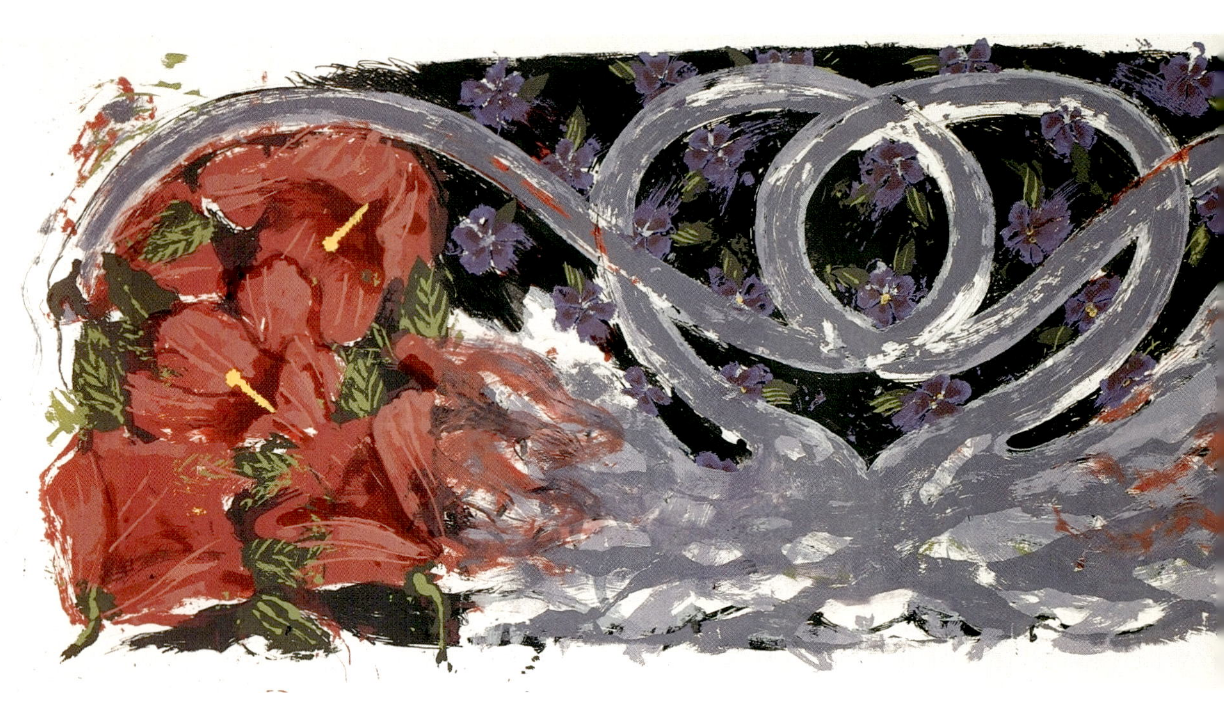

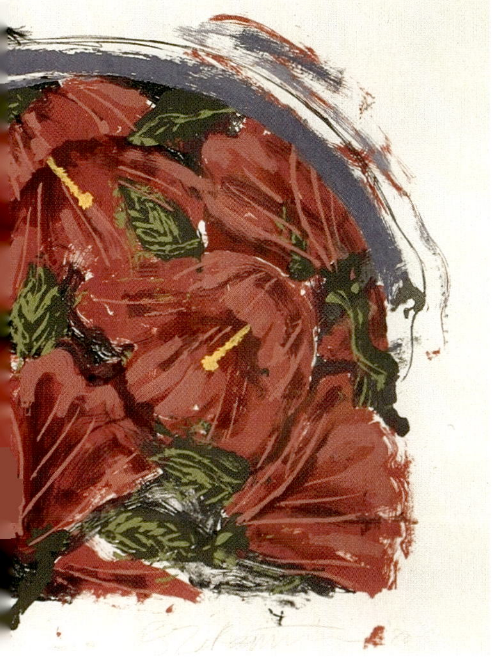

ROBERT RAHWAY ZAKANITCH (American, b. 1935)
How I Love Ya, How I Love Ya, State II, 1981
Lithograph, serigraph, stencil
42 x 120 (106.7 x 304.8)
Tom Strianese, Rodney Konopaki, Kenneth Tyler, Steve Reeves
Tyler Graphics Ltd., Mt. Kisco, New York

Symmetry, flowers, repetition, stencils and luscious color are Zakanitch's tools. This monumental print demonstrates his mastery using interlocking heart motifs. Repetition in the title reinforces the theme.

about fine prints by earl kittleson

WHAT MAKES A PRINT "ORIGINAL"?

An original print is traditionally defined as one for which the artist has made the matrix or object which contains the image to be printed, and that the artist (or his/her printing collaborator) has labored to pull a limited number of prints by using the appropriate mechanical techniques to create an image. Paper is the most common support for prints but plastic, leather, vellum and even sheet lead have been used. In early stages of printing, the printmaker limited the number of images by determining his market and then printed what was feasible under the limitations of time, the cost of paper and the life of the printing plate or block or stone.

HOW IS A PRINT MADE?

There are four basic ways to make prints. These include: (1) cutting away the white or negative areas of the block and inking and printing off of the raised surface (relief); (2) making depressions in a metal plate through cutting or etching and wiping ink into those depressions to print (intaglio); (3) making a stencil of the image and pushing ink through the open cuts to some surface (screen printing); (4) chemically creating images on a surface of stone or grained metal that either attracts or repels applied ink (lithography).

THE PROCESSES

THE RELIEF IMAGE: WOODCUT, WOOD ENGRAVING, LINOLEUM CUT, METAL RELIEF

To produce the WOODCUT relief image, the plan of drawing may be painted on the surface of a plank of wood and the parts of the wood not to be touched with ink are carved away with gouges. The resulting raised areas are inked with a brayer (roller) and printed either with a press or by hand rubbing the back of the paper with a smooth surfaced tool like a spoon. Early woodcuts like those of Albrecht Dürer show great attention to the preservation of the original drawing on which the print was based. Traditional Japanese woodcuts combine a refined linear structure with technically perfect color registration. Late 19th and early 20th century woodcuts made by Paul Gauguin, Ernst Ludwig Kirchner and Emil Nolde display great feeling because of the expressive manner in which the gouges were used.

The WOOD ENGRAVING was a popular reproductive media in the mid-19th century due to its durable nature. Practically, cutting into the end grain of dense wood like (pear or apple) made a sturdy support for long press runs, and the assembling of pieces into type high blocks creates a plane surface from which to print type and illustration simultaneously. The technique of cutting a block for this purpose used gouges and knives of finer design than woodcut tools because the cutting out of white printing depressions needs great care and precision to produce finer linear work and the illusion of gray. Illustrators like Winslow Homer and Thomas Nast had their drawings reproduced exactly in Harper's Magazine in the 1800s. They are collectibles today. A few artists of the 20th century such as Rockwell Kent and Lynd Ward have used this technique as their form of expression.

LINOLEUM CUTS are made using 1/8" thick "battleship" linoleum as the printing matrix (sometimes mounted to type height on plywood for support) which provides an easily cut, grainless surface for the artist's gouges. Prints may be proofed on a press or by inking with a brayer (roller) and pressing paper against the block with a spoon or burin. Pablo Picasso was a 20th century master of the linocut and produced many editions in the later part of his career.

The METAL RELIEF is created by drawing an image directly on a flat metal surface with an acid resist and then etching the plate so that the image is left raised. Ink is then rolled onto the raised surface and printed. The poet William Blake was a late 18th and early 19th century printmaker who used his "Song of Innocence and Experience". Commercially, this is the method long used by printers to produce "line cut" illustrations through photographic means.

THE INTAGLIO (In-TAL-yo) TECHNIQUES: ENGRAVING, ETCHING, MEZZOTINT, DRYPOINT, GRAVURE

To create an ENGRAVING, the printmaker begins with a polished flat piece of copper or other malleable metal and, using a burin, graves lines into the surface in direct proportion to the fineness or boldness of the line desired. To print the image from the engraved plate, the printer wipes ink into the groove thus made and wipes the polished surface clean.

Dampened paper is then pressed into the grooves pulling out the ink which then lies upon the surface of the paper. A characteristic of engravings is that the raised ink lines can be felt with a sensitive finger as ridges. The engravings of Albrecht Dürer and Hendrik Goltzius remain the world's finest examples of the ability to control the burin as it cuts through the surface of a piece of copper. Engravings, like all intaglio prints, may be identified by the mark of the edge of the metal plate impressed into the paper.

Medieval armorers used ETCHING as a way to decorate metal. They waxed polished armor, scratched through the wax and then bathed the piece in acid. The acid ate away the metal in proportion to the time it was left in the bath. It is conjectured that etched prints rose out of the paper proofs that were used to test the armor designs. As a fine art form, the technique of allowing acid to make depressions in a printing plate has enabled the reproductive work of artists like Dürer, Rembrandt, Whistler, Jasper Johns and Colescott.

Several ETCHING techniques may be employed: simply drawing with the etcher's needle through a resist covering the plate; painting directly with the acid resist; using a water-soluble medium to make an image and applying resist over that; and applying a photosensitive emulsion to the plate and exposing a photographic positive or negative to the plate. Resists may be also applied by transferring from other surfaces which might carry a wax-based image.

After etching to the desired degree, the plate is inked thoroughly, the surface wiped clean and the inked image is pulled from the plate on dampened paper with the use of backing blankets and a press.

The artist who seeks tonal qualities in the etched image may use the AQUATINT technique. In this technique, variations in gray are produced through the use of a powdered rosin acid resist dusted and melted onto the plate which is then exposed to acid to varying times. This creates a surface which will accept more or less ink when wiped. A variation on the aquatint known as SPIT-BITE involves the selective application of acid with a brush to areas of a rosin grounded plate, rather than immersing the whole plate.

The quest of 17th century printmakers for tonal development without the use of acid was satisfied in the invention of the MEZZOTINT. The darkest dark required is produced by mechanically creating a surface which will catch and hold a large quantity of black ink. This surface is prepared with the use of a mezzotint rocker which abrades with row upon row of crisscrossing cut points. Lighter values are pulled from the dark surface by smoothing the roughened copper in varying degrees and scraping ultra clean where white is required. Today it continues to challenge artists like Mario Avati and Katsunori Hamanishi who continue to create light out of the darkness in this labor-intensive process.

The artist making a DRYPOINT engraves using only a sharply pointed tool held in the manner of a pen on the polished copper plate. The tool creates scratches of various depths which in turn causes a burr to be raised on the surface. The plate is wiped with ink, the surface wiped clean and dampened paper is pressed against the plate. It is the "soft" or "heavy" quality of the burr produced line which is desirable, and that is worn down in subsequent printing. This makes earlier proofs more interesting and more valuable than later ones. The drypoint proof also exhibits the plate mark as evidence of its trip through the press. Many artists have used this portable sketching media away from the studio. Germany's Max Beckmann and Lovis Corinth used drypoint to achieve expressive results.

GRAVURE is a commercial reproductive process which has been adapted by some artists of today. Also printed with a copper plate, gravure uses a very fine screen of 220 lines per inch or more to etch a tonal image into microscopic pits of varying size which hold ink to proportionate degrees. Printing is through the wipe in and wipe off method of plate printing. Commercially, gravure has been used for extremely fine quality reproductions of artwork and photographs because of its ability to record maximum tonal ranges.

THE STENCIL METHOD

A SCREENPRINT is made by squeegeeing inks through a fine-meshed monofilament cloth stretched over a printing frame placed upon a printable surface. Various methods of blocking out areas of the screen fabric not to be printed include the use of glues, paper stencils, plastic films and photographic emulsions. Artists of the 30s and 40s adapted this poster printing process for multicolor printing. Then, it was called serigraphy or silk screen process because the fabric used was silk. An outstanding example of a revival in the 1960s was the screenprinting success of artist Andy Warhol with his Pop art portraits of "Mao", "Marilyn", "Jackie" and the Campbell's soup can series of paintings.

THE STONE LITHOGRAPH

When Alois Senefelder discovered in 1798 that greasy ink could be attracted to some areas of a flat printing stone (traditionally Bavarian limestone) and repelled from others through the use of water, he laid the ground for the commercial printing of sheet music. This process begins with drawing on a stone with a greasy ink or crayon and sensitizing the surface with a touch of acid and gum solution. Some printmakers substitute more easily portable grained metal plates for the stone, sensitizing and printing in much the same way.

LITHOGRAPHY permits the use of the finest pen or pencil techniques, expressive crayon drawing or the freedom of bold and flowing pigment washes applied by brush. Adopted by French artists of the early 19th century, lithography was mastered by Théodore Géricault, Eugène Delacroix, Honoré Daumier and many others. In the USA, Currier and Ives printed editions of "Pictures for the People" which were later hand colored. Later in the century the technique was used to print the colorful posters of

Toulouse-Lautrec and Alphonse Mucha. Pablo Picasso produced one of the most significant bodies of 20th century lithographic work at Atelier Mourlot, Paris. Contemporary artists who have exploited the range of expressive possibilities of the stone include Jim Dine, Sam Francis, Richard Serra and Susan Rothenberg.

As lithography became more and more of a commercial success, a printing press was invented (Harris, 1906) whereby the image was transferred to a rubber blanket from the stone and then again from that blanket to the surface to be printed. This method of taking a read right image, transferring it to a rotary rubber blanket in reverse so it could be re-deposited onto almost any texture of paper became known as OFFSET printing. Later still, images were taken from photographically produced bendable metal plates which could be fitted to a rotary press and this enabled printing at extremely high speeds.

Because of the huge press runs of commercial plants, their product has not made it into the realm of collectable fine art. Some wildlife and scenic artists have popularized their paintings through the publishing of reproductions, but critics find it hard to ascribe rarity to a hand-signed edition of 3,000 to 10,000 copies.

Because offset advertising posters may be well designed, colorful and decorative they have found success on the lower end of the collectable market as a good thing to put on the wall for a short time, and then easily changed for another when the design style or ink fades. Museums have traditionally popularized their rare works through reproduction sales for souvenir and educational purposes.

ALTERNATIVE TECHNIQUES

COLLAGRAPHS, MONOTYPES, MONOPRINTS and COMPUTER PRINTS. Inventive printmakers have found that they could use cheap materials for their own studio work. An arrangement of textural materials collaged to a board and varnished may be inked and wiped like an intaglio print. This is called a COLLAGRAPH.

Working with a press, a single flat plate of metal or sturdy plastic and an assortment of inks, the MONOTYPE printer paints or draws directly onto the plate and pulls the ink off of the plate with dampened paper in a press as in intaglio printing. This procedure makes one unrepeatable proof of the work. A counterproof may be taken from the first print but the image will be reversed. A second print might also be pulled from the plate which will appear to be a very weak, faded duplicate. Painters Edgar Degas and Maurice Prendergast often used monotypes to embellish with pencil drawing, pastel or watercolor.

MONOPRINTS are made with the same procedure as the monotype with the exception that a printable plate is used as a matrix. Changes made by applying various colors freely on the surface of an etching or engraving plate or doing additional drawing with printing inks on such a plate before printing characterize a monoprint.

The advent of the COMPUTER as a fine art printmaking resource has enabled the growing acceptance of the product of the commercial inkjet as in Iris print proofing technology. The fact that the printer/publisher could "hand print" a piece of fine rag paper by wrapping it around a cylinder has lead to the production of limited editions on machines normally dedicated to pre-press proofing. David Hockney is prominent among artists who work in this manner. The collector may question the long term stability of such production and may wait for future improvements in color stability.

COLLABORATION

Contemporary fine art printing is strongly related to the commercial printing concept of collaboration. All members of a staff of a commercial printing plant find pleasure in working as a team to produce the best possible product. The team of artist, printer and publisher of a fine art print strive to enable each other's success by giving and taking advice and suggestions before and during the varied procedures involved in the production and finishing of the limited edition. The master printer knows what can, could and should be done to produce the artist's concept and is not afraid to confer. The publisher works with both because his money investment and reputation is on the line. The artist trusts his partners because he knows they will help when problems arise, when he changes his mind about a color or process or addition of an image, or another layer of ink or varnish though halfway through printing.

THE FINISHED PRINT: WHAT DO THE MARKS MEAN?

In the production of fine prints for sale to the public, artists and their printer/publishers have invented many ways to identify a printed product as their own work. This procedure is similar to the legal signing of an official document which indicates that the signer has inspected and verifies the truth of the content of the document. In signing a print the artist certifies to the authenticity of the work and to the exclusivity of the edition or number of proofs pulled. Since contemporary prints may be made at a workshop instead of a private studio, often the chop mark of the printer-collaborator and/or publisher is blind embossed on each print.

Writing on a print is preferably done in pencil to avoid the possible blooming and staining which moistened ink may be subject to, and to avoid accidents of dripping or transference. Museum curators are still dismayed by the encroachments of collector's stamps on the image on many rare 14th and 15th century etchings and engravings, put there by ambitious collectors or museums during the 17th or 18th century. These marks may indicate some of the history of the ownership of the work. On the other hand, the penciled Bartch or other catalogue numbers on the verso of a Rembrandt, for instance, are a valued reference. Erasable pencil is recommended for any work on or near fine prints.

The system that has evolved since about 1915 dictates that along with a penciled signature at the lower right margin, and an indication of a title at the lower left margin, a declaration of the number of proofs pulled and the number of the proof in a sequence shall lie somewhere in between. For instance, numbers inscribed as 1/200 indicate the first print in a run of 200.

The Trial, Artist and other special proof labels are NOT considered part of the edition number, therefore the number under the slash on a notation does NOT indicate the total number of the same print in existence. All proofs pulled, however, are listed in the publisher's print documentation record and such information may be made available through the print dealer.

THE PUBLISHER

Generally, print publishers will invite the artist to their establishment because they like the person, the style of work or the fact that the artist is popular. The prints that result from their collaboration may be shared by artist and publisher. A variety of financial arrangements have been developed by print publishers so that artist, printer and publisher remain a happy team.

Since the 1950s, fine print publishers have grown in numbers. Begun by June Wayne under a Ford Foundation grant, the Tamarind Lithographic Workshop was established in Los Angeles and later moved to the University of New Mexico as the Tamarind Institute. Tamarind produced the work of many prominent artists. The University of South Florida gathered artists and printers in the late 1960s and also produced a large volume of contemporary editions, and at Indiana University, Echo Press was begun. Today, Tandem Press of the University of Wisconsin, Madison, follows the tradition of university linkage, as does Normal Editions of the University of Northern Illinois and The Center for Innovative Printmaking at Rutgers University. Today many hundreds of independent workshops carry on the traditions and methods acquired at those studios. Some master printers who have become publishers include Jack Lemon at Landfall Press, Chicago, Kenneth Tyler at Tyler Graphics, Bedford Village, NY, and Kathan Brown at Crown Point Press, San Francisco.

AQUIRING PRINTS

Fine print dealers are a potentially knowledgeable source of information about an artist's background, personal history of success and print values. Learning to identify the processes by visiting art museums to examine prints, reading about history and techniques, and attending auctions where fine prints are sold are activities a collector does to build awareness of the wonders of the artist-made print.

note to the reader

All of the works reproduced in this volume are in the exhibition held jointly at the Milwaukee Art Museum and the Quad/Graphics Gallery.

The works in this catalogue are arranged alphabetically by artist. The data in each entry is organized as follows: artist, country and date of birth, and date of death, if applicable; title of the print, title of portfolio or suite, if applicable, year produced; medium(s); dimensions; printer(s); publisher(s).

Dimensions are in inches, followed by centimeters; height precedes width precedes depth. Dimensions are for image size.

Printers are personally named whenever possible; otherwise, the name of the printing shop is given. The publisher is designated by the name of the firm. In certain instances, information in collection records yields only the name of the publisher.

Every work in the Quad/Collection is listed in the index at the back of this book. The data given is: artist; title; date (if known); medium. All information has been taken from collection records.

glossary

ABSTRACT EXPRESSIONISM

U.S.-originated style descended from Surrealism and concerned mainly with two categories: calligraphy, with freely made scribbles covering the surface of work; or iconic, in which the composition is dominated by a single form.

AQUATINT

An etching process in which tone is created by treating a plate with fine particles of acid-resistant material (like powdered resin) and then placing the plate in an acid bath. The acid bites into the plate between the grains of resin and, when printed, the mass of tiny spots produces a textured area with tonal effects similar to watercolor wash.

ARTIST'S PROOF/EPREUVE D'ARTISTE

Impressions printed especially for the artist and excluded from the numbering of an edition, but exactly like the editioned prints in every other respect. Usually appears as "A.P." or "E.A."

BLINDSTAMP/CHIP

The embossed, inked, or stamped symbol used by printers and print workshops, usually in the margin of the paper as a mark of identification.

BON À TIRER/RIGHT TO PRINT

The proof approved by the artist which establishes the standard for all of the other prints in the edition.

BURR

When using a drypoint needle or other engraving tool to draw directly into a metal plate, small, fine pieces of metal are raised up on both sides of the scored line. This burr holds additional ink during the printing process and gives the lines a velvety or fuzzy texture. Burr is very delicate and consequently is easily worn down during the pressures of the printing process. Early pulls or impressions taken from such plates are characterized by rich burr. In the case of Old Master prints especially, the quantity and evidence of burr can sometimes be used as an aid in determining how early the impression was pulled.

CANCELLATION PROOF

When the edition is complete, the matrix – a block, plate, stone, mylar or other – is effaced, crossed out or otherwise "cancelled." An impression is then taken from this matrix, showing that the plate has been "cancelled." This ensures that no further uncancelled impressions can be pulled.

CARBORUNDUM

The trade name for silicon carbide, Carborundum began its use in printmaking as an abrasive which was used in effacing lithographic stones. The particles, when mixed together with glue can also be used to draw on a plate – sometimes creating a raised surface – which is then inked and printed with the ink being held in the spaces between the particles. The resulting prints are often textured due to the raised areas of the printing surface.

CATALOGUE RAISONNÉ
A scholarly catalogue which should include all the known works by an artist at the time of publication. Essential information by which works are identified is included.

CHICAGO IMAGISM
Usually irreverent, sometimes violent, imagery of the 50s through 70s, Chicago Imagism was, in part, a reaction to the Abstract Expressionism dominant on the East Coast and the West Coast-based Funk and figurative styles.

CHINE APPLIQUÉ/CHINE COLLÉ
A method of adhering a thin paper, sometimes of a different color or texture, onto a larger, heavier sheet during the printing process using glue or water to dampen and coat the papers.

COLOPHON/JUSTIFICATION
A note, usually at the end of a book or portfolio of prints, giving all or some of the following information: name of work, author, printer, place of printing, date, size of edition.

CONCEPTUALISM
Style that consists of at least one of the following principles: the all-important basic idea; the use of language as a basic material of art; and the end-result that may be considered an interim demonstration of a general conclusion made by the artist.

DECKLE EDGE
The natural, untrimmed edge of handmade paper usually slightly uneven and sometimes slightly thinner than the rest of the sheets.

DRYPOINT
An intaglio process in which a plate is marked or incised directly with a needle. The drypoint line can look very much like an etched line but is usually lighter and characterized by the existence of burr.

EDITION
The total number of impressions pulled of a single image or set of images from the same matrix. To this number the artist usually authorizes the addition of a small number of artist's, printer's, publisher's and other proofs.

EMBOSSING
A process used to create a raised surface or raised element, but printed without ink.

ENGRAVING
An intaglio process in which a plate is marked or incised directly with a burin or other metal-marking tool. No acid is used in this process since the design is dug out by hand. An engraved line can range from very deep and wide, to lighter and thinner and is often characterized by a pointed end signaling the exit of the "v" shaped burin from the metal.

ETCHING
An intaglio process in which a plate is treated with an acid-resistant ground. The artist then draws through the ground with various tools to expose the metal. The plate is then immersed in an acid bath where the acid "bites" or chemically dissolves the exposed lines. The metal plate is therefore "carved" or "etched" by the acid rather than by a tool directly in the metal.

FOUL-BITING
When the acid-resistant ground on a metal plate does not keep the acid entirely out, irregularities can appear. These "bitten" areas will, when the plate is printed, catch ink and appear as spots or oddly inked areas.

FRONTISPIECE
Illustration in a book opposite the title page.

HELIOGRAVURE
A method of making a photo-etched or photogravure plate using an aquatint texture directly on the plate to create tone.

HORS-COMMERCE/"H.C."
Meaning "outside of the commercial edition," these proofs, not originally intended for sale, are excluded from the numbering of an edition, but are otherwise exactly like the editioned prints in every other respect.

INTAGLIO
All matrices which have either been cut into or "bitten" into. The resulting "dug out" lines are printed. Intaglio processes include etching, aquatint, engraving, mezzotint and metal engravings, among others.

LINOCUT/LINOLEUM CUT
A relief process, like a woodcut, where the artist carves the design out of the linoleum or linoleum mounted onto wood. What remains is printed, rather than what is cut away.

LITHOGRAPHY
A planographic printing process where a drawing is made directly on a stone or other smooth matrix with greasy materials such as lithographic crayon. The surface is then dampened with water, which is repelled by the greasy areas. The surface is then rolled with greasy printing ink which adheres only to the greasy areas and is itself repelled by the areas which have water. The drawn image is then printed.

MASTER PRINTER
A highly skilled printer who works very closely with the artist to produce the edition.

MATRIX
The base from which the print is made. This can be anything – a standard metal plate or lithographic stone, a potato or vinyl record, a stencil – anything from which you print.

MEZZOTINT
An intaglio method in which the entire surface of the plate is roughened by a spiked tool ("rocker") so that, if inked, the entire plate would print in solid black. The artist then works from "black" to "white" by scraping (or burnishing) out areas to produce lighter tones.

MINIMALISM
Art pared to its essentials, often depicted as geometric shapes used repetitively.

MODERNISM
The philosophy of modern art, including many styles of the 20th century, such as Dadaism and Minimalism. Modernist painting emphasizes refinement of color and flatness.

MONOTYPE
A unique image printed from an unworked, smooth, metal or glass surface painted in ink by the artist.

MONOPRINT
A print which has as its base an etching, lithograph or woodcut and which is then uniquely altered by monotype coloring, unique inking, or choices in paper color.

NEO-EXPRESSIONISM
The expressionist revival of the 70s and early 80s with adherents often turning to gestural, figurative painting.

NEW FIGURATION, NEW REALISM
An art style somewhere between abstraction and figuration, in which the artist attempts to depict the isolation of contemporary man, often with dark humor.

NEW IMAGE
A contemporary style distinguished from other current styles by recognizable images, often seen against abstract backgrounds.

OFFSET PRINTING
Method of printing in which the inked image from a lithographic stone, a metal plate or other matrix is first transferred to an intermediary such as a rubber cylinder or blanket and then to paper, thus creating an image in the same direction as the original.

PATTERN AND DECORATION, PATTERNISM
Predominantly American style of the mid-70s to 80s in which decoration, borrowed from Eastern and Western crafts and decorative art, plays an important role.

PHOTO-ETCHING/PHOTOGRAVURE
An intaglio process in which an image is produced on an etching plate by photographic means.

PHOTO-LITHOGRAPH
A process in which an image is produced on a lithographic plate by photographic means.

PHOTO-REALISM
Style that uses a photograph as a starting point. For many followers it is the effect, not the subject, that interests the artist.

PLANOGRAPHIC PRINT
Printing from a flat surface. Planographic processes include lithography and some forms of commercial printing.

PLATE MARK
The imprint in the paper resulting from the edge of a metal plate being pushed into it during the pressure of the printing process.

PLATE TONE
A veil of ink intentionally left on the surface of the plate during printing which creates delicate areas of tone or shading.

POCHOIR
A printing process using stencils, originally used to simulate hand coloring.

PRINTER'S PROOFS
Impressions printed especially for the printer(s) and excluded from the numbering of an edition, but exactly like the editioned prints in every other respect. Usually appears as "P.P."

PROGRESSIVE PROOFS
Series of proofs taken to show each individual color plate and each combination of them culminating in the final, complete version.

PUBLISHER
The person or entity who subsidizes and often initiates the making of a print edition or portfolio and who also disseminates the prints.

RELIEF PRINTING
When the image is printed from the raised or uncarved portion of the matrix. Relief processes include woodcuts and linocuts, among others.

SCREENPRINT/SERIGRAPH/SILKSCREEN
A printing process using stencils to block out areas which are then printed through silk, other fabric or metal mesh.

SOFT-GROUND ETCHING
An etching technique where a soft ground is laid on the metal plate. The artist draws onto a piece of paper which is laid down on top of the ground. The ground adheres to the paper where the pencil or other tool has pressed down into it through the paper and pulls away when the paper is lifted. The resulting "marked" plate is placed in an acid-bath where the acid "bites" into the more exposed areas where the ground has been "lifted". The line created is often soft and grainy.

STEEL FACING
When a metal intaglio plate is covered with a thin deposit of steel using electrolysis creating a much harder surface which can accommodate larger numbers of printings before wear becomes evident.

TRIAL PROOF
An early proof, often incorporating artist's revisions and changes and generally not identical to the numbered, editioned prints. Also referred to as Working Proof.

TUSCHE
Grease in stick or liquid form used principally for drawing in lithography.

WATERMARK
Design in the paper seen when held against the light. A manufacturer's mark, it is used to trace the origin and date of the paper.

WOODCUT
A relief technique where the image or design is left raised above what is carved out of the wood. What is not carved is printed.

index

LAST NAME, FIRST NAME
Title, Date, Medium

ASHBAUGH, DENNIS
Untitled, 1981, Serigraph

AVERY, MILTON
Pilot Fish, 1952, Woodcut

AYCOCK, ALICE
Miami Proposal I-IV, 1990, Serigraph

BAECHLER, DONALD
Untitled, 1995, Serigraph, printed in color

BAEDER, JOHN
Empire Diner, 1981, Lithograph
Discount Litho, 1979, Etching
Curley's Diner, 1979, Lithograph

BALDESSARI, JOHN
Cliché: Eskimo (Blue), 1995, Lithograph, serigraph
Cliché: North American Indian (Red), 1995, Lithograph, serigraph
Cliché: Japanese (Yellow), 1995, Lithograph, serigraph

BALKIN, ANDREW
Sagitta, 1993, Etching

BARBER, PHIL
Untitled, 1989, Monoprint

BARNET, WILL
The Skaters, 1994, Serigraph, printed in color
Interlude, 1982, Serigraph, printed in color

BARTLETT, JENNIFER
From Rhapsody: House, Trees, Beach, Birds, 1985, Sugar-lift aquatint
In the Garden #116, 1983, Serigraph, printed in color
Chamber Music Society, 1981, Serigraph
Graceland Mansion, 5 pieces, 1978, Drypoint, aquatint, serigraph, woodcut, lithograph

BATES, DAVID
Stringer of Sheepshead, 1994, Woodcut, printed in color
Magnolia Spring, 1991, Woodcut, printed in color
Corpus Christi, 1991, Woodcut, printed in color

BATTENFIELD, JACKIE
Calliope, 1993, Monoprint

BATTLE, GEORGETTE
Collage Elements I-IV, 1979, Serigraph, printed in color

BAYNARD, ED
Still Life with Orchid, 1980, Woodcut, printed in color
The Dragonfly Vase, 1980, Woodcut, printed in color
Dark Pot with Roses, 1980, Woodcut, printed in color
Quarter Moon, 1980, Woodcut, printed in color
The Blue Tulips, 1980, Woodcut, printed in color

BEARDEN, ROMARE
Dreams of Exile, 1973, Serigraph

BECHTLE, ROBERT
34th Avenue, 1987, Soft-ground etching, printed in color
Potrero VW, 1993, Monoprint

BECK & JUNG
Criss Cross #59, 1986, Serigraph
Dendra 1st Day #31, 1986, Computer ink plot
Indian Games #57, 1986, Computer ink plot
Game Quiz, Computer ink plot
Dendra #47, 1985, Computer ink plot
Dendra 3rd Day #25, 1985, Computer ink plot
Indian Games #IV, 1985, Computer ink plot
Indian Games #37, 1985, Computer ink plot
Indian Games #1, 1985, Computer ink plot
Ring Box, 1985, Computer ink plot

BECKER, DAVID
Light Rail, 1993, Etching

BELL, PEGGY
Botanical Study I, 1986, Monoprint
Night Pods, 1986, Etching
Lily Pond II, 1986, Serigraph
Forest Floor, 1986, Collagraph
Botanical Study II, 1986, Monoprint
Snow Buds, 1986, Etching
Sea Foam, 1986, Collagraph
Snow Pods, 1986, Etching

BELLMAN, ERIC
Woman at Table, 1986, Etching
On the Avenue, 1986, Etching
Street Scene II, 1986, Etching
Landscape with Trees, 1986, Etching
Three Houses, 1986, Etching
Main Street, 1986, Etching

BENAIM, RICARDO
Spring Waltz, 1985, Embossed collage print

BENGLIS, LYNDA
Tandem Press Series,1988, Monoprint, relief print with hand coloring and collage
#13, 1987, Monoprint

BENTLEY-SCHECK, GRACE
Profile II Union Stations Series, 1986, Collagraph
Lackawana, 1986, Collagraph
City Nights – Roseland, 1986, Collagraph

BENTON, THOMAS
Hart, Instruction, 1940, Lithograph

BERO, MARY
Portrait, 1993, Etching, asphaltum stop out

BEYER, STEVEN
Four Member Family System, 1979, Drypoint
Untitled II, 1978, Lithograph
White Cross, 1977, Drypoint

BISHOP, ISABEL
Noon Hour, 1935, Etching

BLECKNER, ROSS
Untitled, 1987, Serigraph

BOCHNER, MEL
Untitled, 1984, Serigraph

BOLOTOWSKY, ILYA
Untitled, 1980, Serigraph

BORDETTE, EDWARD
Sandwiches, 1986, Serigraph
Sabrette, 1986, Serigraph
Fragment, 1986, Serigraph

BOROFSKY, JONATHAN
Foot Print (Right), 1986, Serigraph with 3-D ink
Foot Print (Left), 1986, Serigraph with 3-D ink
Berlin Dream (Closeup) at No. 2947838, 1986, Monoprint with hand coloring

BOSMAN, RICHARD
Canis Major/Minor, 1992, Etching and relief, printed in color
Night Lace, 1992, Carborundum etching, printed in color
Night Light, 1992, Aquatint, etching, printed in color
The Edge, 1992, Woodcut, printed in color
Untitled, Lithograph
Sailboat, 1989, Monoprint
Lightning, 1989, Lithograph
Moonrise, 1990, Lithograph, printed in color
The Wave, 1987, Woodcut, printed in color
Green Wave III, 1987, Monoprint
Full Moon, 1986, Woodcut, printed in color

BOTELLO, ANGEL
Girl Arranging Flowers, 1980, Lithograph
Rascandos La Oreja, 1980, Lithograph
Girl with Little Bird, 1980, Lithograph
The Wink, 1980, Linocut

BOURGEOIS, LOUISE
Storm at Saint Honoré, 1994, Engraving, drypoint

BOWDEN, SANDRA
Canyon River Bend, 1986, Collagraph
Stone Wall, 1986, Collagraph
Masada I, 1985, Collagraph
Lava Flow, 1985, Collagraph
Sinai I, II, 1985, Collagraph
From Between the Dunes, 1985, Collagraph
Stretched Out Before Me, 1985, Collagraph

BOWER, GARY
Lenten Trials, 1983, Monoprint with oil crayon

BOWLING, KATHERINE
Double Reflection, 1992, Etching

BOXER, STANLEY
Elephant, 1979, Etching, aquatint, drypoint, with hand coloring
Turtle, 1979, Etching, aquatint, drypoint, with hand coloring
Pauseofnoconcern, 1976, Etching, aquatint, with hand coloring
Askanceglancelongingly, 1976, Etching, aquatint, with hand coloring
Curiousstalking, 1976, Etching, aquatint, with hand coloring

BRADFORD, KATHERINE
Color X, 1993, Collagraph
Lavender, 1993, Collagraph
Dalmatian, 1993, Collagraph
Nature, 1993, Collagraph

BRICE, WILLIAM
Untitled #12 Floating Forms, Color, 1990, Soap-ground and spit-bite aquatint

BRINK, GUIDO
Opera Duo, 1990, Lithograph

BROAD, DEBORAH
The Meek, Lithograph

BROUET, AUGUSTE
The Mattress Makers, 1935, Etching

BROWN, CHRISTOPHER
The Farmer's Almanac, 1994, Color spit-bite, soap-ground aquatint with aquatint and soft-ground etching
Divining Rod, 1994, Color spit-bite, soap-ground aquatint with aquatint and soft-ground etching
Under the Flag, 1991, Spit-bite aquatint and soft-ground etching
Zig Zag I, II, 1991, Woodcut, printed in color
Circles, Smoke and Braid, 1990, Woodcut, printed in color
Little Blue Run, 1990, Woodcut, printed in color
Hole Notes, 1990, Woodcut, printed in color
Seventy-Nine Men, 1991, Soft-ground etching

BROWN, JAMES
Salt Suite (Violet), 1991, 4 Lithographs, 1 monoprint
Japanese Room Drawings 1-10, 1989, Lithograph

BROWN, LARRY
Untitled IV, V, 1989, Monoprint

BROWN, ROGER
Talk Show Addicts, 1993, Hard-ground etching, aquatint

BUCK, JOHN
Tropic of Cancer, 1984, Woodcut
Tropic of Capricorn, 1984, Woodcut
Avenue of the Americas, 1984, Woodcut, printed in color

BURKERT, NANCY
Veriditas, 1994, Lithograph

BURKERT, ROBERT
River Snag, 1993, Lithograph

BURTON, RICHMOND
Untitled, 1992, Linocut
Untitled, 1992, Linocut

BYRON, MICHAEL
Peacock, 1986, Etching

CAGE, JOHN
HV2 1-15, 1992, Etching, printed in color

CALDER, ALEXANDER
Circles and Pyramids, Lithograph

CANNON, T.C
Hopi with Manta, 1978, Woodcut, printed in color

CAPORAEL, SUZANNE
Dissection: Tobacco Flower, 1993, Drypoint etching, printed in color
Dissection: Morning Glory, 1993, Drypoint etching, printed in color
Dissection: Honeysuckle, 1993, Drypoint etching, printed in color
Architecture of Trees (Oak), 1991, Soft-ground aquatint, printed in color
Architecture of Trees (Eucalyptus), 1991, Soft-ground aquatint, printed in color
Seeing Things (Rain), 1990, Woodcut, printed in color
Seeing Things (Shade Trees), 1990, Woodcut, printed in color

CARNWATH, SQUEAK
Sorry Bird (for India), 1993, Woodcut, printed in color
Look See, 1991, Woodcut, etching, printed in color
Striped Bird, 1991, Woodcut, printed in color
Breathe, 1991, Woodcut, printed in color

CASTER, PAUL
To City, 1990, Lithograph
Excision, 1990, Lithograph
Rembrandt Full Face, 1979, Lithograph

CELIS, PEREZ
Rescate-Fuego, 1992, Mixed media on canvas

CELMINS, VIJA
December, 1984-85, Mezzotint
Ocean Surface-Second State, 1985, Drypoint
Untitled, 1990, Woodcut

CHAHINE, EDGAR
Tennis Player, 1899, Drypoint

CHASE, LOUISA
Icarus, 1991, Lithograph with added relief elements, printed in color
Headstand, 1991, Lithograph with added relief elements from plexi-plates, printed in color
Sleepwalker, 1991, Lithograph with added relief elements from plexi-plates, printed in color
Untitled, 1988, Etching
Six Etchings, 1984, Etching
Untitled, 1981, Serigraph

CHIA, SANDRO
Athletes, 1988, Lithograph, printed in color
Boy and His Double, 1983, Etching with soft ground
Untitled, 1983, Etching

CHRISTENSEN, DAN
Untitled, 1983, Serigraph
#11, 1983, Monoprint
Galina Territory 1-3, 1982, Lithograph, printed in color with pochoir
Untitled, 1972, Lithograph, printed in color

CHRISTO
Surrounded Islands 1-4, 1984, Dye-transfer photographs
Wrapped Automobile, 1984, Lithograph with collage
Wrapped Museum Floors, 1983, Lithograph with collage
Package on Handtruck, 1981, Lithograph, collage, printed in color
Wrapped Modern Art Book, 1978, Pliofilm and twine
Tex Mastaba, Project for 500,000 Stacked Oil Drums, 1977, Serigraph
Wrapped Armchair Project, 1977, Lithograph, printed in color
20 Exchange Place, Project for NY S.61, 1973, Serigraph

CHRYSSA, VERDEA
Gates to Times Square 1-20, 1978, Serigraph

CIESLIK, RALPH
Blue Grotto, Capri, 1991, Monoprint
Dénouement, 1989, Monoprint

CLARK, CHARLOTTE
Cahoon Hollow Beach (Right), 1988, Monoprint
Cahoon Hollow Beach (Left), 1988, Monoprint
Waiting, 1988, Monoprint

CLEMENTE, FRANCESCO
Order and Disorder, 1991, Spit-bite aquatint etching
Seed, 1991, Spit-bite aquatint etching
Self-Portrait, 1990, Woodcut, printed in color
Morning, 1982, Woodcut, printed in color

CLOSE, CHUCK
Alex/Reduction Block, 1993, Reduction block
Leslie, 1986, Woodcut, printed in color
Keith Four Times, 1975, Lithograph

COAR, NORLYN
Vivace Con Brio, Monoprint
The Diver, Monoprint
Scherzo, Monoprint

COHEN, ARTHUR
Brooklyn Bridge, 1984, Lithograph, printed in color

COIGNARD, JAMES
Resolution Triangulaire, 1985, Carborundum, pochoir
Architecture au Vert, Oil on canvas
Diagonal Blanche, Oil on canvas
Diagonal Rouge, Oil on canvas
Symetrie Blanche, 1985, Carborundum, pochoir
Deux Rouge en Nomenclature, 1984, Carborundum, pochoir

COLESCOTT, WARRINGTON
Audubon Paints the Birds of Florida, 1994, Lithograph, printed in color
In the Trenches with Otto Dix, 1992, Etching, printed in color
Riding with the Blue Riders and Franz Marc, 1992, Etching, printed in color
At the Cafe de Prave with George Grosz, 1992, Etching, printed in color
Joining the March with Kathe Kollwitz, 1992, Etching, printed in color
Lunch with Albrecht Dürer, 1992, Etching, printed in color
The Hunt: Steenland's Drive, 1981, Etching, printed in color
The Hunt: First Dawn Stakeout, 1981, Etching, printed in color
The Hunt: Counterattack, 1981, Etching, printed in color
Last Day's Drive, 1981, Etching
History of Printmaking 1-11, 1976-78, Etching

COLT, JOHN
Over and Under, 1991, Monoprint, printed in color
Pond Tokens, 1991, Lithograph, printed in color
Sea Moves, 1991, Monoprint, printed in color
Twilight Visitors, 1991, Monoprint, printed in color
Night Sentinels, 1980, Lithograph, printed in color
Tropic Visitors, 1979, Lithograph, printed in color

CONLON, WILLIAM
Untitled, 1985, Serigraph

COTTINGHAM, ROBERT
Art, 1992, Lithograph, printed in color
Rolling Rock Series No. 22 for Bill, 1992, Lithograph, etching, printed in color
Rolling Rock Series No. 7 for Jim, 1991, Lithograph, etching, printed in color
Santa Fe, 1988, Woodcut
Santa Fe, 1987, Lithograph
Barrera Rosa's, 1986, Lithograph, printed in color
Woman/Girls, 1978, Lithograph
Tattoo, 1975, Lithograph, printed in color
Dr. Gibson, 1974, Lithograph, printed in color

COWIN, JACK
Black Pond, 1993, Lithograph, etching, chine collé
Black Earth, 1993, Lithograph, etching, aquatint
Spring Run, 1985, Lithograph, printed in color
Hen Rainbow Trout, 1983, Lithograph, printed in color

CRAGG, TONY
Suburbs I, II, 1990, Aquatint, spit-bite etching, printed in color

CRAMER, GEORGE
Maelstrom, 1994, Monoprint, printed in color
Forest, 1992, Monoprint, printed in color
Gee Whiz, 1992, Monoprint, printed in color
Reaching for a Cause, 1992, Monoprint, printed in color
Flora Bunda, 1992, Monoprint, printed in color
Tropical Leaves, 1992, Monoprint, printed in color
Opening to Flower, Monoprint, printed in color

CRANE, GREGORY
Mandrake's Corner, 1989, Woodcut, printed in color

CRILE, SUSAN
Untitled, 1985, Serigraph
Untitled, 1980, Serigraph

CUEVAS, JOSE LUIS
Coloso, 1987, Lithograph, printed in color

CUMMING, ROBERT
Bee Box, 1992, Monoprint
Non-Specific Table Top IV, IX, 1991, Monoprint
Water Above/Water Below, 1989, Monoprint
Untitled, 1989, Monoprint
Light in Window/Look to Floor, 1989, Monoprint
Berlin/Brazil, 1987, Lithograph, Serigraph
The First Three Minutes, Etc. Series of 9, 1987, Drypoint with hand coloring
Two Frame Arc, 1985, Lithograph, serigraph
One Frame Step, 1985, Lithograph, serigraph

D'ARCANGELO, ALLAN
Untitled, 1976, Serigraph

DANNER, ROBERT
Calendar Capers 1-12, 1990, Serigraph, printed in color
Art Moves, 1987, Serigraph
Brazil, 1986, Serigraph
Hot Air Color Float, 1985, Serigraph

DAUMIER, HONORÉ
After Water, Fire (Apres L'eau Le Feu), 1858, Lithograph

DAVIES, HANLYN
Flip Flop, 1976, Lithograph

DAVILA, CARLOS
Seascape V, 1985, Etching

DAVIS, BRAD
Three Junipers, 1985, Lithograph, serigraph

DAVIS, GENE
Untitled, 1971, Serigraph
Series 2, 1969, Serigraph on canvas

DAVIS, RONALD
Red Brick, 1983, Lithograph, printed in color
Brick, 1983, Lithograph, printed in color

DE FEURE, GEORGE
Paris Almanac, 1894, Lithograph

DE JESUS, NICHOLAS
Day of the Dead/Dia De Los Muertos 1-11, 1991, Etching

DE KOONING, ELAINE
Les Eyzies, 1985, Etching, aquatint, printed in color
Pech-Merle, 1985, Etching, printed in color
Torchlight Cave Drawings 1-8, 1985, Etching

DE SAINT PHALLE, NIKI
NY Film Festival, 1973, Serigraph
Je T' Aime, 1971, Lithograph

DE VINNY, DOUG
Arkansas Melon, 1986, Etching

DELAUNAY, SONIA
Untitled, Serigraph on canvas
Untitled, Lithograph on canvas

DIAMOND, MARTHA
Battery Park City, 1985, Lithograph

DICKSON, JANE
Witness, 1992, Serigraph on sandpaper
Revelers II, 1989, Monoprint
Bogie Down, 1989, Monoprint
Herald II, 1989, Monoprint

DIEBENKORN, RICHARD
Folsom St. Variations I (Black), 1985, Soap-ground aquatint, drypoint
Folsom St. Variations II (Grey), 1985, Soap-ground, flat-bite etching
Folsom St. Variations III (Primaries), 1985, Soap-ground aquatint, drypoint, flat bite
Two Way, 1982, Soft-ground etching
Two Way II, 1982, Color aquatint etching

DILL, LADDIE JOHN
Stage Left, 1982, Lithograph, printed in color
Stage Right, 1981, Lithograph, printed in color
Stage Whispers, 1981, Lithograph, printed in color

DILL, LESLEY
The Poetic Body, 1-4, 1992, Lithograph, letterpress, collage

DINE, JIM
Hearts (Diptych), 1992, Lithograph, with hand coloring
A Robe in Los Angeles, 1984, Lithograph, printed in color
Rachel Cohen's Flags, 1979, Etching, aquatint with hand coloring
Piranesi's 24 Colored Marks, 1976, Etching, with hand coloring
Wall Chart, 1974, Lithograph
Cincinnati III, 1969, Lithograph, printed in color

DI SUVERO, MARK
Brooklyn Bridge, 1983, Lithograph
Centering, 1976, Lithograph, printed in color
Jak, 1976, Lithograph, serigraph

DODSON, JILL
Jacklin Klugman, 1983, Lithograph

DOUGAN, JOHN
Brush and Tape Lines, Lithograph

DUNHAM, CARROLL
Touching Two Sides, 1989, Drypoint etching

DURAND, ELIZABETH
Island Moonrise, 1986, Mixed media monoprint

ENGLANDER, DOROTHY
Double Whammy III, 1985, Monoprint, printed in color
Blue Rift, 1985, Monoprint, printed in color
Red Nettle, 1985, Monoprint, printed in color
Mumbledy Peg, 1985, Monoprint, printed in color

EPSTEIN, YALE
Mystikon II #23, 1986, Monoprint

ERTÉ
Red Dancer, 1983, Serigraph
Trapeze, 1983, Serigraph

ESTES, RICHARD
Escalator, 1979, Serigraph
Venezia, 1979, Serigraph

FANNING, LEE ANN
Spring Fling, 1986, Serigraph, printed in color
Woods Way, 1986, Serigraph, printed in color
Ocean Walk, 1986, Serigraph, printed in color
July (Diptych), 1986, Serigraph, printed in color
Bayside Garden, 1986, Serigraph, printed in color
September (Triptych), 1986, Serigraph, printed in color

FENNELL, PATRICIA
Here and Now Then and There, 1993, Etching, aquatint with hand coloring

FERRER, RAFAEL
Verduras, 1990, Woodcut, printed in color
Amanecer Sobre el Cabo, (Dawn Over the Cape), 1988, Woodcut, printed in color

FINE, DIANE
Curtain Rises on Chairs and Hut, 1985, Viscosity etching, aquatint

FINK, AARON
Cherry Tomato, 1994, Woodcut, printed in color
Green Grapes, 1993, Woodcut, printed in color
Eggplant II, 1991, Monoprint, printed in color
Green Pepper II, 1991, Monoprint, printed in color
Pear I, 1991, Monoprint, printed in color
Juniper Berries III, 1991, Monoprint, printed in color
Steaming Cup, 1990, Woodcut, printed in color

FISCHL, ERIC
Untitled, 1992, Monoprint

FISH, JANET
Daffodils, 1995, Serigraph, printed in color
Waimea, 1993, Serigraph, printed in color
Cerises, 1992, Serigraph, printed in color

FISHER, VERNON
Dark Night Full of Stars, 1985, Lithograph

FIX-MASSEAU, PIERRE
Venice Simplon Orient Express 1-7, 1982, Lithograph, printed in color

FLESCHER, CAROL
Dancing Bones, 1994, Woodcut

FOLON, JEAN MICHEL
Manifesti di Folon 1-15, 1978, Aquatint

FORD, JOHN
Corrosive Force #3, 1990, Monoprint

FÖRG, GÜNTER
Untitled, 3 pieces, 1988, Monoprint

FORRESTER TOBACCO, PATRICIA
Lilies, Lithograph, printed in color
Royal Flush, 1989, Lithograph, printed in color

FRANCIS, SAM
King Corpse, 1986, Serigraph, printed in color
Generated, 1983, Lithograph, printed in color
Untitled (Sfe-001), 1982, Etching, printed in color

FRANK, HELEN
Bird's Nest, 1986, Monoprint
Cactus, 1986, Monoprint
Flea Market, 1986, Monoprint
Hollyhock, 1986, Monoprint
Morning Glory, 1986, Monoprint
Nasturtium, 1986, Monoprint
Owners and Jockeys, 1986, Etching
Balloons, 1985, Monoprint
Fitting Room at Loehmann's, 1985, Etching
Foal, 1985, Monoprint
July, 1985, Monoprint
Sheep, 1985, Monoprint
Woman with Owl, 1985, Monoprint
Carousel (Single Horse, Beige), 1983, Monoprint
Jockeys, 1983, Monoprint
Morning Rider, 1983, Etching
Saratoga in August, 1983, Serigraph
Saratoga Italianate – The Adelphi, 1983, Etching
Skidmore Class of '22, 1983, Etching
The Beach, 1983, Etching

FRANK, MARY
Realm, 1992, Monoprint, printed in color
Untitled, 1992, Monoprint, printed in color
Solar Box, 1992, Monoprint, printed in color
Man in the Water, State II, 1987, Lithograph printed in color
Untitled, 1978, Monoprint, printed in color

FRANKENTHALER, HELEN
Eve, 1996, Serigraph, printed in color
Reflections IX, X, 1995, Lithograph, printed in color
Mary Mary, 1990, Serigraph, lithograph, printed in color
Walking Rain, 1987, Lithograph, engraving, etching, aquatint
Sudden Snow, 1987, Lithograph, printed in color
Blue Current, 1987, Aquatint, etching, engraving

FRIEBERT, JOSEPH
The Models, 1992, Lithograph, printed in color

FRIEDMAN, DEBRA
Whitfield Road, 1991, Monoprint

FRIEDMAN, JON
Untitled, 1986, Serigraph

FRINGS, DENNIS
Untitled, 1986, Monoprint

FUNAKOSHI, KATSURA
After Mirror Reflecting Fingers, 1990, Sugar-lift, spit-bite aquatint, etching with drypoint

GAINES, CHARLES
Color Regression 1-3, 1980, Lithograph, printed in color

GILBERT-ROLFE, JEREMY
Untitled, 1983, Serigraph

GILLESPIE, DOROTHY
Untitled, 1989, Serigraph

GILLIAM, SAM
Untitled #10, 1992, Monoprint, multi-color relief with acrylic
Running Series: Red (Diptych), 1991, Monoprint
Running Series: Orange (Diptych), 1991, Monoprint
Untitled #12, 17, 1992, Monoprint, multi-color relief, with acrylic and gel medium
Coffee Thyme, 1979, Drypoint, etching, cast acrylic, embossing

GINSBERG, ELIZABETH
Alor, 1982, Lithograph

GIPE, LAWRENCE
Elegy, 1992, Etching

GLOECKLER, RAYMOND
The Engraver, Woodcut
Resolute Wren, Woodcut
All My Friends Are Over 50, Woodcut
Spinner, Woodcut

GOEBEL, ROD
Untitled, Monoprint

GOLDBERG, GLENN
Untitled, 1990, Serigraph
Untitled 1-3, 1990, Monoprint, pochoir
Four, 1988, Monoprint, pochoir

GOLDMAN, JANE E.
Evening Tide, 1995, Lithograph
To the Garden, 1989, Serigraph
Mid-Summer Light, 1987, Serigraph

GOLDSTEIN, JACK
Untitled 1, 2, 1983, Lithograph, serigraph

GOLDYNE, JOSEPH
Untitled, 1994, Etching, Drypoint, Monoprint
Floral Trilogy: Cadence into Chaos, 1994, Etching, Drypoint, Monoprint

GRASS, PETER
Untitled, 1994, Monoprint
Lake Park: Path into Shadow, 1994, Etching

GRAVES, NANCY
Approaches the Limit of I, 1981, Lithograph, printed in color
Approaches the Limit of II, 1981, Lithograph, engraving, printed in color
Untitled, 1980, Serigraph
Onon, 1977, Etching, aquatint, drypoint, engraving with hand coloring
Saille, 1977, Etching, aquatint with hand coloring

GREENEBAUM, NANCY
Fire Glyph, 1978, Lithograph

GRONK
Cook, Monoprint
Ear Man, 1995, Monoprint
Bullet Nose, 1995, Monoprint
Perfume, 1995, Monoprint
Mulata de Cordova, 1995, Woodcut, printed in color
36th Street, 1994, Etching on steel
31st Street, 1993, Etching on steel
32nd Street, 1993, Etching on steel
33rd Street, 1993, Etching on steel
34th Street, 1993, Etching on steel
C-Cup, 1993, Etching on steel

GROOMS, RED
Taxi to the Terminal, 1994, Lithograph, printed in color
Holy Hula, 1991, Lithograph, printed in color
Chuck Berry, 1978, Silkscreen with collage

GROSS, MICHAEL
Bowl with Stars, 1985
Nat, Rat, Cat, 1985
Green Skeleton on Red Horse, 1985

GRUENWALD, JOHN
Performer, 1992, Lithograph, printed in color
Lover, Lithograph, printed in color
Morning Light, Lithograph
Buddha Head, Lithograph
Father and Son, 1992, Lithograph
Saltimbanques, Lithograph
Bathers, 1990, Lithograph
Untitled Head, 1990, Lithograph
Tales of the Journey, Lithograph,
Head in Profile, 7 Pieces, 1990, Lithograph
Blue and Red Landscape, Lithograph
Weeping Willow, 1989, Monoprint
Woman in Doorway 1-3, 1988, Etching
Kid, 1986, Lithograph
Walking Man, 1984, Lithograph

GUSTON, PHILIP
August, 1966, Lithograph

GUTIERREZ, MICHELLE
Variations on a June Bug (Blue), 1982, Lithograph, printed in color
Variations on a June Bug (Brown), 1982, Lithograph, printed in color

HAAS, RICHARD
New York Lexington, Looking North-Central Synagogue, 1991, Etching, aquatint, printed in color
Dallas Skyline, 1989, Lithograph, printed in color

HALE, MICHAEL
Barade 5 #28, 1986, Embossed mixed media monoprint
Susp Cadence, 1985, Serigraph
Phygian Cadence, 1985, Serigraph
Trio, 1985, Serigraph
Largo, 1985, Serigraph

HALL, SUSAN
Light on the Headlands I, 1992, Monoprint, printed in color
Red Cottage I, 1990, Monoprint, printed in color
Stones Cottage, 1990, Monoprint, printed in color
Journey by Water, 1990, Monoprint, printed in color
Boats near Marshall, 1990, Monoprint, printed in color
Orange Ball, 1990, Monoprint, printed in color
Red Dahlia, 1989, Monoprint, printed in color
Moving Dream, 1989, Monoprint, printed in color
Dahlia, 1989, Monoprint, printed in color
Jessie's Dream, 1989, Monoprint, printed in color

HAMBLETON, SUSAN
Untitled 1-2, 1989, Monoprint
In the Garden, 1989, Monoprint

HAMMOND, HARMONY
Chicken Lady, 1985, Lithograph
Fan Lady Meets Cactus Lady, 1981, Lithograph

HANAUER, GEORGE
Untitled 1-17, 1988, Printers ink on coated paper

HANNAH, DUNCAN
Under the El, 1991, Lithograph, printed in color
Drugstore, 1990, Monoprint, printed in color
Riverman, 1990, Monoprint, printed in color
Riders, 1990, Monoprint, printed in color
Jumprope, 1990, Monoprint, printed in color
Northern Lights (Slate), 1990, Monoprint, printed in color
Northern Lights (Purple), 1990, Monoprint, printed in color
Wreck of the *Shiloh*, 1989, Monoprint, printed in color
Overseas, 1989, Monoprint, printed in color
Hidden Beach (Green), 1989, Monoprint, printed in color
Boy in Tree, 1989, Monoprint, printed in color

HANSELL, FREYA
Murmur, 1991, Monoprint
Untitled, 1989, Monoprint

HANSEN, HAROLD
Tradition, 1986, Lithograph, with hand coloring
Robins, 1983, Lithograph
Percheron, Lithograph, with hand coloring
Basket, 1982, Lithograph

HARING, KEITH
Apocalypse 1-10, 1988, Serigraph, printed in color

HASHEY, JAN
Bruno with Lei, 1989, Monoprint
Untitled, 1989, Monoprint

HEEKS, WILLY
Pole, 1993, Monoprint, printed in color
Glowing Gate, 1989, Monoprint, printed in color

HELD, AL
Embarcadero, 1994, Spit-bite aquatint
Space Between the Two, 1992, Spit-bite aquatint
Magenta, 1990, Color aquatint, spit-bite engraving, etching
Straits of Malacca II, 1989, Hard-ground etching
Pachinko, 1989, Woodcut, printed in color
Kyoto-Wa, 1985, Woodcut, printed in color

HENDON, CHAM
Musings (Triptych), 1987, Multiple woodcut reduction, printed in color, with acrylic wash

HERNON, PATRICK
Untitled, 1973, Etching, aquatint

HIMMELFARB, JOHN
Kandy Mountain, 1989, Monoprint, printed in color
Grown Woman in the Promised Land, 1989, Monoprint, printed in color
Storyteller, 1981, Lithograph, printed in color

HIRATSUKA, YUJI
Forger II, 1994, Lithograph, chine collé

HITCH, STEWART
Infidel, 1985, Woodcut, printed in color
Slum Goddess, 1985, Lithograph, printed in color

HOCKNEY, DAVID
Views of Hotel Well II, 1985, Lithograph, printed in color
My Pool and Terrace, 1983, Etching, aquatint, printed in color
Stravinsky Poster, 1981, Serigraph
Study of Lightning Medium, 1973, Lithograph
Illustrations for Flaubert's "A Simple Heart," 1-3, 1969-74, Etching, aquatint
Picture of a Landscape in an Elaborate Gold Frame, 1965, Lithograph

HODGKIN, HOWARD
Gossip, 1995, Serigraph, printed in color
Community Holiday Festival Poster, 1992, Serigraph
Untitled, 1989, Serigraph
David's Pool, 1986, Etching, aquatint, with hand coloring
One Down, 1983, Lithograph, with hand coloring
Bleeding, 1982, Lithograph, with hand coloring
Black Moonlight, 1980, Lithograph, with hand coloring
Furnished Room, 1977, Etching, aquatint, with hand coloring
Nick's Room, 1977, Lithograph, with hand coloring
Jarid's Porch, 1977, Lithograph, with hand coloring
More Indian Views (Shutters), 1976, Lithograph
More Indian Views (Window), 1976, Lithograph

HODICKE, KARL
Horst Irish Sheep, 1982, Serigraph, printed in color

HOEFER, WADE
Patriae IV, 1993, Monoprint, printed in color
Riparius, 1993, Woodcut, etching, printed in color
Aestas I, II, 1993, Monoprint
Agrestus III, 1993, Monoprint
Flumina XVI, 1993, Monoprint

HOFFMAN, ARNOLD
For Pleasure, 1986, Computer ink plot
By Way of #18, 1986, Serigraph

HOLLAND, TOM
Tow, 1986, Etching, printed in color
Pamino, 1986, Etching, printed in color
Tetton, 1984, Etching, printed in color

HOLLINGSWORTH, ALVIN
Untitled, 1990, Serigraph, with hand coloring

HOOD, RANCE
Rhythm of the Plains, 1991, Serigraph, printed in color

HUDSON, ROBERT
Green and Red Rhyme, 1987, Etching, printed in color
Out of Orbit, 1986, Etching, printed in color

HUGHTO, DARRYL
Untitled, 1977, Serigraph

HULL, RICHARD
Loamings, 1993, Hard-ground etching
Return, 1986, Lithograph, printed in color
Change, 1986, Lithograph

HUNT, BRYAN
Island, 1992, Soft-ground etching with soap ground, sugar lift, aquatint, printed in color
Sedona Precipice, 1992, Soft-ground etching with soap ground, sugar lift, spit bite, aquatint, printed in color
Window, 1986, Woodcut, printed in color

HURSON, MICHAEL
Frog, Lithograph

IDA, SHOICHI
Between Air and Water No. 7, 1992, Soft-ground etching with spit-bite aquatint and drypoint on chine collé
Between Air and Water No. 3, 1992, Spit-bite aquatint with drypoint on gampi chine collé
Between Vertical and Horizon Descending Triangle D, 1987, Etching, printed in color
Between Vertical and Horizon Descending Triangle C, 1987, Etching, chine collé, printed in color
Between Vertical and Horizon Descending Triangle B, 1987, Etching, chine collé, printed in color
Between Vertical and Horizon Descending Triangle A, 1987, Etching, chine collé, printed in color
Between Vertical and Horizon-Descending Triangle (Square), 1987, Etching, printed in color
Between Vertical and Horizontal San Pablo Ave. #2, 1984, Aquatint etching
Between Vertical and Horizontal San Pablo Ave. #1, 1984, Aquatint etching

INDIANA, ROBERT
Garden of Love 1-6, 1982, Serigraph, printed in color
American Dream #2, 1-4, 1982, Serigraph, printed in color
Mecca III, 1978, Serigraph

IRELAND, PATRICK
Flying Open Cube (Red), 1993, Etching, relief
Flying Open Cube (Blue), 1993, Etching, relief
Flying Open Cube (Purple), 1993, Etching, relief
Flying Open Cube (Orange), 1993, Etching, relief

IRVINE
Feeling Good, 1986, Serigraph
Pow Wow Mesa, 1986, Serigraph

JACQUETTE, YVONNE
Night View Wing I, II, 1992, Serigraph, printed in color
Times Square (Overview), 1987, Woodcut, printed in color

JANKLOW, M.
Untitled, 1985, Serigraph

JANZ, ROBERT
Passover Rose, 1988, Lithograph

JAUDON, VALERIE
Untitled 1-4, 1986, Serigraph

JENKINS, PAUL
Sinclair Red, 1982, Serigraph, printed in color
Sheffield Blue, 1982, Serigraph, printed in color
Vermillion Enigma, Serigraph, printed in color
Cardinal Prism, 1982, Serigraph, printed in color
Continental Divide, 1981-82, Serigraph, printed in color
Moby Dick, 1981, Serigraph, printed in color
York Summer Solstice, Serigraph, printed in color
Cardinal Rain Palace, 1980, Serigraph, printed in color
Light Graphic, 1972, Lithograph, printed in color

JIMENEZ, LUIS
Texas Waltz, 1984, Lithograph, printed in color

JOHNS, JASPER
Ale Cans I, 1975, Lithograph, printed in tones of blue and black
Ale Cans III, 1975, Lithograph, printed in tones of gray and black

JOHNSON, DALE
Ice House, 1989, Monoprint, printed in color
Red Ice House, 1989, Monoprint, printed in color
Ochre Ice House, 1989, Monoprint, printed in color

JONAS, JOAN
Double Lunar Dogs, 1982, Aquatint, printed in color

JONES, ALLEN
Black Feat, Lithograph

JOY, STEVE
Untitled, 1991, Serigraph

JUAREZ, ROBERTO
Barracks, 1993, Monoprint, printed in color
Noche, 1993, Monoprint, printed in color
Calender, 1993, Monoprint, printed in color

JUDD, DONALD
Untitled, 1992, Woodcut
Untitled 1-6, 1992, Woodcut with pochoir
Untitled (3 Diptychs), 1990, Woodcut
Red, 1-10, 1989, Woodcut, printed in color
Untitled, 1980, Aquatint

KAINEN, JACOB
Tblisi Rose, Lithograph
Vladimir, Lithograph

KAPOOR, ANISH
Untitled 10, 11, 1990, Woodcut, printed in color

KAREN, BRUCE
Untitled, Woodcut

KATZ, ALEX
Day Lilies, 1992, Serigraph, printed in color
Swimmer, 1990, Woodcut, printed in color
Red Cap, 1989, Aquatint etching, printed in color
John Ashbery, 1986, Etching, printed in color
The Green Cap, 1985, Woodcut, printed in color

KELLEY, DANIEL
Radishes, Lithograph

KELLEY, JOHN
Andalusia Rose, 1991, Pencil

KELLY, ELLSWORTH
Square with Black (State), 1982, Aquatint
Concorde I-III (State), 1982, Aquatint
Colors on a Grid 1976, 1976, Serigraph, printed in color
Colored Paper Image XIV, 1976, Laminated paper pulp, printed in color
Colored Paper Images XVIII, 1976, Handmade paper
Blue with Black I, 1974, Lithograph, printed in color
Peach Branch, 1974, Lithograph
Red Yellow Blue, Serigraph, printed in color
Yellow over Black, 1964, Lithograph, printed in color
Black over Yellow (No. 21), 1964, Lithograph, printed in color

KENT, JANE
Yt, 1993, Lithograph, printed in color
Starry Night, 1993, Etching, printed in color
Untitled 1-6, 1992, Monoprint, printed in color
String of Pearls, 1992, Lithograph, printed in color
5 PM Suite, 1992, Etching, printed in color
Blue, 1990, Etching, printed in color
Gray and White, 1990, Etching, printed in color
Brown and Black, 1990, Etching, printed in color
Red and Black, 1990, Etching, printed in color
Orange, 1989, Etching, printed in color
Crown, 1989, Etching, printed in color
Purple, 1989, Etching, printed in color

KEPETS, HUGH
Akron, 1989, Serigraph, printed in color
Huron, 1989, Serigraph, printed in color

KERNAN, CATHERINE
Tidewater 1-4, 1995, Etching, printed in color
Srahlagy, 1993, Monoprint
Belderrig Falls #8, 1993, Monoprint
Ballymachugh Falls 9, 10, 1993, Monoprint

KIM, KI-CHANG
Mystic Star of the Orient, 1988, Lithograph, printed in color

KITTLESON, EARL
Figure, 1995, Monoprint

KJAER, RUTH
Blue Collar, 1992, Lithograph, etching, printed in color

KLEIN, LYNN
Untitled, 1992, Lithograph

KOMOSKI, BILL
Untitled, 1987, Serigraph

KOZLOFF, JOYCE
Untitled, 1982, Serigraph

KRAMER, STEVE
Untitled, 1985, Monoprint

KRUGER, BARBARA
Printed Matter Matters, 1989, Lithograph with relief
Savoir c'est pouvoir (Knowledge Is Power), 1989, Lithograph

KUHN, AUDREY
Rose Lake Wilderness I-III, 1986, Serigraph with embossing
Chromatic Variations I-III, 1985, Serigraph with embossing
Transparencies I, II, 1985, Serigraph with embossing
Golden Hills, 1985, Serigraph with embossing
Spectrum 7, 10, 1985, Serigraph with embossing
Gothic Window I, II, 1985, Serigraph with embossing

KUNC, KAREN
A Jaded Nature, 1992, Woodcut, printed in color

KUSHNER, ROBERT
Tropical Bouquet III, 1994, Monoprint
Camellia Pink, 1994, Sugar-lift, spit-bite aquatint, drypoint
Camellia Red, 1994, Sugar-lift, spit-bite aquatint, drypoint
White Anemone, State 1, 2, 1989, Woodcut, printed in color
Black Jade, 1989, Woodcut, printed in color
Red Anemone, 1989, Woodcut, printed in color
Pineapple, 1986, Lithograph with sequins
Maple, 1986, Lithograph with sequins
Daphne II, 1985, Woodcut, printed in color
Another Question, 1981, Lithograph, printed in color
Fruit Plate, 1983, Lithograph with collage, printed in color
Nubiana (Diptych), 1982, Etching, printed in color
National Treasure, 1981, Lithograph, printed in color
Gardening (3 Panels), 1981, Lithograph
The Joy of Ornament, 1980

LACK, STEPHAN
Motorcade, 1988, Monoprint

LANE, LOIS
Untitled, 1989, Linocut

LANG, DANIEL S
Three Windows (Ward's), 1995, Serigraph, printed in color

LANYON, ELLEN
Black Egret, 1984, Lithograph
Eagle Beak, 1984, Lithograph

LARSON, DIANE
The Five Muscians, 1996, Serigraph
Lake Michigan Catch, 1992, Serigraph

LARSON, ED
Parts, 1983, Woodcut, printed in color

LATIMER, SHERIDAN
Untitled, 1974, Serigraph

LATTANZI
Untitled, 1981, Etchings

LAWRENCE, JACOB
The Workshop, 1972, Collage

LAWRENCE, LORI
Icarus Falls in Black, 1986, Etching
Collidescade, 1985, Etching
Untitled (Blue-Green), 1985, Collagraph
Circus I, II, 1985, Etching

LEBADANG
La Comédie Humaine, 1980, Lithograph, handmade paper

LEE, LI LIN
In the Rainy Season, 1989, Woodcut, printed in color
Mirror Image, 1989, Woodcut, printed in color
Sacrament and Sorrow, 1989, Woodcut, printed in color
A Hidden Place, 1989, Woodcut, printed in color

LESLIE, ALFRED
Frank Fata, 1974, Lithograph, printed in color
Richard Bellamy, 1974, Lithograph, printed in color
Alfred Leslie, 1974, Lithograph, printed in color

LEVINE, MARTIN
Catching the 5:15, 1993, Hard-ground etching, aquatint

LEVINE, SHERRIE
Meltdown After Duchamp, Monet, Kirchner, Mondrian, 1989, Woodcut, printed in color
Laundress After Degas #5, 1987, Lithograph

LEVINTHAL, DAVID
Untitled from The Wild West 1-3, 1995, Waterless lithograph on foil

LEWITT, SOL
Color and Black, 1991, Spit-bite aquatint etching
Arcs from Four Corners, 1986, Woodcut, printed in color
Untitled, 1972, Serigraph
Untitled, 1-16, 1971, Lithograph, printed in color

LICHTENSTEIN, ROY
Vertical Apple, 1983, Woodcut, printed in color
I Love Liberty, 1982, Serigraph, printed in color
American Indian Theme, 1980, Etchings, printed in color
Head with Braids
Dancing Figures
Two Figures with Teepee
Night Scene
Head with Feather and Braid
Mirror 5, 7, 1972, Serigraph, printed in color

LICHTNER, SCHOMER
Cow Jar, 1992, Lithograph, printed in color

LINHARES, JUDITH
Cow Girl, 1987, Monoprint

LISIECKI, DENISE
Red Leather Chair, 1983, Lithograph

LOHNER, HAROLD
Vienna, 1986, Lithograph
One Hundred, 1986, Intaglio

LONGO, ROBERT
Men in the Cities II, IV, V, 1990, Lithograph
Red Kiss, 1990, Lithograph
Meryle, 1988, Lithograph
Joanna and Larry From: Men in the Cities, 1983, Lithograph

LUPE, LORI
Seascape, 1986, Serigraph
Fairway, 1986, Serigraph

LYNCH, MICHAEL
Prairie House, 1979, Lithograph

MACHINIST, LESLIE
Untitled (Couple), 1989, Monoprint

MANDIGO, CATE
Parade, 1983, Serigraph
County Fair, 1983, Serigraph
Race Track, 1983, Serigraph
Wilson's General Store, 1983, Serigraph

MANET, EDOUARD
Odalisque, 1877, Etching, aquatint

MANGER, BARBARA
Sacajawea, 1983, Lithograph, printed in color
Leap Out, Lithograph, printed in color

MANGOLD, ROBERT
Five Color Frame, 1985, Woodcut, printed in color
Multiple Panel Paintings, 1973, Serigraph

MANGOLD PLIMACK, SYLVIA
The Pin Oak at the Pond, 1986, Etching, aquatint, printed in color

MARGIS, WILLIAM A
Why Me, Why Me?, Lithograph, printed in color

MARINI, MARINO
Red Horse, 1980, Etching, aquatint

MARIONI, TOM
Finger Print, 1991, Soft-ground, sugar-lift etching with drypoint, chine collé, collage
Flying Yen, 1990, Woodcut, printed in color
Pi, 1988, Woodcut, printed in color

MARLOWE, WILLIE
Minimal Pink, 1986, Monoprint
Untitled, 1986, Monoprint

MARSH, GEORGIA
Blue Riddle, 1993, Lithograph, printed in color
White Sleeve, 1993, Monoprint
Science of the Night, 3 pieces, 1992, Monoprint, printed in color
American Elm IV, 1991, Monoprint, printed in color

MATTA, ROBERTO
Le Gai Venin, Aquatint
Damnepar L'are-En Ciel, 1978, Aquatint

MAURO, GARY
Figure, Monoprint, printed in color
Early Nude, Serigraph, printed in color
Figure, Monoprint, printed in color

MAYO, GRETCHEN
Untitled, Lithograph, printed in color

McCAFFERTY, JAY
#4, 1977, Woodcut

McCANN, TOM
Electric Mountain Triple Feature, 1977, Serigraph

McCOLLUM, SUDI
Ducks, 1983, Serigraph with embossing

McCOY, ANN
Night Sea (Diptych), 1978, Lithograph
Planets for Michael Mears, 1978, Lithograph

McKENZIE, HOWARD
Sideshow, 1986, Etching, printed in color
Clown Band, 1986, Etching, printed in color
Solitude, Etching

McKIE, TODD
Untitled, 1989, Serigraph

McNALLY, BERNARD
Loring Gables, 1978, Lithograph

MECIKALSKI, EUGENE
Panic, 1991, Lithograph

MERKIN, RICHARD
Satchel Paige in Kansas City, 1978, Serigraph, printed in color

MEYER, ELISABETH
Untitled 1-3, 1992, Monoprint, printed in color
III, 1990, Monoprint, printed in color
Untitled 1-4, 1989, Monoprint, printed in color
Dl'e X, 1989, Monoprint, printed in color
Untitled VI, XII, 1989, Monoprint, printed in color
XVIII, 1988, Monoprint, printed in color
XIV, 1988, Monoprint, printed in color

MIKOLOWSKI, ANN
Highway 58, 1995, Serigraph, printed in color

MIRÓ, JOAN
Fusées, 1959, Aquatint with stencil
Untitled, Lithograph

MITCHELL, JOAN
Bedford Series, 1981, Lithograph, printed in color
Sides of a River I, III
Flower I
Bedford I, III

MOMINEE, JOHN
Untitled #3, 1989, Monoprint, printed in color

MOMOSE, HISASHI
Untitled 1-12, 1982, Serigraph, printed in color
Untitled 1-4, 1982, Serigraph, printed in color

MOORE, JOHN
Untitled, 1976, Serigraph

MOORE, W.
Regatta, Serigraph

MORA, FRANCISCO
Los Alegres Compadres, Lithograph, printed in color

MORLEY, MALCOLM
Untitled, 1986, Lithograph
Untitled, 1985, Lithograph
Beach Scene, 1982, Lithograph, printed in color
Devonshire Bullocks, 1982, Lithograph, printed in color
Parrots, 1982, Lithograph, printed in color
Fish, 1982, Lithograph, printed in color
Horses, 1982, Lithograph, printed in color
Devonshire Cows, 1982, Lithograph, printed in color
SS Amsterdam in Front of Rotterdam, 1966, Lithograph, printed in color

MOSKOWITZ, ROBERT
Cadillac Chopsticks, 1985, Lithograph

MOTHERWELL, ROBERT
Mostly Mozart, 1991, Serigraph, printed in color
Yellow Flight, 1987, Etching, aquatint, printed in color
Signs on Copper, 1981, Etching, aquatint
Rite of Passage III, 1980, Lithograph, chine appliqué
Red Sea II, 1979, Etching, aquatint

MUCHA, ALPHONSE
Flirt, Biscuits Lefevre – Utile, 1900, Lithograph

MULHERN, MARK
Vessel Against Red Background 1-6, 1994, Monoprint, printed in color
Floral Landscape 1-7, 1992, Monoprint, printed in color
Untitled, 1990, Lithograph, printed in color
Blue Vase, 1986, Monoprint, printed in color
Gold Vase, 1986, Monoprint, printed in color
Landscape with Mulberry Trees, 1986, Monoprint
Red Vase, 1986, Monoprint, printed in color
Fauvist, 1986, Monoprint, printed in color
Landscape with Plowed Field, 1986, Monoprint, printed in color
Self-Portrait, Lithograph

MULLIN, MARTIN
Arrival of Anselm Kiefer in Bunclody 1-8, 1991, Monoprint, printed in color

MURRAY, ELIZABETH
Untitled, 1993, Serigraph
Snake Cup, 1984, Lithograph, printed in color
Sniff, 1984, Lithograph, printed in color
Untitled, 1979, Serigraph, printed in color

MURRAY, JUDITH
Untitled, 1991, Serigraph on rag paper, printed in color
Untitled, 1986, Serigraph, printed in color
Untitled, 1981, Serigraph, printed in color

MYERS, FRANCES
Les Faveurs de Dieu (The Favors of God), 1994, Lithograph, printed in color
Of Things Past, 1993, Etching
Tending Jan's Garden, 1990, Soft-ground etching, printed in color

NADLER, HARRY
Untitled, 1990, Serigraph

NATKIN, ROBERT
Color Bath Series – Blue, 1978, Lithograph, serigraph, printed in color
Untitled, 1978, Etching

NAUMAN, BRUCE
Floor Drain, 1985, Etching with drypoint, aquatint
Suspended Chair, 1985, Drypoint, printed in color
House Divided, 1985, Drypoint, etching, printed in color
Untitled (Gray), 1971, Lithograph
Untitled (Salmon Pink), 1971, Lithograph

NAZARRO, ANTHONY
Configurations #19, 1986, Monoprint, printed in color
Fantasia, 1986, Monoprint, printed in color
Sea and Sails, 1986, Monoprint, printed in color
Sails and Rigging, 1986, Monoprint, printed in color
Harp String, 1986, Monoprint, printed in color
Masquerade, 1986, Monoprint, printed in color

NECHVATAL, DENNIS
Passage, 1993, Etching, asphaltum , relief, aquatint
Birth, 1990, Woodcut, printed in color
Landscape Drama, 1990, Woodcut

NESBITT, LOWELL
Untitled, 1978, Serigraph, printed in color
Fruit on Rug, 1978, Serigraph, printed in color
Blue Flower, 1974, Lithograph, printed in color
Poppy, 1974, Lithograph, serigraph, printed in color

NEVELSON, LOUISE
Facades 1-12, 1966, Serigraph, photograph, aquatint

NEWMAN, BARNETT
Untitled, 1969, Etching, aquatint

NICE, DON
Trout XIII, 1990, Monoprint, printed in color
Untitled, 1988, Serigraph, printed in color

NICHOLS, BILL
Poppies, 1991, Lithograph, printed in color

NICKSON, GRAHAM
Beach, 1981, Lithograph, printed in color

NIELSEN, STUART
Untitled, 1983, Lithograph, woodcut

NILSSON, GLADYS
The Little Naturalist's Field Trip, 1993, Etching, soft-ground, drypoint, aquatint, printed in color

NORSTEN, TODD
Synousia 1-8, 1994, Intaglio, chine collé, woodcut

NOZKOWSKI, THOMAS
Untitled, 1992, Woodcut, printed in color

OLDENBURG, CLAES
Blue Saxophone, 1992, Lithograph, printed in color
Untitled (Black and White), 1992, Lithograph
Untitled (Black, Yellow, Red), 1992, Lithograph, printed in color
Apple Core, Black and White State, 1991, Lithograph
Bat Spinning at the Speed of Light State II, 1975, Lithograph, printed in color
Spoon Pier, 1975, Aquatint, sugar lift, printed in color
Mitt, 1973, Lithograph, printed in color
The Letter Q as Beach House with Sailboat, 1972, Lithograph, printed in color

OLITSKI, JULES
Mozart Nights, 1992, Serigraph, printed in color

OROPALLO, DEBORAH
Ball and Plane, 1994, Woodcut, etching, serigraph, printed in color
Lessons VII, 1994, Monoprint, with hand painting
Airplane, 1994, Monoprint, with hand painting
Red, 1993, Woodcut, aquatint, etching, printed in color
Number Work, 1990, Woodcut, etching

ORTEGA, TONY
Una Vista at Aztlan, 1992, Monoprint, printed in color
La Pareja at Aztlan, 1992, Monoprint, printed in color
Urban Paletero, 1992, Monoprint, printed in color
Seven Mares at Aztlan, 1992, Monoprint, printed in color
La Chevy at Aztlan, 1992, Monoprint, printed in color
La Troca at Aztlan, 1992, Monoprint, printed in color
La Parado Urbana, 1992, Monoprint, printed in color
La Caratera at Aztlan, 1992, Monoprint, printed in color

OTT, SABINA
Disappearance and Return 1-4, 1990, Woodcut, etching, printed in color

OWEN, FRANK
Know the Elements, 1989, Lithograph, printed in color

PALADINO, MIMMO
Muto, 1985, Etching with aquatint, sugar lift, in colors, with collage

PAOLOZZI, EDUARDO
Quadram Dax

PAPART, MAX
New Orleans Fantasy, 1986, Lithograph
Dreams, 1985, Lithograph, embossing, printed in color
Inca Bird, 1985, Carborundum with collage
Magic Man, 1985
Primavera, 1985, Lithograph
Romeo and Juliet, 1985, Aquatint, Carborundum
Circus Rider, 1982, Aquatint, Carborundum, printed in color
Birds (1-4), 1982, Carborundum with collage, printed in color
Blue Harlequin, 1982, Aquatint, Carborundum printed in color
Oval Bird, 1982, Lithograph, embossing, printed in color
Beautiful Bird, 1981, Lithograph, printed in color
Blue Moon, 1981, Aquatint, Carborundum
Circle, 1981, Lithograph, printed in color
Clown Three, 1981, Lithograph, printed in color
Hello Broadway, 1981, Aquatint, Carborundum, collage, printed in color
Le Cirque (Triptych), 1981, Aquatint, Carborundum
Spanish Bird, 1981, Lithograph, embossing
Trapeze Artist, 1981, Lithograph, printed in color
Trapeze, 1981, Lithograph, embossing, collage, printed in color
Ideal Couple, 1980, Lithograph, printed in color
Marianne, 1980, Lithograph, printed in color
O Douce Fantaisie, 1979, Aquatint, Carborundum, printed in color

PARKE, LESLIE
Passing the Gate (Triptych), 1985

PARKER, JEANNE
Mountain View, 1986, Monoprint, printed in color
Spring Landscape, 1986, Monoprint, printed in color

PASCHKE, EDWARD F
L.A. Ex, 1994, Lithograph, printed in color
George Mills, 1990, Lithograph, printed in color

PEARLSTEIN, PHILIP
Nude with Iron Bench and Mirror, 1978, Lithograph, printed in color

PENCK, A.R.
Dealink, 1993, Monoprint
Mul, Bul, Dang and Sentimentality, 1988, Woodcut, printed in color

PERKINS, LYNNE RAE
What's It Like Here/Country Life, 1992, Etching, with hand coloring

PETERSEN, ROBERT
July 1980, 1982, Etching, collage, with hand coloring
February 1980, 1982, Etching, collage, with hand coloring
Sunday March 27, 1977, Lithograph, chine collé
March 29, 1977, Lithograph, chine collé
October 18, 1976, 1977, Lithograph, chine collé
April 1984, Silkscreen, collage, with hand coloring
September 20, 1976, 1977, Lithograph, chine collé
September 1976, 1977, Lithograph, chine collé

PFAFF, JUDY
Half A Dozen of the Other: Che Cosa E Acqua, 1992, Drypoint, spit-bite aquatint, soft-ground, sugar-lift aquatint, etching

PFISTER, CHRIS
Untitled (Moonscape), 1990, Monoprint

PICASSO, PABLO
Les Saltimbanques, 1905, Drypoint

PICILLO, JOSEPH
Ep I-III, 1992, Photogravure, chine collé
Edge Event I-III, 1982, Lithograph

PIRANESI, GIOVANNI
Villa Albani (Veduta Della Villa Dell'Emo), 1769, Etching
Ponte Molle (From Views of Rome), 1760, Etching

PLAGENS, PETER
Untitled, 1983, Serigraph, printed in color

PLOTKIN, LINDA
Sea Garden, 1994, Lithograph, printed in color
Grey Star, 1992, Monoprint, printed in color
Rising Confluence, 1992, Lithograph, printed in color
Grotto, 1990, Monoprint, printed in color
Cave Window, 1990, Monoprint, printed in color

POEHLMANN, JOANNA
Pheasant Under Glass, 1993, Lithograph, collage, printed in color
A Big Fan of Yours, 1993, Lithograph, printed in color
"... and Something Blue", 1993, Lithograph, printed in color
Something Borrowed, 1993, Lithograph, embossing, printed in color
The Reunion, 1990, Lithograph
Quadratures of the Moon, 1987, Lithograph, embossing, printed in color
Stamp Collection 1-6, 1986, Lithograph, printed in color
Billboard as Lovely as a Tree, 1986, Lithograph, printed in color
Love and Kisses, 1983, Lithograph, collage, with hand coloring
Flight Patterns (Triptych), 1982, Lithograph, with hand coloring

PORTNOW, MARJORIE
Little Verona, Wisconsin, 1988, Lithograph, printed in color

POZZI, LUCIO
Minos Night, 1987, Monoprint, printed in color
Soaligera, 1987, Monoprint, printed in color
Priamos, 1987, Monoprint, printed in color

PRICE, KEN
Chairs, Table, Rug, Cup, 1971, Serigraph, printed in color

PRINCE, PETER
Tranquility, 1986, Monoprint

PROVISOR, JANIS
Star Trap, 1991, Spit-bite aquatint, hard-ground, sugar-lift etching with drypoint, chine collé
Star Throw, 1991, Hard-ground, sugar-lift etching with chine collé
Long Fall, 1989, Woodcut on chine collé, printed in color
Rifle, 1985, Lithograph, printed in color
Parachute, 1985, Lithograph, printed in color

PUTNAM, PAUL
Ace, 1986, Monoprint, printed in color
Z-Xerographic, 1985, Monoprint

QUICK-TO-SEE SMITH, JAUNE
Fish for a Lifetime (State IV), 1994, Lithograph, printed in color

RAFFAEL, JOSEPH
Amethyst, 1989, Woodcut, printed in color
Crystal Lily, 1987, Woodcut, printed in color
Future Memory, 1986, Aquatint, printed in color
Matthew's Lily, 1984, Woodcut, printed in color

RAIMONDI, MARC ANTONIO
Holy Family (Virgin with the Long Thigh), Etching

RAMMELLZEE
Palladium Protractor, Chase to Assassination, 1984, Etching, printed in color

RANDALL, NANCY
Sweet ... Adversity, 1984, Monoprint, printed in color

RAUSCHENBERG, ROBERT
Untitled, 1991, Serigraph
Platter (From Airport Series), 1974, Relief and intaglio on fabric, printed in color
Fuse from Stoned Moon Series, 1969, Lithograph
Earth Crust from Stoned Moon Series, 1969, Lithograph

RHEINGOLD, LOIS
Yellow Stars for Lily Tomlin, 1986, Serigraph, printed in color
Route 9W, 1983, Serigraph, printed in color
Lingam Highway Sunset and Rainbow, 1983, Serigraph, printed in color
Decorative Yellow Plastic Dot Print, 1983, Serigraph, printed in color

RICHARDSON, SAM
Going Unnoticed, 1993, Lithograph, monoprint, collage, pastel, colored pencils
Establish a Reality, 1993, Assemblage variants, printed in color
Through the Greened into, 1988, Relief with chine collé, hand coloring and hand-drawn additions
Through the Magenta'd into, 1988, Relief with chine collé, hand coloring and hand-drawn additions
Through the Chartreused into, 1988, Relief with chine collé, hand coloring and hand-drawn additions

RICHTER, GERHARD
Farbfelder (Color Charts) 1-6, 1974, Lithograph, printed in color

RIDLON, JAMES
Untitled E, I, H, 1986, Embossed monoprint, printed in color

RIFKA, JUDY
Apotheosis in Indigo, 1991, Lithograph, woodcut, printed in color

RIVERS, LARRY
On the Phone (Large), 1981, Lithograph, serigraph, printed in color
Untitled, 1979, Serigraph, printed in color
Blue Line Camel, 1978, Pochoir, printed in color
Boston Massacre 1-11, 1970, Serigraph, printed in color

RIZZI, DAN
Aqua Fria, 1995, Intaglio with sugar-lift aquatint, printed in color

ROBERTS/(JEAN)
GUEQUIERRE, (NATHAN)
Book of Hours – February, 1992, Woodcut
Book of Hours – July, 1992, Woodcut

ROCKBURNE, DOROTHEA
Chamber Music Society of Lincoln Center, 1993, Serigraph, printed in color

ROSENQUIST, JAMES
Glass Wishes, 1986, Lithograph, printed in color
Star Thief, 1986, Lithograph, printed in color
On Stage, 1982, Aquatint, drypoint, printed in color
Derrière l'Étoile (Behind the Star), 1978, Lithograph, printed in color
Plume, 1982, Aquatint, printed in color
Krapp's Banana, 1982, Aquatint, drypoint, printed in color
Highway Trust, 1980, Lithograph, printed in color
Fast Feast, 1978, Lithograph, printed in color
Red Pyramid, 1978, Lithograph, printed in color
Black Tie, 1977, Lithograph, printed in color
Paper Clip, 1974, Lithograph, printed in color
Spaghetti, 1970, Lithograph

ROSSI, BARBARA
Moon Meet May, 1993, Hard-ground etching, aquatint

ROTH, DAVID
Untitled, 1978, Serigraph

ROTH, DEITER
Helvetia, 1972, Lithograph

ROTHENBERG, SUSAN
Breath-Man, 1986, Drypoint engraving, woodcut, printed in color
Tilting, 1986, Woodcut, lithograph, printed in color
Untitled, 1985, Serigraph
Girl/Boy, 1984, Etching with drypoint
Puppet, 1983, Woodcut, printed in color
Untitled, 1977, Lithograph

ROTTERDAM, PAUL
Minnesota II, 1981, Lithograph, intaglio, serigraph

ROWLAND, FRANK
Aero, Lithograph
Stage Left, Lithograph
Stage Right, Serigraph
Square I, Serigraph

RUDQUIST, JERRY
Snake Chair, 1989, Monoprint, printed in color
Owl Chair, 1989, Monoprint, printed in color

RUSCHA, ED
Home with Complete Electronic Security System, 1982, Serigraph, printed in color
Made in the USA, 1974, printed in color

SALLE, DAVID
Untitled, 1991, Linocut

SANTLOFER, JONATHAN
Human Nature, 1991, Serigraph, printed in color

SAYERS, JOHN
Untitled, 1993, Lithograph, printed in color

SCANGA, ITALO
Two Trees, 1992, Woodcut, printed in color
Untitled (Shoe), 1991, Monoprint
Pitcher, 1991, Lithograph, printed in color
Figs, 1991, Lithograph, printed in color
Napoli, 1989, Woodcut, printed in color

SCANLON, MARCIA
Lake of Isles, 1987, Monoprint

SCHACHT, MIKE
Ty Cobb, Serigraph, printed in color

SCHMADER, SUSAN
Factory, 1986, Etching, printed in color
Floating, 1986, Etching, printed in color
Collapse, 1986, Etching, printed in color
Hi Tech, 1986, Etching, printed in color

SCHNABEL, JULIAN
Untitled, 1984, Lithograph, serigraph
For Anna Magnani: State I, 1983, (Diptych), Etching, aquatint, printed in black and blue
Todd, Cage Without Bars 1-9, 1983, Etching, aquatint, printed in color

SCHNEEMANN, GEORGE
Blue Flannel Shirt, 1989, Lithograph, printed in color

SCHONZEIT, BEN
Untitled, 1994, Serigraph, printed in color
Untitled, 1990, Serigraph, printed in color
Untitled, 1988, Serigraph, printed in color

SCHUETTE KRAEMER, PAULA
Leftover Bouquet: Yellow Background, 1995, Etching printed in color

SCHWARTZ, BARBARA
Untitled, 1989, Monoprint

SCULLY, SEAN
Block, 1986, Woodcut, printed in color

SEBASTIAN, JILL
Ang, 1990, Lithograph, printed in color
Anchor, 1990, Lithograph

SERR, JAN
Sky over Land, 1982, Lithograph, printed in color
Seasons of a Chestnut, 1990, Lithograph, printed in color

SERRA, RICHARD
Call Me Ishmael, 1987, Lithograph
Ishmael's Edge, 1987, Lithograph
Spoleto Circle, 1972, Lithograph

SHANNON, TOM
Orbiting Bodies III, IV, 1986, Lithograph

SHAPIRO, DAVID
Suki, 1978

SHAPIRO, JOEL
Untitled E, G, J, L, O, 1995, Hard-ground etching, drypoint
Untitled, 1990, Pochoir
Untitled 1-4, 1989, Woodcut, printed in color

SHARP, JOSEPH HENRY
Indian Portraits 1-14, 1980, Etching

SHATTER, SUSAN
Mirror Image, 1992, Lithograph, printed in color
Iceberg, 1990, Monoprint, printed in color
Four Landscapes, 1989, Lithograph, printed in color
Water Reflections, Lithograph, printed in color
Islemarada, 1989, Monoprint, printed in color

SHEDLETSKY, STUART
First Pass, 1990, Monoprint, printed in color
Untitled (Color), 1990, Lithograph, printed in color
Untitled (Black), 1990, Lithograph, printed in color
Echo Cave, 1990, Monoprint, printed in color

SHIELDS, ALAN
Sushi Bar, Lithograph, printed in color

SHOLINSKI
Serendipity, 1985, Etching

SILER, TODD
Metaphorms, 1988, Lithograph, printed in color

SINGER, CLIFFORD
Mostly Mozart Festival in Tokyo, 1991, Serigraph, printed in color

SINGLETON, SUSAN
Counterpane, Lithograph

SLOAN, JEANETTE PASIN
Red Shift, Lithograph, printed in color
Jeanette Pasin Sloan, 1986, Woodcut, lithograph, aquatint
Bassano Strips, Lithograph, printed in color

SLONEM, HUNT
Toucans, 1994, Serigraph, printed in color
Black and White Toucans, 1994, Serigraph

SLOWE, VICKKI
Three Views of Saturn's Rings I-III, 1982

SMITH, RICHARD
Ouse, 1982, Intaglio, lithograph, printed in color
Ghost, Lithograph
Untitled, 1982, Lithograph

SNYDER, JOAN
Cherry Tree Series, 1994, Monoprint, printed in color
Lavender with Maurice, 1992, Monoprint, printed in color
Art and the Nature of Grief, 1992, Monoprint, printed in color
Lavender Pool, 1992, Monoprint, printed in color
Free to Explore (Every Corner of Your Imagination), 1990, Monoprint, printed in color
Brooklyn Bean Field, 1990, Monoprint, printed in color
Rough Pond, 1990, Monoprint, printed in color
Study for Symphony for A.I., 1990, Monoprint, printed in color

SOLIEN, T.L
Only He Can Wield that Deadly Stroke, 1988, Monoprint, woodcut, printed in color
Ship in Bottle, 1987, Monoprint, printed in color
Husband Lost at Sea, 1985, Lithograph, printed in color

SONNEMAN, EVE
Deep Runners, 1987, Lithograph, printed in color

SORMAN, STEVEN
What's This, What's That (Dyptych), 1982, Lithograph, intaglio, pochoir, woodcut
Letter from Matisse, 1982, Lithograph, serigraph, collage, pochoir, monoprint, woodcut
Which a Partial Memory, 1981, Lithograph
Rax, 1980, Lithograph, collage, printed in color
Which (Necessity), 1979, Lithograph, printed in color

SPALATIN, MARKO
Nautica 8 #60, 1986, Serigraph, printed in color
Hexagon 2 – #5, 1986, Serigraph, printed in color
Parnasos 8 – #36, 1986, Serigraph, printed in color
Uxmal I, III, 1985, Serigraph, printed in color
Rhombus VI, VIII, 1985, Serigraph, printed in color

STACKHOUSE, ROBERT
Approaching Diviner, 1992, Intaglio, printed in color
Soundless, 1992, Spit-bite etching, printed in color

STAMBLER, DON
Palomino Motel, 1992, Lithograph, printed in color

STEINBERG, SAUL
Provincetown, 1984, Etching, drypoint, printed in color
Gogol I, IV, 1984, Etching, drypoint, aquatint, engraving

STEINWORTH, SKIP
Still Life with Pears, 1992, Lithograph, printed in color

STEIR, PAT
Peony, 1993, Soap-ground reversal, with aquatint and spit-bite aquatint, printed in color
Evening, 1993, Soap-ground reversal, with aquatint and spit-bite aquatint, printed in color
Fern, 1993, Soap-ground reversal, with aquatint and spit-bite aquatint, printed in color
Red/Blue Berlin Waterfall, 1993, Serigraph, printed in color
Sepia Rainclouds, 1991, Rosin reversal aquatint etching
Orange and Green, 1991, Soap-ground, sugar-lift and spit-bite aquatint etching
Raindrops, 1991, Soap-ground, sugar-lift and spit-bite aquatint etching
Big Fall, Black and White, 1991
Long Horizontal, 1991, Rosin reversal, soft-ground and spit-bite aquatint etching
Kweilin Dreaming, Part C,#51-66, 1989, Woodcut, printed in color
Kweilin Dreaming, Part A, 1989, Woodcut, printed in color
Sunflower, 1986, Woodcut, printed in color
Untitled, 1983, Serigraph
Form, Illusion, Myth 1-3, 1982, Lithograph, printed in color
Abstraction, Belief, Desire, 1981, Etching, printed in color
Wish #1, 1974, Lithograph, printed in color
Between the Lines, 1974, Lithograph, printed in color

STELLA, FRANK
Shards V, 1982, Lithograph, serigraph, printed in color
Wolfeboro, 1974, Lithograph
Effingham, 1974, Lithograph, serigraph, printed in color
Purple Series, 1972, Lithograph
Charlotte Tokayer
Hollis Frampton
Kay Bearman
Sidney Guberman

STEPHAN, GARY
III, 1990, Airbrush, spit-bite aquatint

STEWART, NORMAN
Harbinger, 1989, Serigraph, printed in color

STONE, CAROLINE
Summer II, 1984, Etching

STONEHOUSE, FRED
El Senor, 1990, Lithograph
Sea of Leisure, 1986, Lithograph

STOREY, DAVID
Untitled 1-3, 1993, Linocut, printed in color
Untitled, 1991, Lithograph, printed in color
Veloxist A, B, 1990, Linocut
Venus and Mars, 1989, Linocut
Mars and Mars, 1989, Linocut
Untitled, 1-3, 1988, Monoprint
Untitled, 1988, Linocut

STORY, AGNES
Pelicano Club, 1984, Lithograph, collage, printed in color

STRAUTMANIS, EDVINS
Untitled, Monoprint, printed in color

SULTAN, DONALD K.
Untitled, 1993, Serigraph, printed in color
Roses, April 20, 1992, Serigraph, printed in color
Playing Cards (Joker), 1990, Aquatint
Playing Cards (Four of Spades), 1990, Aquatint
Playing Cards (Four of Hearts), 1990, Aquatint
Playing Cards (Four of Diamonds), 1990, Aquatint
Playing Cards (Four of Clubs), 1990, Aquatint
Water Under the Bridge, 1979, Etching

SUMMERS, CAROL
Kali Gandaki, 1983, Woodcut, printed in color
Hellespont, 1978, Woodcut, printed in color
Sonoma, 1977, Woodcut, printed in color
Untitled, 1975, Serigraph, printed in color
Himalaya, Woodcut, printed in color

SUPPLEE, SARAH
Christiana's Pond, 1991, Soft-ground etching, aquatint

TAJIMA
Glass Studio, 1977, Woodcut
Yellow and Yellow Green, Woodcut, printed in color
The Door, 1975, Woodcut

TAMAYO, RUFINO
Iron Cross, 1988, Lithograph, printed in color

TANIKAWA, KOICHI
Forest Memories, 1991, Serigraph

TANNING, DOROTHEA
Untitled, 1992, Lithograph, printed in color
Anabella, 1992, Lithograph, printed in color

TAYLOR, RICHARD
Btu #2, #5, 1991, Etching, aquatint

TERRY, EVELYN
My Son Out to Play "With My Heart", 1988, Etching, monoprint

THIEBAUD, WAYNE
Valley Farm, 1993, Soft-ground, spit-bite aquatint with drypoint, printed in color
Dark Cake, 1983, Woodcut, printed in color
Recent Etchings I: Bird, 1979, Soft-ground etching, aquatint, printed in color
Clown, 1979, Etching, printed in color

THOMAS, LARRY
Desert Circle I, 1989, Monoprint, printed in color

THORNE, JOAN
Salu II, 1983, Lithograph, printed in color
Untitled, 1982, Serigraph, printed in color

THUSIUS, ANGELIKA
Man and Pole, 1987, Lithograph, printed in color

TOBEY, MARK
Mandarin, 1973, Lithograph, printed in color

TOBIASSE, THEO
Circus 1-5, 1985, Lithograph, printed in color
Jacob, Rachel, Lea, 1983, Lithograph, printed in color
Bellerophon, 1983, Carborundum gravure, printed in color
Lorsque Le Jour Entier Devient Fruit, 1983, Aquatint with Carborundum, printed in color
Le Fruit Qui Retient Les Songs, 1982, Aquatint and Carborundum, printed in color
Poupée Gigogne, 1982, Carborundum gravure, printed in color
Femme Foraine, 1981, Carborundum gravure, printed in color
Fleur de Cantique, 1980, Lithograph, printed in color

TRACHTMAN, PAUL
Untitled, 1992, Monoprint, etching, ink and oil

TRAVANTI, LEON
Performance Ritual #1, 1983, Lithograph, printed in color

TROVA, ERNEST
Falling Man/Study "A", 1977, Serigraph, printed in color

TRUE, DAVID
Fragile Wings, 1989, Woodcut, printed in color
Open Channel, 1987, Etching, printed in color

TULIS, SPENCER
Opus Paralleled, 1986, Woodcut
Closed for the Holidays, 1986, Aquatint
Vent #3, 1986, Aquatint

TURNER, ALAN
Tree Felled by Storm, 1-3, Lithograph, printed in color

TUTTLE, RICHARD
Trans Asian, 1993, Watercolor, woodcut on silk, chine collé
Perceived Obstacles, 5 pieces, 1991, Lithograph, printed in color

TWADDLE, RANDY
Untitled, 1985

TWORKOV, JACK
Tworkov 1-3, 1979, Aquatint, printed in color

UGLOW, ALAN
Untitled, I, II, 1980, Lithograph

USLE, JUAN
Untitled, 1992, Lithograph, printed in color

UTTECH, TOM
Kasakokweg Shoreline, 1991, Lithograph printed in color
Windigo Falls, 1986, Lithograph, printed in color

VAN VLIET, CLAIRE
Wheeler Mountain Bowl (Triptych), 1989, Lithograph

VENET, BERNAR
Angles, Arcs, Line, 1981, Lithograph with collage, printed in color

WADDELL, THEODORE
Crazy Mountains 2, 3, 1990, Monoprint, printed in color
Snowy Mountains 18, 1990, Monoprint, printed in color
Wind Series #3, 1986, Monoprint, printed in color
Untitled #6, 1985, Monoprint, printed in color
Africa Series #5, 1988, Monoprint, printed in color

WAGONER, GERALD
Love Lock, 1985, Lithograph
Untitled, 1985, Lithograph
Untitled, 1985, Monoprint
Inscape, 1985, Lithograph

WALKER, JOHN
Untitled, 1992, Monoprint

WARHOL, ANDY
General Custer, 1986, Serigraph, printed in color
Cow, 1977, Serigraph on wallpaper, printed in color
Mao, 1972, Serigraph, printed in color

WATERHOUSE, MONA
Cross Land, 1985, Mixed media
Night I, 1985, Mixed media
Going Home the Long Way Around, 1985, Mixed media

WEAVER, ROBERT
E-12, 1981, Lithograph, printed in color

WEEGE, WILLIAM
Desert, the Desert, 1994, Woodcut, printed in color
Ducks Unlimited, 1993, Woodcut, printed in color
Mother Nature Never Loses Series, 1989-91, Woodcut, printed in color
Don't Cry Wolf
Frying Pan Effect
It Came to Me Out of the Blue
Acid Rain in the Red Room
Polluted Fantasy

WEGMAN, WILLIAM
Composer Series, 1993, Photogravure, lithograph, printed in color
Scriabin
Janacek
Fauré
Smetana
Chopin
Aeronautical Landscape, 1991, Monoprint, printed in color
Endless Column, 1990, Assembled woodcut, printed in color
Ray Cat, 1988, Lithograph, printed in color
Doguerreotype, 1988, Lithograph, printed in color

WELLIVER, NEIL
Untitled, 1984, Serigraph, printed in color

WESSELMANN, TOM
Study for Nude Painting, 1980, Aquatint, printed in color

WILDE, JOHN
Boxed Fruit, 1992, Lithograph, chine collé

WILEY, TAD
Semaphores, 1991, Monoprint
Untitled, 1988, Monoprint

WILEY, WILLIAM T
Once Upon a Time When All Was Flawless, 1982, Lithograph on silk, printed in color
#4, Monoprint, printed in color
Three Mile Island/Three Years Later, 1980, Lithograph, printed in color
Torturer, 1989, Soft-ground etching, printed in color

WILLIS, THORNTON
Untitled, 1981, Lithograph

WINTERS, ROBIN
Robots, 1985, Lithograph

WINTERS, TERRY
Glyphs I-VI, 1995, Indigo-dyed linocut

WOFFORD, PHILLIP
Untitled, 1989, Monoprint, printed in color

WOODMAN, BETTY
On the Way to India, 1988, Lithograph, printed in color

YOUNG, PETER
Untitled, 1973, Serigraph, printed in color

YOUNGERMAN, JACK
Untitled Suite A-H, 1980, Serigraph, printed in color

YUNKERS, ADJA
A Moment into Eternity I, 1982, Intaglio, lithograph, serigraph, printed in color
Les Pendus II, 1980, Intaglio
Falling Birds, 1978, Lithograph, serigraph, printed in color

ZAKANITCH, ROBERT RAHWAY
Dragon Flower Shaker Salt, 1994, Monoprint, printed in color
Dragon Flower Shaker Pepper, 1994, Monoprint, printed in color
Nina, 1986, Lithograph, printed in color
Untitled, 1983, Serigraph, printed in color
Hearts of Swan (Red), 1981, Serigraph, lithograph, printed in color
Double Geese Mountain, 1981, Serigraph, stencil, printed in color
Hearts of Swan (Black), 1981, Serigraph, stencil, lithograph, printed in color
How I Love Ya, How I Love Ya, State II, 1981, Serigraph, stencil, lithograph, printed in color
Untitled, 1977, Serigraph, printed in color

ZAPKUS, KES
Untitled, 1979, Serigraph

ZOELLICK, SCOTT
Untitled, Lithograph

ZUCKER, JOSEPH
Untitled, 1979, Serigraph, printed in color

photo credits

Photography courtesy of:

A.G.B. Graphics, Madison, Wisconsin, p. 68

© 1996 Louise Bourgeois
Licensed by VAGA, New York, New York, p. 26

Brooke Alexander Editions, New York, New York, p. 75, 94, 118, 119

Cirrus Editions, Los Angeles, California, p. 22

Warrington Colescott, Hollandale, Wisconsin, p. 41

Crown Point Press, San Francisco, California, p. 27, 31, 36, 37, 38, 43, 47, 50, 51, 65, 69, 74, 76, 77, 78, 81, 84, 88, 100, 111, 112, 113, 117

© 1996 Robert Cumming
Licensed by VAGA, New York, New York, p. 43

Derrière l'Étoile Studios, New York, New York, p. 28, 29, 32, 40, 43, 48, 57, 58, 59, 61, 63, 64, 74, 80, 81, 83, 89, 90, 109, 116,

Mark di Suvero
Centering
Printed and published by Tyler Graphics Ltd.
© Mark di Suvero/Tyler Graphics Ltd. 1976, p. 49

Éditions de la Tempête, Paris, France, p. 26

Editions Schellmann, Inc. Munich, Germany, p. 87

© 1996 Richard Estes
Licensed by VAGA, New York, New York,
Marlborough Gallery, New York, p. 56

Experimental Workshop, San Francisco, California, p. 18, 19, 25, 68

Gemini GEL, Los Angeles, California, p. 24, 46, 60, 73, 95, 102, 105, 108

Graves, Nancy
Approaches the Limit of I
Printed and published by Tyler Graphics Ltd., 1981
© Estate of Nancy Graves, p. 62

© 1996 Al Held
Licensed by VAGA, New York, New York, p. 65

Hockney, David
Views of Hotel Well II
Printed and published by Tyler Graphics Ltd.
© David Hockney/Tyler Graphics Ltd. 1985, p. 66

© 1996 Jasper Johns
Licensed by VAGA, New York, New York, p. 73

© 1996 Alex Katz
Licensed by VAGA, New York, New York,
Marlborough Gallery, New York, p. 78

Kelly, Ellsworth
Colors on a Grid, Screenprint, 1976
Printed and published by Tyler Graphics Ltd., p. 79

Landfall Press, Chicago, Illinois, p. 10, 11, 14, 15, 30, 35, 42, 125

Lincoln Center Print Program, New York, New York, p. 67

Mitchell, Joan
Bedford I
Printed and published by Tyler Graphics Ltd.
© Joan Mitchell/Tyler Graphics Ltd. 1981, p. 91

Morley, Malcolm
Devonshire Bullocks
Printed and published by Tyler Graphics Lts.
© Malcolm Morley/Tyler Graphics Ltd. 1982, p. 92

Motherwell, Robert
Rite of Passage III
Printed and published by Tyler Graphics Ltd., 1980
© Dedalus Foundation, p. 93

Multiples Inc., New York, p. 17, 104

Pace Prints, New York, New York, p. 54

Parasol Press, New York, New York, p. 56

© 1996 Robert Rauschenberg
Licensed by VAGA, New York, New York, p. 102

Sharks Inc., Boulder, Colorado, p. 63

Solo Impression Inc., New York, New York, p. 16, 52, 53, 124

Stewart and Stewart, Bloomfield Hills, Michigan, p. 72

Tamarind Institute, Albuquerque, New Mexico, p. 101

Tandem Press, Madison, Wisconsin, p. 20, 21, 31, 33, 61, 62, 110

Vermillion Editions Ltd., Minneapolis, Minnesota, p. 13, 23, 64, 92, 97

Diane Villani Editions, New York, New York, p. 107

Zakanitch, Robert
How I Love Ya, How I Love Ya
Printed and published by Tyler Graphcs Ltd.
© Robert Zakanitch/Tyler Graphics Ltd. 1981, p. 126, 127